FOUR SEMINAL THINKERS IN
INTERNATIONAL THEORY

Also by Martin Wight

The Development of the Legislative Council 1606–1945 (1946)

Power Politics (1946)

The Gold Coast Legislative Council (1947)

Attitude to Africa, with W. Arthur Lewis, Michael Scott, and Colin Legum (1951)

British Colonial Constitutions 1947 (1952)

Diplomatic Investigations, edited and contributed to, with Herbert Butterfield (1966)

Systems of States, edited by Hedley Bull (1977)

Power Politics, expanded version edited by Hedley Bull and Carsten Holbraad (1978)

International Theory: The Three Traditions, edited by Gabriele Wight and Brian Porter (1991)

FOUR SEMINAL THINKERS IN INTERNATIONAL THEORY

Machiavelli, Grotius, Kant, and Mazzini

Martin Wight

Edited by
Gabriele Wight and Brian Porter

Foreword by Sir Michael Howard, C.H.

Introduction by David S. Yost

OXFORD
UNIVERSITY PRESS

Great Clarendon Street, Oxford OX2 6DP

Oxford University Press is a department of the University of Oxford.
It furthers the University's objective of excellence in research, scholarship,
and education by publishing worldwide in

Oxford New York

Auckland Bangkok Buenos Aires Cape Town Chennai
Dar es Salaam Delhi Hong Kong Istanbul Karachi Kolkata
Kuala Lumpur Madrid Melbourne Mexico City Mumbai Nairobi
São Paulo Shanghai Taipei Tokyo Toronto

Oxford is a registered trade mark of Oxford University Press
in the UK and in certain other countries

Published in the United States
by Oxford University Press Inc., New York

© Gabriele Wight 2005
Introduction © David S. Yost 2005

The moral rights of the author have been asserted
Database right Oxford University Press (maker)

First published 2005

All rights reserved. No part of this publication may be reproduced,
stored in a retrieval system, or transmitted, in any form or by any means,
without the prior permission in writing of Oxford University Press,
or as expressly permitted by law, or under terms agreed with the appropriate
reprographics rights organization. Enquiries concerning reproduction
outside the scope of the above should be sent to the Rights Department,
Oxford University Press, at the address above

You must not circulate this book in any other binding or cover
and you must impose this same condition on any acquirer

British Library Cataloguing in Publication Data
Data available

Library of Congress Cataloging in Publication Data
Data available

ISBN 0-19-927367-7

1 3 5 7 9 10 8 6 4 2

Typeset by Newgen Imaging Systems (P) Ltd., Chennai, India
Printed in Great Britain
on acid-free paper by
Biddles Ltd., King's Lynn, Norfolk.

Foreword

Martin Wight was, if not the greatest, then certainly the most influential twentieth-century British thinker about international relations. Whether he founded something called 'the English School', or indeed whether there was anything that deserved to be called an 'English School' is a matter of some doubt. What is certain is that he transformed thinking about international relations in this country at least; and if he has been ignored or downgraded in the United States, the result has been the impoverishment, not only of American thinking but, disastrously, of American practice in the conduct of foreign affairs.

When Wight began teaching in the 1950s, 'international relations' extended little beyond, on the one hand, the study of diplomatic history and international law, and on the other the aspirational work of such Wilsonian idealists as Alfred Zimmern, Lionel Curtis and Philip Noel Baker; men who were concerned rather to change the world than to understand it. Those thinkers had grown up in the shadow of the First World War, and saw it as their mission to prevent such a catastrophe from ever happening again. Wight grew up in the shadow of the Second and of the Cold War that followed it, and his generation had learned that idealism was not enough. 'Realist' thinkers such as E. H. Carr in the United Kingdom and Hans Morgenthau in the United States thus taught that international relations was

Foreword

inescapably about power, and the management of power; not its abolition.

Wight came late to the teaching of the subject, having studied history and taught it as a schoolmaster and then serving an apprenticeship at Chatham House (the Royal Institute for International Affairs) at a time when the inchoate hopes of the immediate post-war period were hardening into the frigid hostilities of the Cold War. His heart lay with the idealism of Chatham House, but his observation of the world in which he lived convinced him it could not work. The genial anarchy of Charles Manning's Department of International Relations at the L.S.E. gave him the opportunity to think the whole subject through from the beginning, taking his pupils with him on a voyage of discovery in the famous lectures most of which, like those in this volume, were to see the light only long after his death.

Two qualities distinguished Wight as a teacher and thinker. One was a depth and range of learning that was rare even in his generation and has now almost disappeared; learning that gave him a profound knowledge of the entire ancient world and a continuum of European history and thought from the Renaissance onward. This depth, so some of his critics have argued, was bought at the expense of width. The thinkers he studied, it must be admitted, were male, dead, white, and above all European; but female, live and coloured scholars had as yet made little contribution to the subject, and the thinkers Wight did study, from Aquinas to Mazzini, constituted a rich seam of ideas that is still far from exhausted. The 'systems of states' whose structure and relationship he studied, whether those of the classical world, or the Italy of the Renaissance, or of Europe since the fifteenth century, were admittedly parochial *sub specie eternitatis*, but they have provided a template for the global society that was developing in his own lifetime, and no alternative had as yet—and arguably has as yet—replaced it. Wight did not see it as his business to provide such an alternative: he was one of

Foreword

those philosophers dismissed by Marx as being more concerned to understand the world than to change it. But attempts to change the world before one has understood it normally result in disaster, as contemporary events show only too clearly.

The second quality was a profound moral commitment. Wight was a deeply committed Christian, although he never allowed his faith to distort the clarity of his thinking. He could never see his subject as a branch of the social sciences. Implicit in his thinking was the belief that the state is an imperfect instrument to enable imperfect people to live a good life, and so has to be taken seriously as a moral entity. The same moral commitment inspired the work of Herbert Butterfield, who invited Wight to help him initiate the discussions sponsored by the Rockefeller Foundation by a small group that the Foundation, termed, a little misleadingly, 'The British Committee on the Theory of International Politics'—'British' to distinguish it from an American body that had been founded under similar auspices. It was an unfortunate title. It suggested both a distinctively national approach to the subject, and, worse, an acceptance of the concept that there was, or should be, such a thing as a 'theory' of the subject. In his first contribution to our discussions Wight sardonically suggested that "international theory is the theory of survival",* which, in the context of the Cold War, did not seem so wildly far-fetched.

I have slipped into the first person, since I was a member of the British Committee; invited, I suppose, as a historian of war and a thinker about nuclear war, to provide an input about the place of force in international relations. As a Christian and one-time pacifist Wight agonised over the problem of nuclear weapons, but never allowed it to dominate his thinking. He put it in the context of international order and justice which were the framework of his thought and of our discussions. Nor did he press us towards any conclusions about contemporary international affairs.

---

* Butterfield & Wight, *Diplomatic Investigations* (London, 1966) p. 33.

Foreword

He invited men of affairs to join our deliberations, but rather so that we could learn from their experience than because we had anything to teach them. (While agreeing with Kant that bureaucrats should listen to philosophers, he believed no less profoundly that philosophers should listen to bureaucrats). What mattered to him was not so much what we thought, but the clarity, the cohesion and above all the moral quality of our thought.

I can think of nobody who has had greater influence on my own thinking, and thus, I hope, on those I have myself taught. I believe that the same can be said of his own pupils, and their pupils *in saeculo saeculorum*. As Burckhardt said of History, Wight saw his object as being, not to make people clever for next time, but wise for ever.

Michael Howard

May 2004

Preface

Martin Wight (1913–72), who was Reader in International Relations at the London School of Economics from 1949 to 1961, left among his papers a great number of lecture notes dealing with political ideas. These fell into two groups. The larger group was of notes for the lectures on 'International Theory', which he had given in the 1950s. These lectures so impressed all who heard them, and became so celebrated, if only by reputation, throughout the international relations profession, that we decided to undertake the formidable task of editing and publishing them as a readable text. The result, after several years' work, was *International Theory: The Three Traditions*, published by Leicester University Press in 1991. Our confidence in the lasting value of Martin's achievement proved to be well founded, for this book, even though the lectures themselves had been delivered more than a generation earlier, at once took its place as a notable contribution to the literature of international relations.

This left the smaller group of notes, on the political thinking of Machiavelli, Grotius, Kant, and Mazzini. They were something of a mystery, for the one of us who as a graduate student had attended the 'Three Traditions' lectures in the 1950s had no knowledge of other lectures devoted to these four thinkers. When, and where, were they delivered? And how did they relate to the main series? The answers to these questions were provided by Martin's diaries. The lectures had been composed

Preface

and delivered at the London School of Economics in 1959–60, Martin's last teaching year there before his appointment in 1961 to the post of Professor of History and Dean of European Studies at the University of Sussex. It seems therefore that he lectured from these notes once only, and so far as is known he never made subsequent use of them.

Yet they were clearly related to the 'Three Traditions' lectures in that Machiavelli, Grotius, and Kant had been central to an understanding of these traditions, and indeed Martin Wight had come to prefer to his original 'Realism', 'Rationalism', and 'Revolutionism' the terms 'Machiavellianism', 'Grotianism', and 'Kantianism' as titles for them. In view of this we briefly considered publishing these notes as either a prolonged introduction or an extended appendix to the rest. Yet this would have been a mistake. It would have made the book too long and spoilt the essential unity of 'The Three Traditions'.

The alternative course was to publish these four lectures as a short work on their own. They have their own character. They are both more discursive, and more biographical, than the 'Traditions' lectures. They may be read no less for their intrinsic interest as studies of four key figures in the history of Western thought, than as a companion to *International Theory: The Three Traditions*, leading, perhaps, to a fuller understanding of why Martin chose the three thinkers he did to illustrate and personalize the three categories or traditions he discerned in nearly all political thought and behaviour.

The 'traditions', however, focused only upon Machiavelli, Grotius, and Kant, so his introduction of Mazzini needs a word of justification. The reasons for doing so are presumably to be found partly in a 'philosophical genealogy' which accompanied the notes, and which we have included as an Appendix, and partly in the character of Mazzini himself. The 'genealogy' shows him as occupying a key place in one of those lines of descent into which Martin Wight liked to arrange significant historical figures: a Revolutionist but also a democrat and a

Preface

nationalist, one in the tradition less of Lenin and Khrushchev than of Woodrow Wilson, Nehru, and, in some ways, Nasser. But Martin was clearly fascinated by a man who was not only, like himself, a moralist of a religious temperament (one of very few Western post-Enlightenment revolutionaries who were), but also, again like himself, a radical traditionalist steeped in the long heritage of European history and culture.

The process by which these lecture notes have been turned into a book has been identical to that described in the preface to the earlier volume, although this time without the help of personal notes and memories. This has not, however, been too much of a disadvantage, for the essential structure, consisting of the careers and thoughts of four men, has been easier to follow. It remains to thank Barbara Wight once again for her patience and interpretative skill in turning her father's bare notes into prose, as well as, at a later stage, her sister Susannah for further refining the text and typing it up in Word format. We are indebted also to those several scholars who generously gave of their time and learning to read through and comment upon all or part of the typescript: notably Dr D. O. Thomas of Aberystwyth; Professor Howard Williams of the University of Wales, Aberystwyth; and Professor David Yost of the Naval Postgraduate School, Monterey, California. The last, moreover, not only undertook to write the Introduction, but brought the Bibliography up to date and tracked down some rare publications. This help much lightened our task.

The responsibility for any imperfections there might be in the interpretation or the presentation rests, however, with us. In particular, not all cited passages conform strictly to their textual sources. Martin Wight often adapted these for lecturing purposes and his limited and judicious paraphrasing we have usually followed.

G. W.
B. E. P.

17 September 2003

Contents

Foreword by Sir Michael Howard, C.H.	v
Preface	ix
Introduction: Martin Wight and Philosophers of War and Peace by David S. Yost	xvii

1 Machiavelli	**3**
Introduction	3
The Inductive Method	4
Historical Method	5
Methodological Critique	6
The Badness of Human Nature	7
Self-regard, Self-interest, Struggle for Power	8
Primacy of Contradiction	10
Power is Antecedent to Law, Custom, and Justice	14
Causal Complexity of Politics	17
Notes	24

2 Grotius	**29**
Life and Achievement	29
Ambiguity and Inaccessibility	31
Richness and Complexity	32
Reconciler: The Middle Way	34
Restrain Evil: Lessen Suffering	34
Natural Law	36
Prescription	44

Contents

Political Variety: Multiformity versus Uniformity	46
Beyond Natural Law: Hierarchy of Moral Life	49
Individual Moral Responsibility	53
Notes	55

3 Kant — 63

Life and Influence	63
Was Kant a Revolutionary?	65
The Categorical Imperative: Duty	67
The Kantian Type of International Theory: Revolutionary Presumption	71
Federation of Republican States	72
Cosmopolitanism	74
Harmony of Interests	75
Doctrine of Progress	77
Perfectibility of Man	80
Eradication of Suffering and Sin	81
Diagram of Kantians	83
Kant's Universality	83
Notes	84

4 Mazzini — 89

Bibliographical Inaccessibility	89
A 'Victorian'	90
Mazzini and Religion	91
God in Politics: Providence and Progress	92
God in Politics: Duty	96
His Political and Social Theory	98
Nationalism and Internationalism	100
Nationality	102
The Revolutionary Situation	104
Revolutionary Methods	108
Humanity	109
Power and Morality	110
A Traditionalist Revolutionary	115
Notes	116

Contents

Appendix I: A Philosophical Genealogy   121

Appendix II: The Three Traditions in Christianity   123

Appendix III: The International Theory of Grotius   124

Bibliography I: From Martin Wight's Notes and Reading Lists, 1959–72   129

Bibliography II: Selected Publications since 1972   133

An Anatomy of International Thought   **141**

Index   157

Introduction: Martin Wight and Philosophers of War and Peace

David S. Yost

Martin Wight (1913–72) was, as Sir Adam Roberts has noted, 'perhaps the most profound thinker on international relations of his generation of British academics'.[1] A man of wide-ranging interests and great learning, with a command of Greek and Latin as well as modern European languages, Wight wrote about British colonial history, European studies, the history and sociology of states-systems, the philosophy of history, religious faith and history, and the theory and philosophy of international politics (notably with regard to ethics, ideology, the balance of power, and the causes of war), among other subjects. While Wight served as professor of history and founding dean of the School of European Studies, University of Sussex (1961–72), much of his influence has stemmed from his lectures on the theory and philosophy of international politics at the London School of Economics and Political Science in the 1950s.[2]

Wight's continuing prominence has also derived from the attention accorded to the 'English School' since the 1980s. The term 'English School' did not arise until nine years after Wight's death, when it was given currency by Roy Jones in a polemical article in 1981. The term is usually construed as signifying an approach to the study of international politics more rooted in historical and humanistic learning than in the social sciences.[3] *Four Seminal Thinkers* is characteristic of a scholar steeped in such learning. Wight was more interested in analysing moral

Introduction

and philosophical questions raised by international politics than in debating immediate policy decisions. The lectures reproduced in this volume illustrate his ability to bring insights from philosophy, biography, and literature to bear upon political thought and behaviour. Wight's literary references range from Virgil and Shakespeare to Ian Fleming, and his many interests are happily combined in the present work.

During his lifetime Wight's most extensive publications concerned the history of British colonialism,[4] and his other publications were limited to a pamphlet and some articles and book chapters.[5] Only one book chapter—his classic essay, 'Western Values in International Relations'—outlined Wight's path-breaking organization of the history of Western thinking about international politics into three categories, or traditions; and it focused on what Wight called the Rationalist, or Grotian, tradition. In addition to the present volume, three books by Wight have been published posthumously: *Systems of States* in 1977,[6] *Power Politics* in 1978,[7] and *International Theory: The Three Traditions* in 1991, the last based on Wight's notes for the widely discussed lectures given in the 1950s.[8] Wight published relatively little, Hedley Bull observed, because he was 'a perfectionist . . . one of those scholars—today, alas, so rare—who (to use a phrase of Albert Wohlstetter's) believe in a high ratio of thought to publication'.[9]

Wight's lectures won the enduring admiration of his listeners. As Bull testified in 1976, 'These lectures made a profound impression on me, as they did on all who heard them. Ever since that time I have felt in the shadow of Martin Wight's thought—humbled by it, a constant borrower from it, always hoping to transcend it but never able to escape from it'.[10]

Similarly, recalling her studies at the London School of Economics in 1950–4, Coral Bell wrote in 1989 that Martin Wight 'still seems to me the finest mind and spirit I ever knew well, looking back over what is now almost a full lifetime of knowing many people of the highest intellectual caliber'.

Introduction

In Bell's view, Wight's most valuable teaching concerned the history of ideas about international politics.

He made his students see the history of thought in the subject from Thucydides to Henry Kissinger as a sort of great shimmering tapestry of many figures, a tapestry mostly woven from just three contrasting threads, which he called realist, rationalist, and revolutionist. What made him such a charismatic teacher, and those lectures so fascinating, was the elegance of his analysis, and the breadth and depth of his learning, literary as well as historical.[11]

Four Seminal Thinkers consists of four lectures Wight delivered at the London School of Economics in 1959–60, plus 'An Anatomy of International Thought', Wight's lecture in 1961 at the Institut Universitaire de Hautes Études Internationales.[12] The volume thus makes available Wight's most extensive (and previously unpublished) discussions of four political philosophers he considered especially influential or representative of the traditions of thinking about international politics in the West. This makes possible a fuller understanding of Wight's remarkable vision of the enduring challenges and dilemmas—moral and practical—in international politics.

This introduction considers the distinctive elements of Martin Wight's approach and the role of these four political philosophers in his analysis. Because one of Wight's greatest contributions is his elucidation of what he called the three traditions, it is important first to clarify what he meant by 'traditions' and the significance of specific thinkers in them.

Wight's Distinctive Approach

Wight was a historian who grounded his findings about theory and philosophy in solid scholarship about how specific thinkers and policy-makers interpreted events in concrete historical contexts. His analysis—compact, aphoristic, and richly documented—provides a robust and unequalled guide to the history

Introduction

of Western thought about the fundamental questions of international politics. Wight's work vividly evokes the central conceptual frameworks of Western statecraft, including recurrences, adjustments, and never-resolved dilemmas and paradoxes. His analysis teaches humility about 'originality' and the limits of the theoretical enterprise.

Wight held that 'international theory is the political philosophy of international relations'.[13] He described the *International Theory* lectures as 'in the first place an experiment in classification, in typology, and in the second an exploration of continuity and recurrence, a study in the uniformity of political thought; and its leading premiss is that political ideas do not change much, and the range of ideas is limited'.[14]

Wight concluded that thinkers in the period since Machiavelli could be placed into three traditions: Realists, Rationalists, and Revolutionists, names that 'do not sacrifice accuracy in any degree to the charms of alliteration'.[15] Realists, or Machiavellians, emphasize the anarchical elements of international politics: 'sovereign states acknowledging no political superior, whose relationships are ultimately regulated by warfare'. Rationalists, or Grotians, concentrate on 'diplomacy and commerce' and other institutions for 'continuous and organized intercourse between these sovereign states'. Revolutionists, or Kantians, underscore the 'concept of a society of states, or family of nations' and pursue the realization of an imperative vision of the moral unity of mankind.[16]

Realist views have been advanced by philosophers such as Bacon and Hobbes and by policy-makers such as Frederick the Great and Napoleon. Realists have tended to deny the existence of international moral and legal obligations based on natural law, and have appealed—implicitly, if not explicitly—to principles of expediency such as justification by success.

Rationalists have been closely associated with Western traditions of constitutional government. Philosophers such as Aristotle, Grotius, and Locke and politicians such as Burke,

Introduction

Gladstone, Lincoln, and Churchill have usually taken Rationalist positions, holding that moral obligations rooted in natural law (and discernible by reason) should be respected. Rationalists have also emphasized the moral tensions and difficulties involved in limiting power and in identifying the lesser evil in specific situations.

The most prominent examples of Revolutionist thinking include the Protestants and Catholics of the religious wars of the sixteenth and seventeenth centuries, each asserting rights and duties to intervene in other states to promote the success of their own doctrines; the intellectual forefathers of the French Revolution, such as Rousseau, and its leaders, particularly the Jacobins; the champions of 'ideological uniformity' as a path to international order and security, such as Kant, Mazzini, and Woodrow Wilson; the proponents of a gradual convergence of interests through commerce and a consensus of world public opinion, such as Cobden and Bright; and totalitarian ideologues, both Communist and Fascist, that have tried to impose their conceptions through conquest and coercion. Revolutionists have tended to argue that the end justifies the means or that political ethics must be identical to those of private life.

Wight suggested that Realists generally view history as cyclical and repetitive and hence a reliable source of lessons for the guidance of astute policy-makers. Revolutionists are prone 'to see history as linear, moving upwards towards an apocalyptic denouement' and 'messianic fulfilment', the triumph of the true faith, conceived in religious, political, and/or economic terms. Rationalists appeal to reason and moral obligations and advocate prudent attempts to pursue constructive international cooperation; but they are usually 'cautious and agnostic' about any pattern or ultimate meaning in history, aware of the unpredictable and contingent and manifesting no confidence in the permanence of any apparent progress in political institutions.[17]

These philosophical approaches to history are, Wight argued, consistent with each tradition's methodological inclination.

Introduction

Realists are prone to make sociological statements on the basis of an empirical analysis of history. 'For example: Machiavelli's "armed prophets [Moses, Hitler] conquer; unarmed prophets [Savonarola, Trotsky] are destroyed" and Carr's "international order . . . will always be the slogan of those who feel strong enough to impose it on others." '[18] Revolutionists are attracted to imperative prescriptions, whether of church doctrine, the Rights of Man, the proletariat, or another cause, such as 'Workers of the world, unite', in the Communist manifesto.[19] Rationalists tend to make ontological, or *a priori*, assertions about the nature and purpose of international obligations, such as the preamble to the United Nations Charter, written by Field-marshal J. C. Smuts: 'We the peoples of the United Nations determined . . . to reaffirm faith in fundamental human rights, in the dignity and worth of the human person, in the equal rights of men and women and of nations large and small.'[20]

What Wight Meant by 'Traditions'

It is essential to clarify what Wight meant by the word 'traditions' and the extent to which, in his judgement, each tradition displays intellectual continuity. It is the Realists and Rationalists, he held, that have drawn on coherent intellectual traditions. The Rationalists have travelled 'the road with the most conscious acknowledgment of continuity', beginning with 'the Greeks and especially the Stoics' and proceeding down a broad path with many representatives, including Aquinas, Grotius, Madison, Tocqueville, and Lincoln.[21] The Realist tradition is 'virtually as self-conscious and as continuous as the Rationalist', with Machiavelli's approach an example for Bacon, Hobbes, Frederick the Great, Bismarck, E. H. Carr, and others.[22] In contrast, 'the Revolutionist ancestry of ideas and continuity of thought is ambiguous or uncertain. The Revolutionist tradition is less a stream than a series of waves . . . [or] disconnected illustrations of the same politico-philosophical truths ... It is characteristic of Revolutionism ... to deny its past, to try to start from scratch, to jump out of history and begin again'.[23]

Critics have repeatedly charged that Wight's exposition of the three traditions is Procrustean and cannot do justice to individual philosophers and policy-makers. The *International Theory* lectures, published in 1991, revealed that Wight made the same point in the 1950s: 'Machiavelli was inspired to write by a passion foreign to the principles of his theory—a passion which breaks out in the last chapter of *The Prince*.'[24] Furthermore, Wight cited examples of 'how far Machiavelli was from cheap Machiavellianism, and how his recommendations are more penetrating, and one jump ahead, of his self-appointed disciples'.[25] Wight began the lecture on Machiavelli published in this volume with a similar observation: 'All individual thinkers transcend typology; and in social studies, generalizations are abstractions, mental conveniences, and to that extent unreal. They must be contrasted with the concrete, historical person in all his richness and possible inconsistency.'[26]

Wight repeatedly noted that 'the three traditions are not clear-cut pigeon-holes, but can overlap'.[27] He compared the traditions to primary colours that might be mixed across a spectrum[28] and to 'streams, with eddies and cross-currents, sometimes interlacing ... They both influence and cross-fertilize one another, and they change, although without, I think, losing their inner identity.'[29] In other words, his work was 'an attempt to pin down and define the *central* principles and *characteristic* doctrines of each of the three traditions'.[30] After one particularly incisive summary of the essential differences among the three traditions, Wight declared that

all this is merely classification and schematizing. In all political and historical studies the purpose of building pigeon-holes is to reassure oneself that the raw material does *not* fit into them. Classification becomes valuable, in humane studies, only at the point where it breaks down. The greatest political writers in international theory

Introduction

almost all straddle the frontiers dividing two of the traditions, and most of these writers transcend their own systems.[31]

In the lectures published in *International Theory: The Three Traditions*, as well as in other works, Wight gave many examples of how the thinking of great philosophers cannot be confined to a single tradition. As Wight noted, 'It is ideas and assumptions we are concerned with, and their logical interdependence; and this commits us to the dangerous method of tracing ideas through a variety of writers and politicians without dwelling on their place in each's complex aggregate of doctrine.'[32]

Furthermore, to be faithful to the historical evidence, Wight identified subcategories and anomalies in the three main traditions. For instance, he distinguished 'soft' Revolutionists, such as Kant and Wilson, from 'hard' Revolutionists such as the Jacobins and Marxist–Leninists; in contrast with the gradual and legalistic approach of the former, the latter have championed the use of violence to bring about a transformation of world politics.[33] He also suggested that 'if Realism is defined by the classic Realists—Machiavelli, Richelieu, Hobbes, Hume, Frederick II, Hegel—then contemporary Realists appear as much Rationalist as Realist'; and he gave statements by George F. Kennan and Hans Morgenthau as examples.[34]

Wight also discussed a fourth tradition, historically of lesser importance, that he called 'inverted Revolutionism'—a tradition 'of whom pacifists are the chief, although not the only, example'.[35] The goal of this approach, notably as expounded by the Quakers, is 'evoking the latent power of love in all people, and transforming the world by the transformation of souls'.[36] 'It is "inverted" because it repudiates the use of power altogether; it is "Revolutionist" because it sees this repudiation as a principle of universal validity, and energetically promotes its acceptance.'[37] Wight maintained that inverted Revolutionism usually partakes of 'a Realist analysis of politics', giving examples such as Tolstoy's *War and Peace* and early Quaker statements comparing men to 'raging lions'.[38]

Introduction

By 'tradition', in other words, Wight did not mean that new adherents to a way of thinking have always been strongly influenced and even guided by the analyses formulated by their predecessors, with certain sets of ideas developed with great continuity and deliberation over centuries. The Revolutionist tradition in particular has been marked by profound discontinuities. Even within the traditions with a greater degree of cohesion (the Realists and the Rationalists), individual analysts and policy-makers have rediscovered and rethought old principles for themselves and have devised approaches extending beyond the notional limits of the tradition. Thus, the traditions are not straitjackets, but organizing frameworks used to group closely related and often interdependent ideas together. The *Four Seminal Thinkers* lectures complement *International Theory: The Three Traditions* by further illustrating Wight's point that truly great thinkers cannot be pigeonholed, because they straddle categories devised for analytical and pedagogical purposes.

In short, the criticism that Wight's exposition of the traditions is too rigid to represent individual thinkers fairly is misplaced. Wight himself explicitly rejected 'pigeonholes' and pointed out the risks of distortion in any classificatory system, and he carefully circumscribed the functions of the traditions he identified.

However, it may be regretted that Wight chose eponymous terms for each of the traditions—calling the Realists Machiavellians, the Rationalists Grotians, and the Revolutionists Kantians. Sometimes Wight himself inadvertently illustrated the awkwardness of using the names of specific thinkers to label the traditions. For example, in *International Theory: The Three Traditions* he said that 'the Revolutionary Kantian principle (not Kant's!) is that the end justifies the means'.[39] Why did Wight call this a 'Kantian principle' if (as Wight rightly emphasized) Kant himself would not have endorsed it? Since the Revolutionist tradition long precedes Kant, and is at any rate much less conscious and coherent than the other two main traditions in Wight's account, why did Wight name it after Kant? Was it because Kant

Introduction

was the most prominent thinker associated with this tradition, and perhaps the most influential in recent centuries?

Similarly, in the lecture on Kant published in this volume Wight observed that 'belief in progress leads to the type of international theory I am calling Kantian'.[40] Would it not have been more apt to call it simply 'Revolutionist' or 'progressivist', given that many believers in progress have held views at variance with those of Kant? Would it not have been more precise to reserve the term 'Kantian' for the views of Kant and people who explicitly profess to be his followers?

In the same lecture, Wight observed that beyond faith in progress 'the Kantian school' has 'a deeper root in the passionate desire to abolish suffering and sin'. Yet, Wight promptly added, 'The passion to abolish suffering and sin cannot really be found in Kant; he was a puritan, concerned positively with duty; "suffering" and "sin" are words that appear little, if at all, in his writings.'[41] This leads the reader to wonder (1) whether Kant was a member of the Kantian school and (2) why Wight assigned people with this passion to 'the Kantian school'.[42] Such questions, to say nothing of objections and misunderstandings, could have been avoided if Wight had employed only the abstract terms Rationalist, Revolutionist, and Realist as names for the traditions he discerned.

In *International Theory: The Three Traditions*, Machiavelli, Grotius, and Kant serve largely as symbols or types representative of traditions of political thought or practice, whereas in *Four Seminal Thinkers* they appear as once-living men confronting specific problems, and with their own idiosyncrasies, strengths, and weaknesses. These lectures foreshadow Wight's career at the University of Sussex as a historian of European thought.

Wight on Machiavelli

Wight's lecture offers a valuable complement to his comments on Machiavelli in other works, even though it is less coherent

Introduction

and offers less biographical insight than the others in this volume. Indeed, at times in the lengthy and absorbing digressions about related or opposed ideas and incidents one almost loses sight of the Florentine. In Wight's view,

> The only political philosopher of whom it is possible to argue whether his principal interest was not in the relations between states rather than—or even more than—the state itself, is Machiavelli. With him, the foreign and domestic conditions for the establishment and maintenance of state power are not distinguished systematically; and this alone—without other reasons—would have justified his being annexed, by detractors and admirers alike, as the tutelary hero of International Relations.[43]

Yet Wight saw other reasons to identify Machiavelli as a pivotal thinker. While Machiavelli was not alone in making 'a self-conscious, decisive break with the scholastic method', as Wight noted in this lecture, '*The Prince* was the first political pamphlet to reject transcendentalism'.[44] By this Wight evidently meant rejecting the ancient search for the principles of divine and natural law and instead observing actual behaviour and drawing conclusions of expediency. Wight called Machiavelli

> the first man (since the Greeks) to look at politics without ethical presuppositions. He was in a real sense the inventor of Realism. He made a conscious break away from the theologico-ethical Rationalism dominant in the Middle Ages, and equally from the latent Revolutionism (or its antecedents) which ran back to the origins of Christianity.[45]

> He conceived of politics as the practical art of obtaining and preserving state power as an end in itself; political power in itself was the natural and sufficient end of government. For Rationalists, the art of government and the business of politics is a means to an end—the security and comparative freedom of the rational man. For Machiavelli, the individual is the raw material of government, from which the ruler manufactures state power. This is implicit in . . . the whole development of the modern sovereign state in defiance of supra-national religious loyalties. Realism asserts the finality of politics: of all human

Introduction

institutions the political category contains the ultimate meaning; politics is for politics' sake ... The essence of the Realist doctrine of political obligation is that politics is the source of morality and law, that power is therefore self-justifying, and the category of politics contains the ultimate meaning.[46]

It is therefore logical that Wight discussed Hegel and Marx and their followers at some length in his lecture on Machiavelli in this volume. Realists and Revolutionists share, Wight noted, a tendency to locate ultimate meaning within politics and history instead of religion and moral convictions. Because they make results the 'chief criterion of action', Realists—and some Revolutionists—emphasize 'immediate utility' over permanent moral obligations.[47] As Wight once pointed out,

The fifteenth century saw the Ottoman menace through the haze of heroism and piety engendered by the crusading ideal ... In the twentieth century policies have on the whole become cooler and more pragmatic, reflecting the spirit of Machiavelli, who advocated a rational approach to politics even more clearly than an economical use of unscrupulousness.[48]

Wight chose Machiavelli as the eponym for the Realist tradition and referred to authors 'whom it is convenient to call the Machiavellians: the succession of writers on *raison d'état* of whom Meinecke is the great interpreter'.[49] As in the Machiavelli lecture in this volume, however, Wight often quoted Hobbes as representative of the Realists and linked the Florentine and the Englishman as kindred spirits, with many ideas in common:

If we are all realists nowadays, it is because we have all been influenced by the political philosophy of Machiavelli and Hobbes, as it has been refurbished by Professor [E. H.] Carr in this country and Professor [Hans] Morgenthau in America, pre-eminent among a host of lesser writers.[50]

Ever since Machiavelli and Hobbes there have been those who take the view that there is no such thing as international society: that international relations constitute an anarchy whose social elements are negligible.[51]

Introduction

Wight also discerned parallels between elements of Machiavelli's thinking and that of Hitler.

And though Hitler moved by intuition, and lacked anything resembling Napoleon's intellectual clarity over a wide horizon, he made power politics the object of his study; he understood the theory of it; and he has left dicta thereon as penetrating and enduring as Machiavelli's, like the principles that the masses fall victims more readily to the big lie than the small lie, and that a shrewd conqueror will enforce his exactions by stages.[52]

Hitler, as befitting the Borgia of an age of universal semi-literacy and popular journalism, was both Cesare and Machiavelli in one; and had expressed very early in his career, under a transparent veil of detachment, the consciousness of being the rare combination of practical politician and political thinker.[53]

An aggressive Power tends to independent action; it is cautious about association with other Powers except upon its own terms; if it enters into engagements they will be bilateral, not multilateral. 'I principi debbono fuggire quanto possono lo stare a discrezione d'altri.' Like Napoleon, Hitler aimed at separate transactions with every Power, and avoided general negotiations.[54]

Wight held, however, that Hitler represented an extreme version of the Machiavellian preoccupation with power. As Wight observed in the lecture in this volume, Machiavelli himself could be rather 'unMachiavellian', at least in the popular sense of the term, in his interest not only in what was expedient but also in what was honourable and in his passionate desire for Italy's liberation from foreign dominance. In contrast, Wight held, Hitler lacked any positive principles of morality or any political purpose beyond the accumulation of power.

Virtù and *fortuna* are opposite sides of the Machiavellian coin. Hitler's policy, having no principle except the extension of German power, was in practice completely opportunist . . . Power becomes opportunist in expression the more it is emancipated from morality; it becomes destructive in character in proportion as it has no purpose save its own

Introduction

expansion. Thus opportunism passes over into nihilism. Hitler's opportunism was carried to an extent that probably was without parallel in previous Western history. Since his aims were limitless, and his methods unqualified by conformity to any exterior standard, his power tended, when checked in its operation, to destroy both itself and the field in which it was exercised.[55]

Wight also cited Machiavelli frequently with reference to the balance of power. As Wight pointed out, 'The original meaning of the phrase [balance of power] is *an even distribution of power*, a state of affairs in which no power is so preponderant that it can endanger the others. When Machiavelli said that, before the French invasion of 1494, "Italy was in a way balanced," he was describing such a condition of things.'[56] Wight nonetheless highlighted the limitations of Machiavelli's thinking about the balance of power:

Machiavelli is the analyst of how a balance of power collapses, and shows little understanding of how it is maintained . . . Machiavelli describes a policy of divide and rule, though not under that name, as one of the arts of peace whereby a faction-ridden state may be brought voluntarily to submit. He also mentions it as a means of breaking up a hostile coalition. He discusses the related issue of the problem of a neutral's policy in a neighbour's war, and gives equivocal advice: usually it is better to side *against* the stronger Power, but in times of necessity to side *with* him may pay off. He assumes that states are normally on the offensive.[57]

If we go back to 1494 [for the origins of the modern states-system, signified for many by the French invasion of Italy in that year], though Machiavelli writes the foreword to the story, it quickly moves into a chapter he neither foresaw nor was capable of understanding, and we watch the states-system being shaped by the strains of four generations of doctrinal conflict, and of a bipolar balance of power.[58]

That is, Machiavelli could not have anticipated the wars of the Reformation and Counter-Reformation or the bipolar balance of power between France and the Habsburgs from the late fifteenth century into the seventeenth century.

Introduction

Wight on Grotius

The lecture on Grotius in this volume richly supplements Wight's previously published reflections on a thinker he greatly admired and frequently quoted. Wight acknowledged that it can be difficult to find one's way through 'the baroque thickets of Grotius's work, where profound and potent principles lurk in the shade of forgotten arguments and obsolete examples like violets beneath overgrown gigantic rhododendrons'.[59] In Grotius's defence, Wight suggested, 'the fruitful confusion of his terminology corresponds to the fruitful confusion of the facts of international life'.[60]

Moreover, Grotius is 'usually taken as the great exemplar' for 'those who accept the states-system as constituting a valid society of mutual right and obligations'.[61] Indeed, 'Grotius' whole work was an attempt to restate and revive the criteria of just war. This inaugurated the modern development of international law, which has tended increasingly to seek legal criteria for a just war.'[62]

Tocqueville, Wight noted, was among the first to identify Grotius and other 'classical international lawyers' as pioneering theorists of international politics.[63] Wight and other historians have linked the Dutch thinker's fame to the Peace of Westphalia in 1648, marking the end of the Thirty Years' War.

The prestige of Westphalia was buttressed by that of Grotius, whose reputation as father of international law was due to a work prompted by the same general war that Westphalia ended. It seems to have been Grotius, incidentally, who brought the word 'system' into the vocabulary of international politics, though not yet in the sense of the whole diplomatic community.[64]

For Wight, however, the main contributions of Grotius resided in his well-balanced articulations of the Rationalist tradition in Western diplomatic history. In Wight's view,

[T]here may be reasons for thinking that the tradition we are at present considering is specially representative of Western values. One is its explicit connection with the political philosophy of constitutional government. The other is its quality of a *via media*. This pattern of ideas

Introduction

usually appears as the *juste milieu* between definable extremes, whether it is Grotius saying: 'A remedy must be found for those that believe that in war nothing is lawful, and for those for whom all things are lawful in war' or Halifax's classic exposition of the balance of power in *The Character of a Trimmer*, or Gladstone's conception of the European Concert seen as a middle way between the radical non-interventionism of Cobden and Bright and the *Realpolitik* of Beaconsfield and Bismarck ... The golden mean can be an overcautious and ignoble principle as a guide to action, but it may also be an index to the accumulated experience of a civilization which has valued disciplined scepticism and canonized prudence as a political virtue. The disposition to think of true policy as a difficult path between seductive but simplified alternatives is a likely, though not of course an infallible, sign of the tradition we are concerned with.[65]

Wight repeatedly contrasted the Grotian, or Rationalist, *via media* to the extremes endorsed by Revolutionists and Realists.

Fiat justitia et pereat mundus marks an extreme position. The opposite extreme has many landmarks, from the Athenian case in the Melian Dialogue to Fisher's dictum at the Hague Conference, 'If the welfare of England requires it, international agreements can go to the Devil', and Salandra's *sacro egoismo per l'Italia*. Between lies the moral sense we are considering. It can reach the point of uttering a moral prohibition in politics. But it assumes that moral standards can be upheld without the heavens falling. And it assumes that the fabric of social and political life will be maintained, without accepting the doctrine that to preserve it any measures are permissible. For it assumes that the upholding of moral standards will in itself tend to strengthen the fabric of political life.[66]

As Wight noted, Revolutionists have characteristically rejected Grotius and other exponents of international law. 'The Rights of Man were transformed into universal conquest without, it seems, any theorizing more sophisticated or less negative than the statement by Genêt which Fox quoted in the House of Commons: "I would throw Vattel and Grotius into the sea whenever their principles interfere with my notions of the rights of nations." '[67]

Introduction

Wight underscored the importance of Grotian thinking by drawing attention to its absence in antiquity.

Hellas for the Greeks was a community of blood and language and religion and way of life; but the Greeks never developed the theory of a society of states mutually bound by legal rights and obligations. There was no Greek Grotius. And the international experience of Rome, first in the consolidating of Italy, and then in the Mediterranean world at large, was that of conqueror, aggressive ally and patron of clients—never of equal intercourse between states . . . Such thought as the ancients gave to international ethics found little middle ground between the statesman's personal honour on the one side, and on the other, the justification of what we should describe as humane action on grounds of pure expediency . . . Perhaps it is a characteristic of medieval and modern Europe that, in contrast to classical civilization, it has cultivated this middle ground, and developed the conception of a political morality distinct equally from personal morality and from *Realpolitik*.[68]

Grotius's first great work, *De Jure Praedae*, concerned whether Dutch investors could rightfully benefit from the forcible seizure of an enemy's property, even in a just war. Accordingly, Wight observed,

At the very beginning of the classical literature of international law there is this dramatic confrontation between the state that is law-abiding even in war and the delinquent state (it is also a confrontation between the state with constitutional processes and the despotic state). The *De Jure Praedae* argued that in international society there could be a robber or bandit, *praedo* or *latro*, whose crime even according to the established law of nations deserved punishment; that it was in the interest of the international community and of unconcerned nations that violation of the law should not pass unnoticed; that a penal code for states was as indispensable as a penal code for citizens. This was the central doctrine of Grotius's bigger and more famous book, published twenty-one years later, when he was no longer pleading the cause of the Seven Provinces against Portugal, but of international society at large against all the Great Powers. If there is an international society at all, then its members have duties, and the duties are enforceable.[69]

xxxiii

Introduction

Grotius's thinking, Wight pointed out, emphasized sociability and social obligations involving custom as well as moral and legal obligations.

'There is no state so powerful that it may not some time need the help of others outside itself, either for purposes of trade, or even to ward off the forces of many foreign nations against it,' said Grotius. 'In consequence, we see that even the most powerful peoples and sovereigns seek alliances.' He was arguing that the essential sociability of human nature shows itself in the connections formed even by states and princes, and moreover that all these connections are governed by universal law.[70]

Grotius likewise conceded that the social condition was inaugurated by the social contract but argued that the pre-contractual state of nature was the condition of sociability—the capacity for becoming social ... Sovereign states, they [the Grotians] will say, do form a society; they do not exist in a political or cultural vacuum, but in continuous political relations with one another. It is a society which must be understood on its own terms and not by comparison with domestic society, a society governed less by force, as the thinkers of the first group [the Machiavellians] may hold, than by custom. It is a society with a system of law that is crude and not centrally enforced but still true law, a society without a government but regulated by certain special institutions such as diplomacy, the balance of power, and alliances.[71]

If 'international society' is the conception preferred by Grotians, as opposed to the 'international anarchy' discerned by the Machiavellians, how should this society be described?

In Grotius's description of international society there is a fruitful imprecision. *Communis societas generis humani, communis illa ex humano genere constans societas, humana societas, magna illa communitas, magna illa universitas, magna illa gentium societas, mutua gentium inter se societas, illa mundi civitas, societas orbis*—such is his range of language. Are kings or peoples or individuals the members of this ambiguous society? exclaims the positivist in irritation. All were. Nor was this tradition entirely eclipsed by the orthodox doctrine of state-personality. Perhaps it might be said that it survived among the lawyers who saw international law rather as a legitimate child of political philosophy than as a recalcitrant vassal of legal science.[72]

The wide array of members in international society, as conceived by Grotius, means that rulers face difficult and complex choices in trying to meet their moral obligations. Wight cited Grotius with regard to both intervention and neutrality.

'Kings,' said Grotius, 'in addition to the particular care of their own state, are also burdened with a general responsibility for human society,' and the idea has been repeated in many ways. Intervention, therefore, may present itself as an exercise, not simply of the right of self-preservation, but of the duty of fellow-feeling and co-operation. Seen in this light, the theory of the rightful occasions for intervention falls at once into the same pattern as the theory of the just causes of war...

Humanitarian grounds for intervention were conceived first of all in terms of protection against tyranny, and the right of intervention followed the right of rebellion. Here is one of the explicit links between constitutionalist political theory and the tradition of international theory under present consideration. Grotius was surprisingly cautious about the right of rebellion (perhaps, as Carlyle suggested, because he was a Roman lawyer and a political refugee in the French monarchy): he refused to allow oppressed subjects to take up arms in their own behalf, but permitted a foreign Power to intervene for them, as an application of the principle of trusteeship: 'quod uni non licet, alteri pro eodem liceri potest.'[73]

In the sixteenth and seventeenth centuries, when international law was in its earliest development, and the very word 'neutrality' was a new coinage, the right of neutrality was limited by the doctrine of the just war. Thus Grotius laid down that a state which wishes to be impartial in a conflict must not hinder the belligerent whose cause is just nor help the belligerent whose cause is unjust... The three great international constitutional instruments of the twentieth century—the League Covenant, the Kellogg–Briand Treaty for the Renunciation of War, and the United Nations Charter—have not abolished the institution of neutrality but they have transformed it back into something resembling the status outlined by Grotius—they have transformed it

Introduction

back from a duty of absolute impartiality into a neutrality that must not be indifferent to the moral issues involved.[74]

Wight frequently found in Grotius examples to illustrate the *via media* approach he deemed representative of the Rationalist tradition.

It has generally been recognized that there is a point of change from international fair weather to storm, where the art of political navigation must discard some methods and take on others, and diplomacy becomes occupied less with seeking agreement than with arranging coercion. It is the point, in Sir Harold Nicolson's precise language, 'where diplomacy ends and foreign policy begins.' Grotius was concerned with it, when he sought to define the justifiable causes of war as defence, recovery of rights, and punishment; it was later described in terms of rectifying the balance of power; it was at the heart of the doctrine of collective security. That the point of change is difficult to define in general terms does not bear out those who deny its reality, asserting on the one side that all foreign policy is potential war, or on the other side that diplomacy is nothing but conciliation.[75]

For all his admiration of Grotius, Wight recognized certain limitations in his thinking. For example, Wight pointed out,

Grotius presents the dual or concentric conception of international society. There is an outer circle that embraces all mankind, under natural law, and an inner circle, the *corpus Christianorum*, bound by the law of Christ. The inner circle is unique. Grotius still accepts implicitly the traditional Christian view of history, and does not have sufficient knowledge of the non-European world to develop a more complex picture.[76]

The conception of Christendom as a 'common cause' led Grotius to champion unity in combat against the Ottoman Turks. In Wight's words, 'Grotius came off his naturalistic fence and asserted the obligation of all Christians to join an alliance against the enemies of Christianity, "an impious enemy raging in arms . . . All Christians ought to contribute men or money, according to their capacity, *ad causam hanc communem*."'[77]

Introduction

All Christian kings and peoples should form an alliance as was once made, Grotius declared, by unanimous consent under the Holy Roman Emperor. At this point, Wight noted, by 'using a faulty historical argument', Grotius 'momentarily degrades Christendom to make it fit one of his political categories'.[78]

Furthermore, Wight acknowledged that the Dutch thinker's influence on actual state behaviour was at best limited and indirect.

The old view that Grotius had a humanizing influence on the later stages of the Thirty Years' War no longer has any credit. 'Undoubtedly, the general picture of international relations in the two centuries which followed the publication of *De Jure Belli ac Pacis*,' Lauterpacht has written, 'was not one pointing to any direct influence, in the sphere of practice, of the essential features of the Grotian teaching.'[79]

Wight on Kant

Wight's lecture on Kant in this volume enriches understanding of how his respect for the celebrated German philosopher magnified his disappointment regarding the philosopher's work on international politics. Kant was hardly alone among Enlightenment thinkers in condemning standing armies, national debts, and other instruments of 'the rivalries of power politics'.[80]

In the time of William III and Louis XIV, it had seemed that constitutional states, states acknowledging a principle of balance in their internal affairs, were predisposed towards the balance of power in foreign policy, while absolute monarchs tended to pursue their own glory or even universal empire. But the doctrines of democracy, growing up in the generation of Kant and Tom Paine, condemned impartially all the ancient regimes, along with the traditional states-system compounded of the balance of power, secret diplomacy, *raison d'état*, and militarism. The balance of power now seemed to have produced its final fruits in the Partitions of Poland.[81]

Introduction

Nor was Kant particularly singular in looking beyond the balance of power to the notion of a peaceful and expanding federation of constitutional states.

Kant's treatment of the balance of power perhaps shows the intellectual rejection of the idea consolidating itself. In the *Idee zu einer allgemeinen Geschichte* (1784) he seems to see 'ein Gesetz des Gleichgewichts,' for the regulation of the wholesome antagonism of contiguous states as if springing up out of their freedom, as a half-way house to the international federation which he advocates. In the *Verhaeltnis der Theorie zur Praxis im Voelkerrecht* (1793) he wrote:

'The maintenance of universal peace by means of the so-called Balance of Power in Europe is—like Swift's house, which a master-builder constructed in such perfect accord with all the laws of equilibrium, that when a sparrow alighted upon it, it immediately collapsed—a mere figment of the imagination.'

The doctrines of the American and French Revolutions seemed to offer an alternative principle for international society, fraternal, uncompetitive, above all simple. For all who were touched by these doctrines the balance of power was condemned as an obsolete principle of the Ancien Regime, the diplomatic counterpart of hereditary absolute monarchy.[82]

Kant was exceptional, however, in arguing that Nature and impersonal historical factors would bring about positive changes in international politics and ultimately eliminate war.

There are two historical agencies which, in this pattern of thinking, promote desirable international change. Kant, who is responsible for so much else in modern thought, was as far as I know the first to describe these historical agencies in this context. First was what he called 'the commercial spirit,' 'which cannot exist along with war, and which sooner or later controls every people.' We should probably translate it as the growing material interdependence of mankind, due to the economic unification of the world and industrialization . . . Second was what Kant called 'the spirit of enlightenment.' 'Enlightenment . . . must ever draw mankind away from the egoistic expansive tendencies of its rulers once they understand their own advantage.' We might translate it as the growing moral interdependence of mankind due to education, cultural exchange, and intellectual standardization. It is manifested in the formation of a world public opinion, which some see as the animating principle of the United Nations. Kant's imaginary treaty of Perpetual Peace contained a secret article, that before going to war, governments must consult the maxims of the philosophers. It is not to be expected (he says) that kings should philosophize or philosophers become kings, but kings can let philosophers speak freely, 'because this is indispensable for both in order to clarify their business.' . . . This 'secret article' is the expression and possibly the direct inspiration of the Wilsonian belief that enlightened public opinion, instructed public opinion in all countries, will promote peace and goodwill in international affairs.[83]

The twin Kantian demiurges engaged in creating peace are the increased power of public opinion, and the increased administrative control of increasingly cautious and responsive state-machines over the means of violence.[84]

Wight professed some respect for Kant's analysis of public opinion and 'open diplomacy', and called the two lengthy appendices on 'publicity' and on harmonizing politics and morals 'the profoundest part' of the essay on 'Perpetual Peace'.[85] Wight evidently found Kant's reasoning in this regard astute and even shrewd.[86] He nonetheless concluded that at least one element of Kant's theory failed to pass the test of empirical experience. For all the differences between the states-system of ancient Greece and that of the contemporary world, Wight judged, one of the similarities that 'stands out is the total inability of international public opinion to affect the march of events. In practical terms, Isocrates failed to influence policy as definitely as did the post-Kantian peace movements of the nineteenth and twentieth centuries.'[87]

More fundamentally, Wight was disappointed by Kant's argument that 'peace will take care of itself . . . , [that] there is a fundamental historical trend, in the development of modern society and of collective psychology, towards the containment

Introduction

and obsolescence of war'.[88] Wight rejected the automaticity implied in some of Kant's declarations and upheld a Grotian perspective of 'bringing war under political control, and strengthening the rudiments of international government'.[89] As Wight wrote in one of the last works he prepared for publication before his death in 1972, 'The belief that the nuclear deterrent has abolished war revived the Kantian illusion of a guarantee of perpetual peace beyond the responsibility of man; the *deus ex machina* now being not commercial interdependence but weapons development.'[90]

Kant also disappointed Wight because he combined his 'slide-over into theodicy'[91]—his argument for God's holiness and justice, despite His having allowed the existence of physical and moral evils—with an 'argument from desperation' that disregarded historical evidence.

In progressivist international theories, the conviction usually precedes the evidence. And when the conviction is analysed or disintegrates, one is apt to find at the centre of it what might be called the argument from desperation. This is already used by Kant, who first channelled the doctrine of progress into international theory through his *Eternal Peace*. Having established the three definite articles of an eternal peace, he argues that such a peace is guaranteed by Nature herself, who wills that we should do what reason presents to us as a duty; *volentem ducit, nolentem trahit*. And she effects this by means of the commercial spirit, which cannot coexist with war, and sooner or later controls every nation. 'In this way Nature guarantees the conditions of perpetual peace by the mechanism involved in our human inclinations themselves.' But a little later, in discussing the disagreement between morals and politics in relation to eternal peace, he seems to reach the ultimate point of his argument, and to take a flying leap beyond it:

'The process of creation, by which such a brood of corrupt beings has been put upon the earth, can apparently be justified by no theodicy or theory of Providence, if we assume that it never will be better, nor can be better, with the human race ... We shall thus be inevitably driven

Introduction

to a position of despair in consequence of such reasonings . . . , if we do not admit that the pure principles of right and justice have objective reality and that they can be realized in fact.'

It is surely not a good argument for a theory of international politics that we shall be driven to despair if we do not accept it. But it is an argument that comes naturally to the children of Hegel (and Kant) when they are faced with defeat.[92]

Indeed, Wight regarded Kantian and Hegelian assumptions about inevitable progress as potentially dangerous because they implied a divinization of politics.

Whereas the Rationalist denies the ultimacy of politics and finality of human institutions, the Revolutionist condemns the existing system of power by a standard external to that system of power but drawn from within the political category. He resembles the Realist in finding the ultimate meaning within the realm of politics; indeed he divinizes the political category: it is politics which prescribe human goals, the right of moral judgement and duty of action.[93]

It is for this reason, Wight suggested, that followers of Kantian ideals—contrary to Kant's own practical prescriptions—could be merciless and unrestrained in overturning the old order; they could see themselves as righteous agents of historical necessity bringing about a better world.

A hundred years before Hitler came to power, Heine, in the most astonishing political prophecy of the nineteenth century, foretold a German Revolution which would make the French Revolution seem like an innocent idyll, when Thor and the old stone gods would arise from the forgotten ruins and wipe from their eyes the dust of centuries, there would appear 'Kantians as little tolerant of piety in the world of deeds as in the world of ideas, who will mercilessly upturn with sword and axe the soil of our European life in order to extirpate the last remnants of the past,' and there would be aroused again the ancient German eagerness for battle, which Christianity had not entirely quenched, and 'which combats not for the sake of destroying, not even for the sake of victory, but merely for the sake of the combat itself.'[94]

Introduction

Wight on Mazzini

Mazzini's thinking paralleled that of Kant, Wight noted, in that both advocated adapting 'all existing states, members of international society, to a pattern of conformity which alone confers legitimacy'.[95] While Kant proposed that every state have a constitutional regime, Mazzini carried the principle 'to a more extreme point than with Kant: that there would be no valid international society till all its members were nation-states. This was the principle of national self-determination which triumphed in 1919.'[96] In Wight's incisive and illuminating account, Mazzini served as a prophet of a new doctrine of international legitimacy and order.

> Mazzini preached that the Vienna Settlement of 1815 had no moral validity and that it was necessary to reconstruct the map of Europe 'in accordance with the special mission assigned to each people.' ... A new doctrine of international legitimacy was modifying the foundations of international society, replacing tradition by consent, prescription by national self-determination . . . The doctrine that there are no valid members of international society save those born of national self-determination triumphed when in the shock of the First World War, the military multinational empires of Eastern Europe—German, Habsburg, Russian and Ottoman—collapsed. The Versailles Settlement was the final victory in Europe of the French Revolution over the Holy Alliance.[97]

Wight illustrated the Revolutionist thrust of Mazzini's thinking in various ways.[98]

> We all know that Engels described insurrection as an art, and expounded its principles; it is less often remembered that Mazzini, the Gandhi of nineteenth-century liberalism, wrote a set of 'Rules for the Conduct of Guerrilla Bands.'[99]

> The first impulse of a revolutionary power is to abolish diplomacy altogether, even to abolish foreign policy. ... It was in the same spirit that Mazzini, the conspirator and propagandist of the Italian Risorgimento, argued against Cavour the politician that an honest faith in ideals and

principles was worth more than the calculations, indecisions and dishonesties of diplomacy.[100]

Thus, Mazzini's argument that the principle of non-intervention could only be justified if the international system that is not to be intervened against is itself already perfectly just, which it isn't.

'What does this non-intervention principle in real fact now mean? It means precisely this—Intervention on the wrong side; Intervention by all who choose, and are strong enough, to put down free movements of peoples against corrupt governments. It means co-operation of despots against peoples, but no co-operation of peoples against despots.'

Mazzini's doctrine has become the doctrine of the anti-colonialist campaign in the United Nations.[101]

Wight suggested that Mazzini's teaching contributed to a complex dialectic of intoxicating and antagonistic ideas, with particularly potent effects in Eastern Europe, where new nation-states were built out of the ruins of the collapsed multinational empires.

Democratic nationalism, like all great political forces, supplied also the dominant conception of political justice of its time; and its fruition in the collapse of the eastern empires had the character, for those involved in it, of a tremendous act of emancipation. Like its great predecessors 1789 and 1848, the year 1918 brought the sense of revolutionary fulfilment, the beginning of a new age, the bliss of springtime or of dawn. This intoxication was itself perhaps the most important political circumstance of the Peace Conference, especially in its dealings with Eastern Europe, and the reaction from it was one of the most important aspects, cause as much as effect, of the rise of Nazi Germany. The same dialectic that had led from the Festival of the Federation to the Terror and the Empire, and from Lamartine and Bakunin and Mazzini to Louis Napoleon and Bach and Cavour, led also from the liberated Eastern Europe whose most splendid figure was Masaryk to the Eastern Europe of March 1939, dominated by the Eastern European expatriate who had become Führer of the German Reich.[102]

The most significant shortcoming identified in Mazzini's thinking, as in the analysis of Kant's approach, resided in the

Introduction

Italian prophet's refusal to recognize what Wight called 'the intractable difficulties of international order'. While the leading powers would have to accept responsibility for the enforcement of that order, including maintaining the balance of power, to offer any prospect of its becoming coherent and reliable, the notion of an enduring harmony of interstate relations was but a 'Mazzinian dream'.

The belief that the dismantling of empires would increase world stability, since the emergent states, their political grievances satisfied by the withdrawal of their colonial rulers, would become absorbed in economic development and in giving a moral lead to the Great Powers, revived the Mazzinian dream of a harmony of nations. There has been a desire to repudiate the intractable difficulties of international order.[103]

The balance of power had been a system of keeping international order. Kant and Cobden, Mazzini and the Peace Societies, assumed in their different ways that the enforcement of international order was unnecessary. The conflicting tendencies ripened simultaneously in the Versailles Settlement. On the one hand, the system of the balance of power, as formulated by its more reflective exponents, foreshadowed the collective security advocated by a majority (having all the member countries in view) of the adherents of the League of Nations. Collective security meant giving the system of the balance of power a legal framework, to make it more rational, more reliable, and therefore more effectively preventive. On the other hand, collective security failed largely because of those who believed that international order was not dependent so much upon maintaining the balance of power as upon satisfying claims to national justice.[104]

In other words, Mazzini's dream was to imagine that competing claims to national justice could be satisfied without recurrent conflict, and that the satisfaction of these claims would readily provide international order and peace. Furthermore, as Wight pointed out, Mazzini 'assumed that nationality meant democracy'.[105] In his enthusiasm for overthrowing Habsburg rule in Italy, Mazzini asserted that the achievement of valid national aspirations in Europe would bring democracy in domestic politics and lasting

Introduction

concord in international politics. He evidently gave little thought to how anti-democratic political movements could exploit nationalism or to how desires for national self-determination could inspire separatist minorities within established states and also far beyond Europe. Nor did he consider conflicts between two peoples asserting passionate national claims to the same territory.

The Merits of Wight's Approach

Perhaps the most fundamental question raised by Wight's work concerns the kinds of knowledge that can be achieved in theoretical inquiry in international relations. Kenneth Waltz has complained that 'Among the depressing features of international-political studies is the small gain in explanatory power that has come from the large amount of work done in recent decades. Nothing seems to accumulate, not even criticism.'[106] In response to a similar lament, Stanley Hoffmann wrote that 'Waltz seems to blame the theorists, rather than asking whether the fiasco does not result from the very nature of the field. Can there *be* a theory of undetermined behavior, which is what "diplomatic-strategic action," to use [Raymond] Aron's terms, amounts to?'[107]

The free wills, differing priorities, and ultimately contingent choices of the many decision-makers in international politics place severe limits on the aspirations towards 'prediction' and 'explanation' held by some scholars. As Hoffmann noted, Aron has 'demonstrated why a theory of undetermined behavior cannot consist of a set of propositions explaining general laws that make prediction possible, and can do little more than define basic concepts, analyze basic configurations, sketch out the permanent features of a constant logic of behavior, in other words make the field intelligible'.[108]

From this perspective, as Bull observed, theoretical work in international relations is 'philosophical in character. It does not lead to cumulative knowledge after the manner of natural

Introduction

science ... All of this must follow once we grant Wight's initial assumption that theoretical inquiry into International Relations is necessarily about moral or prescriptive questions.'[109] Indeed, Wight argued that 'historical interpretation' is the counterpart of political theory for international politics, and wrote that he was tempted to say that 'there is no international theory except the kind of rumination about human destiny to which we give the unsatisfactory name of philosophy of history'.[110] Wight added that 'judging the validity of ... ethical principles ... is not a process of scientific analysis; it is more akin to literary criticism. It involves developing a sensitive awareness of the intractability of all political situations, and the moral quandary in which all statecraft operates.'[111] To develop such an awareness, Wight recommended the study of history, starting with Thucydides, and of works of literature by authors such as Conrad, Hardy, Koestler, Orwell, Swift, and Tolstoy.[112]

As the lectures published in this volume demonstrate, Wight had a talent for grasping each thinker's core principles, with great empathy and lucidity, yet with an awareness of the thinker's limitations and historical context. Wight could elucidate links among the principles articulated by seminal philosophers while simultaneously drawing sharp distinctions.

Kant and Grotius agreed, for example, in demanding respect for the rules of warfare. They also agreed on ruling out a world state as improbable, but with some differences. Grotius saw a world government as likely to be ineffective and disadvantageous. Kant judged governments probably unwilling to accept a world state, or 'a *Universal Republic*', and considered a federation of states a '*negative* surrogate' superior to 'a Universal Monarchy' established by force.[113] Unlike Grotius, Kant had a vision of 'a universal *Cosmopolitical Institution*'.[114]

Kant and Mazzini both rejected competitive balance-of-power politics and advocated an international order of consensus and cooperation—in Wight's words, an 'ideal of a federation of republican states, of free self-determining national democracies'.[115]

Kant and Mazzini also shared what Wight termed a 'revolutionary presumption' questioning the legitimacy of existing political regimes and international orders.[116] Yet this presumption was held inconsistently by Kant, who denied the right of rebellion while professing to be a republican and supporting the American and French Revolutions. Similarly, both Kant's notion that 'the only rightful Constitution' is 'Republican'[117] and Mazzini's belief that only national self-determination provides legitimacy are at odds with Grotius, who recognized a variety of legitimate political regimes.

For all their similarities, Kant and Mazzini differed in key ways beyond the fact that, as Wight put it, Mazzini 'thought like a member of a resistance movement in an occupied country'[118] and exhorted patriots to take action, whereas Kant maintained detached and abstemious professorial routines and composed works of systematic philosophy. Mazzini advocated intervention by external powers on moral and ideological grounds, and championed revolutions to overturn unjust regimes and throw off foreign control in the name of national self-determination. One of the articles of Kant's imaginary treaty of Perpetual Peace was, however, that 'No State shall intermeddle by force with the Constitution or Government of another State.'[119]

Kant lacked Mazzini's romantic convictions about the moral purpose, mission, and destiny of specific nations. Kant held that

> if happy circumstances bring it about that a powerful and enlightened people form themselves into a Republic—which by its very nature must be disposed in favour of Perpetual Peace—this will furnish a centre of federative union for other States to attach themselves to, and thus to secure the conditions of Liberty among all States, according to the idea of the Right of Nations.[120]

However, Kant did not name the nation destined to perform that role.[121] In contrast, Mazzini believed that Providence had assigned a special primacy among nations to Italy and particular missions in service to humanity to other European nations.[122]

Introduction

Kant also lacked Mazzini's antipathy to Irish nationalism and deep distrust of French diplomacy. Nor was Kant concerned about the risk of 'nationalist imposters' that Mazzini anticipated—as Wight put it, 'that nationalist societies without a moral aim might force their way to membership of international society'.[123]

Kant's belief that Nature (a term he often preferred to God or Providence) is benevolently guiding the march of history to a fulfilment unknown to men and 'even against their will'[124] stands at variance with his own call to individual duty and with the views of Machiavelli, Grotius, and Mazzini, who all emphasized the responsibilities of individual decision-makers, especially those holding high government offices.[125] Machiavelli's conception of the political arena offers little scope for protection by a benign Providence, with its emphasis on fortune as 'the ruler of half our actions'.[126]

Grotius and Machiavelli shared a disbelief in progress, if that means the Perpetual Peace foreseen by Kant and, in somewhat different form, by Mazzini. Kant's expectation of 'a great future political Body, such as the world has never yet seen'[127] and his admonition that 'We must work for what may perhaps not be realized' and thus 'put an end to the evil of wars'[128] stands in contrast with the Grotian assumption that the abolition of war is infeasible and Machiavelli's view that struggle and conflict are normal.

Grotius and Machiavelli both attached importance to 'a sense of honour' as a determinant of proper behaviour, and had in common a fondness for examples drawn from ancient Greece and Rome. However, they differed fundamentally in their moral viewpoints. Machiavelli appealed to arguments of expediency and necessity:

> [A] prince, and especially a new prince, cannot observe all those things which are considered good in men, being often obliged, in order to maintain the state, to act against faith, against charity, against humanity, and against religion . . . [I]n the actions of men, and especially of princes, from which there is no appeal, the end justifies the means.[129]

Introduction

A prince should therefore have no other aim or thought, nor take up any other thing for his study, but war and its organisation and discipline, for that is the only art that is necessary to one who commands, and it is of such virtue that it not only maintains those who are born princes, but often enables men of private fortune to attain to that rank.[130]

Machiavelli even suggested that 'a wise prince ought, when he has the chance, to foment astutely some enmity, so that by suppressing it he will augment his greatness'.[131]

In contrast, Grotius rejected 'personal or collective self-aggrandizement' as a justification for war,[132] and also questioned the justice of undertaking war

to weaken a growing power which, if it become too great, may be a source of danger. That this consideration does enter into deliberations regarding war, I admit, but only on grounds of expediency, not of justice. . . . [T]hat the possibility of being attacked confers the right to attack is abhorrent to every principle of equity. Human life exists under such conditions that complete security is never guaranteed to us. For protection against uncertain fears we must rely on Divine Providence, and on a wariness free from reproach, not on force.[133]

Grotius appears in this passage to have had preventive war in mind—that is, war undertaken to avert a plausible but hypothetical future risk, such as an adverse imbalance of power, a position of increased vulnerability, or even potential subjugation. His position regarding pre-emptive attack—that is, action on the basis of evidence that an enemy is about to strike—seems unclear. Grotius held that war must be declared, but added that 'no interval of time is required after the declaration' before conducting military operations.[134]

Grotius acknowledged several just grounds for war, such as self-defence, the recovery of property, and the infliction of deserved punishments. Moreover, the principle that 'kings, and those who possess rights equal to those kings, have the right of demanding punishments not only on account of injuries committed against themselves or their subjects, but also on account of injuries which do not directly affect them but excessively violate the law of nature or of nations in regard to any persons whatsoever'[135] affirms the justice of using force in support of collective security and humanitarian obligations.[136]

At the same time, however, Grotius considered at length 'Rules dictated by prudence' in deliberating about 'ultimate ends' and 'the means which lead thereto'.[137] In view of the profound evils and uncertainties in war, Grotius found several grounds for holding that 'war is not to be undertaken for every just cause' and that it may be wiser and 'more upright and just' in particular circumstances 'to forgo punishments', even if one has been wronged.[138] The proposition that 'a cause for engaging in war which either may not be passed over, or ought not to be, is exceptional'[139] makes clear the distance between Machiavelli and Grotius with regard to 'necessity' as a justification for war.

The Florentine was fascinated by what Wight called 'the unfathomable complexity, the multiple causes, the cross-currents, accidents, unintended results, the ironies of politics',[140] while the Dutchman was determined to look beyond accidental and paradoxical upheavals to identify moral and legal standards for the guidance of statesmen from various sources, including natural law, historical practice, and divine revelation.

Indeed, of the four thinkers examined by Wight, Grotius alone was clearly committed to what the Dutchman termed 'the truth of the Christian religion'.[141] Machiavelli may have focused on antiquity as a way of expressing his rejection of Christianity.[142] As Wight pointed out, Kant's metaphysics discarded the 'traditional philosophy' of Plato, Aristotle, and Christian scholasticism; and Kant recommended what he termed *Religion within the Limits of Reason Alone*, a book that provoked royal censure for 'undermining Christianity'.[143] Mazzini was raised a Catholic, knew the New Testament well, and respected Christian morality; but he stopped believing in the divinity of Christ and professed to belong to 'a still purer and higher Faith'.[144]

Introduction

For Machiavelli, as Wight noted, 'it is pointless to make moral judgements about human nature', and *virtù* may dictate a 'bias in favour of extremism and ruthlessness, of firm, decisive action'.[145] At the opposite pole, Kant underscored the uncompromising commands of his 'categorical imperative', and Mazzini employed wording similar to Kant's in insisting on respect for unqualified and indivisible moral standards, whatever the circumstances. Grotius, however, emphasized 'the golden mean, or Aristotelian moderation', in his approach to political morality, and thereby earned Wight's strongest admiration. As Wight observed in the lecture on Grotius,

This is the maze in which we are lost. Grotius reflects more accurately this morally multi-dimensional character of our experience than, arguably, any other writer on the subject ... He reproduces an endless dialectic of the real and ideal, the actual and permissible, with all its tensions and facets, hesitations, and qualifications. To simplify crudely: if you are apt to think the moral problems of international politics are simple, you are a natural, instinctive Kantian; if you think they are non-existent, bogus, or delusory, you are a natural Machiavellian; and if you are apt to think them infinitely complex, bewildering, and perplexing, you are probably a natural Grotian.[146]

Some of the most valuable passages in *Four Seminal Thinkers* involve what might at first glance seem to be extraneous digressions, as when Wight announced, with reference to Machiavelli, 'Underlying this view of politics as a struggle for power there is an issue of pure philosophy.' Beyond defining security, the issue concerns nothing less than 'the ultimate ... essence of the universe', whether harmony or conflict and contradiction.[147]

Wight concluded his lecture on Grotius with a magisterial contrast of Plato's argument that the just man must rule the elements of his soul, including his appetites and passions, with reason and wisdom 'in well-tempered harmony' before the just state can be established[148] and Kant's thesis that 'The problem of the institution of a State ... would not be insoluble even for

Introduction

a race of devils, assuming only that they have intelligence.'[149] In the lecture on Kant, however, Wight pointed out 'a necessary conjunction... between a belief in progress and pessimism about man',[150] and took note of Kant's famous caveat that 'Out of such crooked material as man is made of, nothing can be hammered quite straight.'[151]

Wight's work is so thoroughly rooted in classical Western philosophy, theology, and literature, and his capacity for discerning paradoxes and pitfalls in the arguments of seminal thinkers is so profound that one is reminded of the closing words of the lecture on Mazzini: 'if he has lasting value or interest, it is not because he was an interpreter of his times, or because he wrenched and pummelled history into new channels, but because he drew his spiritual strength from timeless sources'.[152]

Notes

The views expressed are the author's alone and do not represent those of the US Department of the Navy or any US government agency. Special thanks are owed to Pierre Hassner, Brian Porter, and Gabriele Wight for their comments on earlier drafts of this introduction, which draws on the author's essay, 'Political Philosophy and the Theory of International Relations', *International Affairs*, vol. 70 (April 1994), pp. 263–90.

1 Adam Roberts, 'Foreword', in Martin Wight, *International Theory: The Three Traditions*, ed. Gabriele Wight and Brian Porter (Leicester and London: Leicester University Press for the Royal Institute of International Affairs, 1991), p. xxiv.

2 Wight graduated in 1935 from Hertford College, Oxford, with first class honours in modern history. His professional career may be summed up in a few lines: research staff at the Royal Institute of International Affairs, 1936–8; senior history master at Haileybury College, 1938–41; research staff at Nuffield College, Oxford, 1941–6; diplomatic and United Nations correspondent for *The Observer*, London, 1946–7; research staff at the Royal Institute of International Affairs, 1946–9; reader in international relations, London School of

Introduction

Economics, 1949–61; visiting professor, University of Chicago, 1956–7; professor of history and founding dean of the School of European Studies, University of Sussex, 1961–72.

3   See Roy E. Jones, 'The English School of International Relations: A Case for Closure', *Review of International Studies*, vol. 7 (January 1981). There seems to be no generally accepted definition of the English School. While some observers trace its origins to the work in the late 1950s of the British Committee on the Theory of International Politics (to which Wight made major contributions, along with Hedley Bull and others), Tim Dunne's informative study devotes a chapter to E. H. Carr, who was not a member of this committee. Carr was the originator of a distinctive 'English' approach to international relations theory, owing to his classic work, *The Twenty Years' Crisis 1919–1939: An Introduction to the Study of International Relations* (London: Macmillan, 1939). See Tim Dunne, *Inventing International Society: A History of the English School* (Basingstoke and London: Macmillan Press in association with St Antony's College, Oxford, 1998). Hedley Bull listed Wight among scholars pursuing a 'classical approach' to theorizing about international politics, but Wight himself appears to have refrained from categorizing his methodology. See Hedley Bull, 'International Theory: The Case for a Classical Approach', in Klaus Knorr and James N. Rosenau, eds., *Contending Approaches to International Politics* (Princeton, NJ: Princeton University Press, 1969), pp. 20–1. Bull's famous article was first published in *World Politics*, vol. 18 (April 1966), pp. 361–77.

4   Martin Wight, *The Development of the Legislative Council, 1606–1945* (London: Faber and Faber, 1946); *The Gold Coast Legislative Council* (London: Faber and Faber, 1947); and *British Colonial Constitutions 1947* (Oxford: Clarendon Press, 1952).

5   See especially: Martin Wight, *Power Politics* (London: Royal Institute of International Affairs, 1946); 'Germany', 'Eastern Europe', 'The Balance of Power', and other chapters in Arnold Toynbee and Frank T. Ashton-Gwatkin, eds., *The World in March 1939* (London: Oxford University Press for the Royal Institute of International Affairs, 1952); 'Western Values in International Relations', 'The Balance of Power', and 'Why Is There No International Theory?' all in Herbert Butterfield and Martin

Introduction

      Wight, eds., *Diplomatic Investigations: Essays in the Theory of International Politics* (Cambridge, MA: Harvard University Press, 1966, and London: George Allen and Unwin, 1966); and 'The Balance of Power and International Order', in Alan James, ed., *The Bases of International Order: Essays in Honour of C.A.W. Manning* (London: Oxford University Press, 1973).

6 Martin Wight, *Systems of States*, ed. Hedley Bull (London: Leicester University Press in association with the London School of Economics and Political Science, 1977). For background, see David S. Yost, 'New Perspectives on Historical States-Systems', *World Politics*, vol. 32 (October 1979), pp. 151–68.

7 Martin Wight, *Power Politics*, ed. Hedley Bull and Carsten Holbraad (London: Leicester University Press for the Royal Institute of International Affairs, 1978). This is a revised and expanded version of the 1946 pamphlet with the same title, which was unfinished at the time of Wight's death. Subsequent references in this essay concern the 1978 edition.

8 Martin Wight, *International Theory: The Three Traditions*, ed. Gabriele Wight and Brian Porter (Leicester and London: Leicester University Press for the Royal Institute of International Affairs, 1991).

9 Hedley Bull, 'Martin Wight and the Theory of International Relations', *British Journal of International Studies*, vol. 2 (July 1976), p. 101. This essay is reproduced at the beginning of *International Theory: The Three Traditions* in a slightly abridged form. The citations here refer to the complete original version.

10 Hedley Bull, 'Martin Wight and the Theory of International Relations', p. 101.

11 Coral Bell, 'Journey with Alternative Maps', in Joseph Kruzel and James N. Rosenau, eds., *Journeys through World Politics: Autobiographical Reflections of Thirty-four Academic Travelers* (Lexington, MA: Lexington Books/D.C. Heath and Company, 1989), p. 342.

12 This lecture was posthumously published as a journal article: Martin Wight, 'An Anatomy of International Thought', *Review of International Studies*, vol. 13 (July 1987), pp. 221–7. See below, pp. 143–56.

13 Wight, *International Theory: The Three Traditions*, p. 1.

Introduction

14 Ibid., p. 5.
15 Ibid., p. 7.
16 Ibid., pp. 7–8.
17 Ibid., pp. 29, 161.
18 Ibid., p. 21. The first quotation, from ch. VI of *The Prince*, may be found (in a slightly different translation) in Niccolò Machiavelli, *The Prince and the Discourses*, tr. Luigi Ricci, rev. E. R. P. Vincent (New York: The Modern Library, 1950), p. 22. The other quotation derives from E. H. Carr, *The Twenty Years' Crisis 1919–1939: An Introduction to the Study of International Relations* (London: Macmillan, 1939), p. 110.
19 Wight, *International Theory: The Three Traditions*, pp. 22–3.
20 Ibid., p. 22.
21 Ibid., pp. 14–15.
22 Ibid., pp. 16–17.
23 Ibid., p. 12.
24 Ibid., pp. 259–60.
25 Ibid., p. 151.
26 See below, p. 3.
27 Wight, *International Theory: The Three Traditions*, p. 15.
28 Ibid., p. 216.
29 Ibid., p. 260. Wight also prepared tables and diagrams to clarify his exposition of the traditions. See ibid., pp. 47, 158–60, and 274–8.
30 Ibid., p. 258; italics in the original.
31 Ibid., p. 259; italics in the original.
32 Wight, 'Western Values in International Relations', p. 90.
33 Wight, *International Theory: The Three Traditions*, pp. 46–7, 267.
34 Ibid., p. 267. For a comparable judgement about the moral as well as pragmatic concerns of some contemporary realists, see the incisive essay by Robert G. Gilpin, 'The Richness of the Tradition of Political Realism', in Robert O. Keohane, ed., *Neorealism and Its Critics* (New York: Columbia University Press, 1986).
35 Wight, *International Theory: The Three Traditions*, p. 254.
36 Ibid., p. 257.
37 Ibid., p. 108.
38 Ibid., pp. 19–20, 109–10.
39 Ibid., p. 162.

Introduction

40 See below, p. 76.
41 See below, pp. 81–2.
42 As Wight noted in his lecture on Grotius, the Dutch thinker 'was deeply sensitive to human suffering' and hoped 'to canalize war and restrain its brutality'. Grotius, however, 'did not imagine war could be abolished'—unlike Kant. See below, pp. 34, 35.
43 Wight, 'Why Is There No International Theory?' p. 20.
44 See below, p. 5.
45 Wight, *International Theory: The Three Traditions*, pp. 16–17.
46 Ibid., pp. 103–4.
47 Ibid., p. 248.
48 Wight, 'East and West over Five Centuries', *The Economist*, 30 May 1953, pp. 580–1. This essay was published anonymously.
49 Wight, 'Why Is There No International Theory?' p. 19; italics in the original. The reference is to Friedrich Meinecke, *Machiavellism: The Doctrine of Raison d'État and Its Place in Modern History*, tr. Douglas Scott (London: Routledge & Kegan Paul, 1957), first published as *Die Idee der Staatsräson* in 1924.
50 Martin Wight, 'Is the Commonwealth a Non-Hobbesian Institution?' *The Journal of Commonwealth and Comparative Politics*, vol. XVI, no. 2 (July 1978), p. 123.
51 Wight, 'Western Values in International Relations', p. 92. Wight offered similar observations on Machiavelli and Hobbes in *Systems of States* (p. 39) and *International Theory: The Three Traditions* (p. 26).
52 Wight, 'Germany', p. 317. (See Note 5 above)
53 Ibid., p. 320.
54 Ibid., p. 343. Wight's footnote for the quotation reads: 'Niccolò Machiavelli, *Il Principe*, ch. xxi, ed. L. A. Burd (Oxford, Clarendon Press, 1891), pp. 343–4.' The passage quoted has been translated as 'princes must avoid as much as possible being under the will and pleasure of others'. Machiavelli, *The Prince and the Discourses*, p. 84.
55 Wight, 'Germany', p. 348. Wight's observation about Hitler's objectives could be qualified, in that Hitler pursued specific aims beyond 'the extension of German power', such as the annihilation of the Jews and others according to Nazi doctrines of racial superiority. Wight himself pointed this out in *International Theory: The Three Traditions*, pp. 54–5, 61.

Introduction

56 Wight, *Power Politics*, p. 173; italics in the original. Wight made the same point in 'The Balance of Power', in Butterfield and Wight, eds., *Diplomatic Investigations*, p. 152, and in *International Theory: The Three Traditions*, pp. 19, 164.
57 Wight, 'The Balance of Power and International Order', pp. 88, 91; italics in the original. (See Note 5 above)
58 Wight, *Systems of States*, p. 114.
59 Ibid., p. 127.
60 Wight, *International Theory: The Three Traditions*, p. 37.
61 Wight, *Systems of States*, p. 39.
62 Wight, *International Theory: The Three Traditions*, p. 217.
63 Wight, 'Why Is There No International Theory?' pp. 18–20. (See Note 5 above)
64 Wight, *Systems of States*, p. 113.
65 Wight, 'Western Values in International Relations', pp. 90–1.
66 Ibid., pp. 130–1.
67 Wight, 'Why Is There No International Theory?' pp. 24–5. See also Wight, 'Western Values in International Relations', p. 95.
68 Wight, 'Western Values in International Relations', pp. 126–7.
69 Ibid., p. 105.
70 Wight, *Power Politics*, p. 123.
71 Wight, 'An Anatomy of International Thought', pp. 146, 147 below. See also Wight, *International Theory: The Three Traditions*, pp. 38, 103.
72 Wight, 'Western Values in International Relations', p. 102.
73 Ibid., pp. 116, 119.
74 Wight, 'The Idea of Neutrality', *London Calling*, 11 October 1956, p. 4.
75 Wight, 'Brutus in Foreign Policy: The Memoirs of Sir Anthony Eden', *International Affairs*, vol. 36, no. 3 (July 1960), p. 302.
76 Wight, *Systems of States*, p. 128. See also Wight, *International Theory: The Three Traditions*, pp. 72–3.
77 Wight, *Systems of States*, pp. 121–2. The passage that Wight cited may be found in Hugo Grotius, *The Law of War and Peace, De Jure Belli ac Pacis Libri Tres*, tr. Francis W. Kelsey (Indianapolis and New York: Bobbs-Merrill Company, 1962), p. 403 (bk II, ch. XV, sec. XII). It should be noted that this 1962 edition is a reprint of the 1925 edition (quoted frequently by Wight) published in Oxford by the Clarendon Press with a different title: *De Jure Belli ac Pacis Libri Tres, Volume II: The Translation: On the Law of War and Peace*. The 1925

Introduction

     edition was given this title because vol. I, published by the Carnegie Institution of Washington in 1913, consists of a reproduction of the Latin edition of 1646.

78 Wight, *Systems of States*, p. 128.

79 Wight, 'Why Is There No International Theory?' pp. 29–30. The quotation is from Lauterpacht, 'The Grotian Tradition in International Law', *British Year Book of International Law* (1946), p. 16.

80 Wight, *Power Politics*, p. 252.

81 Wight, 'The Balance of Power and International Order', p. 109; italics in the original.

82 Wight, 'The Balance of Power', in Butterfield and Wight, eds., *Diplomatic Investigations*, pp. 170–1. See also Wight, *International Theory: The Three Traditions*, p. 173.

83 Wight, 'An Anatomy of International Thought', pp. 149, 150 below.

84 Wight, 'Does Peace Take Care of Itself?' *Views*, no. 2 (Summer 1963), p. 95. This is a review-essay about F. H. Hinsley, *Power and the Pursuit of Peace: Theory and Practice in the History of Relations between States* (Cambridge: Cambridge University Press, 1963).

85 Wight, *International Theory: The Three Traditions*, p. 199.

86 Ibid., pp. 199–201. See also Wight, *Systems of States*, p. 72.

87 Wight, *Systems of States*, p. 71.

88 Wight, 'Does Peace Take Care of Itself?' p. 93.

89 Ibid., p. 95.

90 Wight, 'The Balance of Power and International Order', p. 113; italics in the original.

91 Wight, 'Why Is There No International Theory?' p. 33.

92 Ibid., pp. 27–8. The quotation is from Immanuel Kant, 'Perpetual Peace', first published in 1795, in *Kant's Principles of Politics*, tr. and ed. W. Hastie (Edinburgh: T. & T. Clark, 1891), p. 136. See also Wight, *International Theory: The Three Traditions*, p. 115.

93 Wight, ibid. p. 105. Wight discussed the Rationalist tradition's reliance on natural law theory and other non-political sources of moral guidance and inspiration in 'Western Values in International Relations', pp. 120–31.

94 Wight, 'Germany', p. 302. Wight's footnote reads as follows: 'Heinrich Heine: *Religion and Philosophy in Germany*, trans. by John Snodgrass (London, Trübner, 1882), pp. 159–62. This was first

Introduction

published in 1834. Heine's perception that "the German revolution will not prove any milder or gentler because it was preceded by the 'Critique' of Kant, by the 'Transcendental Idealism' of Fichte, or even by the Philosophy of Nature" (p. 158), was independently elaborated by George Santayana in *Egotism in German Philosophy*, 2nd ed. (London, Dent, 1939).' In *International Theory: The Three Traditions* (p. 265), Wight wrote that 'Fichte and Hegel were the great transformation points of Prussian Realism into German Revolutionism, as Kant was the transformation point of eighteenth-century pietistic Rationalism into idealistic Revolutionism.'

95 Wight, 'An Anatomy of International Thought', p. 150 below. See also Wight, 'International Legitimacy', *International Relations*, vol. IV (May 1972), p. 27.
96 Wight, 'An Anatomy of International Thought', p. 151 below. See also Wight, *International Theory: The Three Traditions*, p. 42.
97 Wight, *Power Politics*, pp. 84–5.
98 Although he frequently highlighted the Revolutionist implications of Mazzini's thought, Wight suggested that Mazzini also shared some ideas (at least intermittently) with Rationalist thinkers. See Wight, *International Theory: The Three Traditions*, pp. 14–15.
99 Wight, *Power Politics*, p. 142.
100 Ibid., pp. 117–18. See also Wight, *International Theory: The Three Traditions*, pp. 155–6 and 247–8.
101 Wight, 'Western Values in International Relations', p. 114. The quotation is from 'Non-intervention', *Life and Writings of Joseph Mazzini* (London: Smith, Elder, 1870), vol. vi, pp. 305–6. See also Wight, *International Theory: The Three Traditions*, pp. 134–5.
102 Wight, 'Eastern Europe', pp. 226–7. (See Note 5 above)
103 Wight, 'The Balance of Power and International Order', pp. 113–14.
104 Ibid., p. 110.
105 Wight, *Systems of States*, p. 41.
106 Kenneth N. Waltz, *Theory of International Politics* (Reading, MA: Addison-Wesley Publishing Company, 1979), p. 18.
107 Stanley Hoffmann, 'An American Social Science: International Relations', in Stanley Hoffmann, *Janus and Minerva: Essays in the*

Introduction

      Theory and Practice of International Politics (Boulder and London: Westview Press, 1987), p. 15; italics in the original. This essay was originally published in *Daedalus: Journal of the American Academy of Arts and Sciences*, vol. 106, no. 3 (Summer 1977).

108 Stanley Hoffman, 'An American Social Science: International Relations'. See also Hoffmann's essay, 'Raymond Aron and the Theory of International Relations', in *Janus and Minerva*, pp. 52–69. Wight expressed unqualified admiration for Aron's masterwork *Peace and War* in his review, 'Tract for the Nuclear Age', *The Observer*, 23 April 1967.

109 Bull, 'Martin Wight and the Theory of International Relations', p. 114. For a similar view, see Arnold Wolfers, 'Political Theory and International Relations', in *Discord and Collaboration: Essays on International Politics* (Baltimore and London: Johns Hopkins University Press, 1962), p. 249. This essay was originally published as the introduction to *The Anglo-American Tradition in Foreign Affairs*, ed. Arnold Wolfers and Laurence W. Martin (New Haven, CT: Yale University Press, 1956).

110 Wight, 'Why Is There No International Theory?' p. 33.

111 Wight, *International Theory: The Three Traditions*, p. 258.

112 Wight's reading suggestions regarding history may be found in 'Why Is There No International Theory?' p. 32. His literature suggestions may be found in *International Theory: The Three Traditions* (p. 258), which also contains a bibliography for these traditions of political philosophy in international relations (pp. 269–72).

113 Kant, 'Perpetual Peace', in *Kant's Principles of Politics*, second definitive article and first supplement, pp. 100, 114; italics in the original.

114 Kant, 'Idea of a Universal History from a Cosmopolitical Point of View', in *Kant's Principles of Politics*, eighth proposition, p. 25; italics in the original.

115 See below, p. 73.

116 See below, p. 71.

117 Kant, *Rechtslehre*, quoted in Charles E. Vaughan, *Studies in the History of Political Philosophy Before and After Rousseau*, ed. A. G. Little, vol. II, *From Burke to Mazzini* (Manchester: Manchester University Press, 1925), p. 83.

Introduction

118 See below, p. 108.
119 Kant, 'Perpetual Peace', in *Kant's Principles of Politics*, fifth preliminary article, p. 84.
120 Ibid., second definitive article, p. 98.
121 Wilson's thinking displayed many similarities with Kant's conceptions of international order, as Wight pointed out; but Wilson went beyond Kant in claiming the redemptive role for a specific nation—the United States. In urging the public and the Senate to support ratification of the Treaty of Versailles, including the Covenant of the League of Nations, Wilson declared that America 'has said to mankind at her birth, "We have come to redeem the world by giving it liberty and justice." Now we are called upon before the tribunal of mankind to redeem that immortal pledge.' Woodrow Wilson, 'At the Coliseum,' St. Louis, Missouri, 5 September 1919, in *War and Peace: Presidential Messages, Addresses, and Public Papers (1917–1924)*, edited by Ray Stannard Baker and William E. Dodd (New York and London: Harper and Brothers, 1927), vol. I, p. 645.
122 As Wight pointed out, Mazzini's vision of international affairs was for the most part limited to Europe; he was 'a colonialist' with regard to non-European regions. Mazzini's ideas were nonetheless employed by Asian and African campaigners against European colonialism, as Wight noted in *International Theory: The Three Traditions* (pp. 42, 134–5) and 'An Anatomy of International Thought' (p. 151 below).
123 See below, p. 103.
124 Kant, 'Perpetual Peace', in *Kant's Principles of Politics*, first supplement, p. 105. Kant added, 'When I say of nature that she *wills* a certain thing to be done, I do not mean that she imposes upon us a duty to do it, for only the Practical Reason as essentially free from constraint, can do this; but I mean that she does it herself whether we be willing or not. "*Fata volentem ducunt, nolentem trahunt.*" [The fates lead the willing and drag the unwilling.]' Kant, 'Perpetual Peace', in *Kant's Principles of Politics*, first supplement, p. 111; italics in the original.
125 Pierre Hassner has incisively summarized the tension in Kant's thinking in this respect: 'Kant of course does not exculpate the tainted means; indeed he proscribes the use of such means more uncompromisingly than any other philosopher. He is, however,

Introduction

       willing to see a benefit in them retrospectively, and thereby shows history as overcoming the antinomy of ends and means. It is nature which somehow takes responsibility for the violence and immorality of politics, making use of the maxim "The end justifies the means" that is so strictly forbidden to individuals by practical reason. Thus, when Kant takes up such subjects as the French Revolution, rebellion against tyrants, or wars of liberation, he arrives at a troublesome dual judgment: retrospective vindication by history and unconditional condemnation by morality.' Pierre Hassner, 'Immanuel Kant', in Leo Strauss and Joseph Cropsey, eds., *History of Political Philosophy*, 3rd edn. (Chicago and London: University of Chicago Press, 1987), p. 602.

126   Machiavelli, *The Prince and the Discourses*, p. 91 (ch. XXV of *The Prince*).

127   Kant, 'Idea of a Universal History from a Cosmopolitical Point of View', in *Kant's Principles of Politics*, eighth proposition, p. 24.

128   Immanuel Kant, *The Philosophy of Law*, tr. W. Hastie (Edinburgh: T. & T. Clark, 1887), p. 230.

129   Machiavelli, *The Prince and the Discourses*, pp. 65–6 (ch. XVIII of *The Prince*).

130   Ibid., p. 53 (ch. XIV of *The Prince*).

131   Ibid., p. 79 (ch. XX of *The Prince*).

132   Richard H. Cox, 'Hugo Grotius', in Leo Strauss and Joseph Cropsey, eds., *History of Political Philosophy*, 3rd edn. (Chicago and London: University of Chicago Press, 1987), p. 393.

133   Grotius, *The Law of War and Peace*, p. 184 (bk II, ch. I, sec. XVII).

134   Ibid., p. 640 (bk III, ch. III, sec. XIII). The application of certain Grotian principles—or of classical collective security theory—to circumstances involving modern military technologies may be problematic. See in this regard Inis L. Claude, Jr., *Power and International Relations* (New York: Random House, 1962), pp. 192–4.

135   Grotius, *The Law of War and Peace*, p. 504 (bk II, ch. XX, sec. XL).

136   Mazzini also expressed a sense of shared moral responsibility regarding injustice abroad, 'the principle of mutual involvement', as Wight termed it; and, like Grotius, Mazzini prescribed a discriminating empirical approach in dealing with such cases. See below, pp. 107–8.

Introduction

137 Grotius, *The Law of War and Peace*, pp. 571–3 (bk II, ch. XXIV, sec. V).
138 Ibid., pp. 567–70 (bk II, ch. XXIV, secs. I–III).
139 Ibid., p. 575 (bk II, ch. XXIV, sec. VIII).
140 See below, p. 17.
141 Grotius wrote various works to defend and propagate the faith, including *De veritate religionis Christianae*. As Hedley Bull notes, this book 'is thought to have been written to assist seamen to carry out this task when visiting infidel countries'. Bull, 'The Importance of Grotius in the Study of International Relations', in Hedley Bull, Benedict Kingsbury, and Adam Roberts, eds., *Hugo Grotius and International Relations* (Oxford: Clarendon Press, 1990), p. 82.
142 Leo Strauss argued that Machiavelli's 'praise of the religion of ancient Rome implies . . . a critique of the religion of modern Rome'. Strauss pointed out that the only New Testament quotation in either *The Prince* or *The Discourses* (the reference to Luke 1:53 in bk I, ch. XXVI, of *The Discourses*) is 'used for expressing a most horrible blasphemy'. The quotation from the Magnificat ('He hath filled the hungry with good things; and the rich he hath sent empty away'), intended to celebrate the workings of Divine justice, is employed by Machiavelli as a prescription for a conqueror or new prince to secure his own power by overturning the existing social structure, thus creating new rich (dependent upon him) and new poor. In this context the quotation suggests, Strauss noted, that 'God is a tyrant.' Strauss also observed that Machiavelli's analysis of the duration of 'sects' in history implies 'that all religions, including Christianity, are of human, not heavenly origin'. Leo Strauss, 'Niccolò Machiavelli', in Leo Strauss and Joseph Cropsey, eds., *History of Political Philosophy*, 3rd edn. (Chicago and London: University of Chicago Press, 1987), pp. 308, 312, 314. See also Leo Strauss, *Thoughts on Machiavelli* (Chicago and London: University of Chicago Press, 1958), pp. 48–52.
143 See below, pp. 64–6. Manfred Kuehn's new study, *Kant: A Biography* (Cambridge: Cambridge University Press, 2001), includes an analysis of Kant's rejection of various traditional Christian beliefs and practices; see especially pp. 366–72 and 375–85.

Introduction

144 Mazzini quoted in Bolton King, *The Life of Mazzini* (London: J.M. Dent and Sons, and New York: E. P. Dutton and Co., 1912), p. 230.
145 See below, pp. 8, 21.
146 See below, pp. 33–4.
147 See below, pp. 10–11.
148 *The Republic of Plato*, tr. Francis MacDonald Cornford (Oxford: Clarendon Press, 1941), pp. 136–9.
149 Kant, 'Perpetual Peace', in *Kant's Principles of Politics*, first supplement, p. 112.
150 See below, p. 79.
151 Kant, 'Idea of a Universal History from a Cosmopolitical Point of View', in *Kant's Principles of Politics*, sixth proposition, p. 15.
152 See below, p. 115.

All great thinkers, while historically conditioned, are philosophically contemporaneous. At least Grotians and Machiavellians would accept this; it is Kantians who believe that philosophers are superseded.

M. W.

Chapter 1

Machiavelli

3 May 1469–22 June 1527

Introduction

It is the least of Machiavelli that is most familiar. All individual thinkers transcend typology; and in social studies, generalizations are abstractions, mental conveniences, and to that extent unreal. They must be contrasted with the concrete, historical person in all his richness and possible inconsistency. It seems true that, when a proper name becomes used adjectivally of a school or way of thought, it falsifies the man possessing the name. Grotius was not a Grotian, nor Keynes a Keynesian; Freud was not a Freudian, nor Marx a Marxist. Machiavelli was not a Machiavellian simply; his name became a byword in the sixteenth century for the slick, unprincipled trickster in politics, the sneaking assassin with a stiletto, or the masterly diplomatic operator, aiming at success. Of course the seed of all this can be found in Machiavelli but there is much more; if he was a Machiavellian, he was a Machiavellian *plus*. Here is the answer to popular Machiavellianism: 'You cannot call it political skill to massacre your subjects, to let down your allies, to be untrustworthy, and ruthless, and altogether unscrupulous. These methods may help you build an empire, but they do not win glory.'[1] Also, whereas in general a prudent rule of power politics is not to ally with a stronger power that will treat you as Russia treated Romania in 1878, Germany treated Italy during the Second World War, or Stalin treated Czechoslovakia in 1948, contrast Machiavelli:

> But when a state declares itself gallantly in favour of one side in a war, in time to help it win, though the victor will be so powerful that it has its allies at its mercy, yet it will have an obligation towards *this* ally, and a bond of regard.
>
> And men are never so shameless that they would give an example of ingratitude by oppressing you. Victories are never so complete that the victor must not show some regard, especially towards justice.[2]

Here is the unMachiavellian Machiavelli:

> May Italy at last see her liberator! One cannot describe the love with which he would be received in all those provinces which have suffered so much from this foreign scum, with what thirst for revenge, with what stubborn faith, with what devotion, with what tears. What door would be closed to him? Who would refuse him support? What envy would hamper him?... To all of us this barbarous dominion stinks.[3]

This is the language of passion, with no sense of proportion, the language of Bandung and Accra in the 1950s [later of West Belfast and the West Bank –Eds.].

The Inductive Method

Machiavelli replaced the *a priori* method with the inductive method. He started from the is, not the ought; from facts, not ideals.

> Since I want to write something that shall be useful to the person who grasps it, it seems to me better to follow up the real truth of the matter than imaginary ideas about it. Many writers have described states which have never been known or seen in fact. But how men live is so

different from how they ought to live, that he who neglects what is done for what ought to be done is more likely to achieve his own ruin than his self-preservation.[4]

This marks a self-conscious, decisive break with the scholastic method, although one that Machiavelli shares with Guicciardini and Vettori.[5] The appearance of Renaissance humanism in politics brought with it the fundamental assumption that 'man is the measure of all things'. *The Prince* was the first political pamphlet to reject transcendentalism. In *The Discourses* Machiavelli argues that the revolutionary ruler must retain the appearance of ancient institutions: 'This he must do because men in general are more affected by what a thing appears to be than by what it is, and are frequently influenced more by appearances than by the reality.'[6] That is to say, the masses follow illusions and will-o'-the-wisps like nuclear disarmament, but the statesman must be a 'realist'.

Historical Method

It was not his inductive method, however, that Machiavelli prided himself on as novel. The preface to *The Discourses* opens with one of his loftiest claims to be blazing a new trail; one of the most sublime expressions of consciousness, of doing something new, in all political thought. He compares himself to Columbus discovering new continents: 'Although owing to the envy inherent in man's nature it has always been no less dangerous to discover new ways and methods than to set off in search of new seas and unknown lands ... I have decided to enter upon a new way, as yet untrodden by anyone else.'[7] This 'new way' was to draw the laws of politics out of historical precedents. Antiquity, he said, was held in great honour in the fields of art, law, and medicine; old statues were copied, the decisions of ancient civil jurists were upheld, and ancient experiments and prescriptions were repeated; but in politics 'one finds neither prince nor republic who repairs to antiquity for examples'.[8] So Machiavelli adopted the extraordinary expedient of writing a commentary on the Roman historian, Livy. 'It will comprise what I have arrived at by comparing ancient with modern events... so that those who read what I have to say may the more easily draw those practical lessons which one should seek to obtain from the study of history.'[9]

History is a great storehouse of relevent precedents, Machiavelli maintains, because history consists in mechanically recurring cycles.[10] States are governed by predestined laws of rise and decay, so the lessons of political experience are true lessons, and have an almost scientific validity; political situations can be classified into a number of recurrent problems with theoretically adequate solutions. It is a method characteristic of the way of thought of Machiavelli's followers. 'I think that history is philosophy teaching by examples', said Bolingbroke.[11]

Methodological Critique

Machiavelli's methodology can be contrasted to the deductive method in Kant and Rousseau, and the blend of deductive (*a priori*) and inductive (*a posteriori*) found in Grotius. Machiavelli and Grotius both had a historical method. Grotius is sometimes censured for his uncritical accumulation of, and reliance on, authorities, but mark his great reservation about Aristotle:

Among the philosophers Aristotle deservedly holds the foremost place, whether you take into account his order of treatment, or the subtlety of his distinctions, or the weight of his reasons. Would that this pre-eminence had not, for some centuries back, been turned into a tyranny, so that Truth, to whom Aristotle devoted faithful service, was by no instrumentality more repressed than by Aristotle's name!

For my part... [I swear allegiance to no philosopher] because there... [is] no philosophic sect whose vision had compassed all truth, and none which had not perceived some aspect of truth...

Our purpose is to make much account of Aristotle, but reserving in regard to him the same liberty which he, in his devotion to truth, allowed himself with respect to his teachers.[12]

Or, as was reported of Aristotle himself: *'Amicus Plato, sed magis amica veritas.'* (Plato is dear to me, but dearer still is truth.)[13]

Machiavelli, however, used his historical method uncritically. His examples are abstracted from historical contexts and applied crudely to current politics; he worshipped Rome and Roman precedents. It is possible to argue that Machiavellians as a school tend to be methodologically uncritical: social Darwinists applied the evolutionary theory in biology uncritically to the 'struggle for existence'; Freudians applied psychoanalysis uncritically to civilization and its discontents; and linguistic analysts apply linguistic analysis uncritically to political philosophy. The same methodological device has been applied to international politics which simplifies it: the device in Carr's *Twenty Years' Crisis* might be said to be in the conceptual framework itself, in the antithesis of utopia and reality, free will and determinism, theory and practice.[14] But Morgenthau reproduces Machiavelli's uncritical historical method, presenting the Holy Alliance as the ideology of the Congress system, and Castlereagh as actuated by national interest alone. Kantians, on the other hand, start by repudiating any authority and any methodology save the principles of pure thought, but then become enslaved to sacred books—the Jacobins to Rousseau, the Communists to Marx.

The Badness of Human Nature

Turning from the cyclic movement of historical societies to the behaviour of individuals, Machiavelli argues that man in isolation is essentially bad. There are famous assertions of this in *The Prince*: 'This is to be said in general of men, that they are ungrateful, fickle, false, cowards, covetous...'[15] And a little later: 'If men were entirely good it would be desirable to keep faith, but because they are bad, and will not keep faith with you, you should not feel bound to keep faith with them.'[16] Again, in *The Discourses* he says: 'Nothing is more futile and more inconstant than are the masses—*la moltitudine.*'[17] 'It should be noted, too... how easily men are corrupted and in nature become transformed... however well brought up.'[18]

But it seems likely Machiavelli might have demurred from this formulation; the word 'bad' is being used in different ways. Machiavelli is not standing outside politics, as a judge or spectator, making a moral valuation, but *inside* politics, trying to describe the human material of politics and its possibilities.

For him, it is pointless to make moral judgements about human nature. Human nature is what it is, the supreme datum of politics, and the only meaningful statements to be made about it are about what can be done *with* it, how it can be moulded and manipulated. The point has been made by one of Machiavelli's modern followers, James Burnham, using a different term—tragedy:

> There will be those who will find in this thesis [that capitalism will change into managerial society] a renewed proof of what they will call the essential tragedy of the human situation. But I do not see with what meaning the human situation as a whole can be called tragic, or comic. Tragedy and comedy occur only *within* the human situation. There is no background against which to judge the human situation as a whole. It is merely what it happens to be.[19]

Compare Oakeshott in the *Cambridge Journal*: 'Human life is not "tragic", either in part or as a whole; tragedy belongs to art, not to life.'[20]

Self-regard, Self-interest, Struggle for Power

These are the mainspring of politics, as shown in an important passage in *The Discourses*:

> ...whenever there is no need for men to fight, they fight for ambition's sake; and so powerful is the sway that ambition exercises over the human heart that they never relinquish it, no matter how high they have risen. The reason is that nature has so constituted men that,

though all things are objects of desire, not all things are attainable; so that desire always exceeds the power of attainment, with the result that men are ill content with what they possess... Hence arise the vicissitudes of their fortune. For, since some desire to have more and others are afraid to lose what they have already acquired, enmities and wars are begotten, and this brings about the ruin of one province and the exaltation of its rival.[21]

The language here is curiously close to that of Hobbes, who says in *The Leviathan*:

Felicity is a continual progress of the desire, from one object to another... So that in the first place, I put for a general inclination of all mankind, a perpetual and restless desire of power after power, that ceaseth only in death. And the cause of this, is not always that a man hopes for a more intensive delight, than he has already attained to; or that he cannot be content with a moderate power: but because he cannot assure the power and means to live well, which he hath present, without the acquisition of more. And from hence it is, that kings, whose power is greatest, turn their endeavours to the assuring it at home by laws, or abroad by wars.[22]

Thus men prey upon men, states upon states: 'For men, as King Ferdinand used to say, resemble certain little birds of prey in whom so strong is the desire to catch the prey which nature incites them to pursue, that they do not notice another and a greater bird of prey which hovers over them ready to pounce and kill.'[23] This can be contrasted with Grotius' postulate of the sociability of man. Grotius never mentions Machiavelli, surprisingly, but he is supposed to have him in mind when he argues against Carneades (*c*.215–129 BC) and once against Gabriel Vásquez, SJ (1551–1604). Vásquez said that men desire the security of the state in their own interest, each putting his individual welfare above that of the whole, but Grotius argued:

We do desire, in our own interest, that our state be safe, yet not merely for our own sake but for the sake of others as well.... [Some argue that friendship originates in need alone, but] we are drawn to friendship spontaneously, and by our own nature. Regard for others often warns me, sometimes commands me, to put the interest of many above my own.[24]

He holds that most people would be more satisfied to have averted disaster for their country than from themselves, and that most people, given a deliberate choice, would prefer to lose their homes than to keep them at the price of general catastrophe.[25] For Grotius altruism is an autonomous impulse of human nature; for Machiavelli, it is self-regard projected into another's situation. For utilitarian theory (J. S. Mill) it is intelligently extended self-regard.[26]

Primacy of Contradiction

Underlying this view of politics as a struggle for power there is an issue of pure philosophy. It has two levels: the first is that criteria are negative, not positive. For example, how does one define 'security'? The Machiavellian will say that the essential experience of international politics is insecurity; there is in fact no such condition as 'security', only degrees of insecurity. Thus one defines security in relation to the fact of insecurity, as the relative absence of insecurity. Similarly, peace can be defined only in relation to war, good in relation to evil, and fulfilment in relation to frustration. Thus James Bond, in his first adventure, argues that the good life of a peaceable patriotic citizen has shape and meaning only by contrast with the international crooks whom he tracks down. Having killed Le Chiffre, the French racketeer and Communist agent, Bond reflects: 'By his evil existence, which foolishly I have helped to destroy, he was creating a norm of badness by which, and by which alone, an opposite norm of goodness could exist.'[27] So criteria, and maybe norms, are negative. At the logical end of this path is the proverbial lunatic who beats his head with a mallet because it is such a relief when he leaves off.

But there is a profounder level, of pure metaphysics: the *primacy of contradiction*. What is the ultimate nature of things, of the essence of the universe? Pythagoras apparently answered: harmony, melody, rhythm, or number, because numbers mysteriously reflect the innermost harmony of the universe. That is a religious philosophy, and if the question above is answered by the word 'God', then one is committed to harmony as the ultimate reality. But, if it is harmony, then why does anything grow, change, and decline; move, collide, and conflict? Why is there not an unaltered unending stability? Heraclitus, a generation or so earlier, gave another answer. The essence of things was itself change, motion, and flux.

There seem to be two ideas in Heraclitus: the first is 'Πάντα χωρεί οὐδέν μένει.' (Everything flows and nothing stays.)[28] One cannot step into the same river twice. (How can one step into it once? For it is not for one instant the same river. How can one have knowledge of anything?) This theme was taken up by Plato, Heraclitus' pupil's pupil.[29]

The second of Heraclitus' ideas is that of conflict, mutual tension. Everything is a battleground of opposing forces, there is fundamental impermanence; and only relative permanence when the balance of opposing forces is momentarily achieved. 'War is the father of all things.'[30] Heraclitus was the 'weeping philosopher', according to tradition, because he always found in human life matter for tears.

What has this to do with Machiavelli? Nothing: Machiavelli was not a metaphysician; but some of his successors have explored these heights. Hegel is the great Clapham Junction of political philosophy where a main-line from Machiavelli joins a main-line from Kant and the two run on together.

Not all Kantians pass through the Hegel junction nor all Machiavellians, but the joint line carries high-powered traffic. In *Science of Logic* Hegel deals with the theory of contradiction: it is a prejudice of ordinary imagination that contradiction has less essence and immanence than identity, but in any question of ranking, 'Contradiction would have to be taken as the profounder and more fully essential'. For identity only determines 'the simple immediate' or 'dead Being', 'while Contradiction is the root of all movement and life, and it is only in so far as it contains a Contradiction that anything moves and has impulse and activity'.[31]

This idea fascinated nineteenth-century revolutionaries. Ferdinand Lassalle (1825–64) was the son of a Jewish merchant in Breslau. Edmund Wilson describes him thus:

> [at] the University of Berlin . . . he saturated himself with Hegel, got up at four in the morning to read him, [and] became transported by the feeling that he was realizing himself as the Idea of the Hegelian World Spirit. 'Through philosophy', he wrote to his father, 'I have become self-comprehending reason—that is to say, God aware of himself'.[32]

He spent years on a book on Heraclitus (published 1858), whom he saw as the forerunner of Hegel. He founded the General Union of German Workers in 1863, treated Bismarck as the head of a rival Great Power and was a forerunner of fascism. He was shot in a duel in 1864.[33]

Mikhail Bakúnin (1814–76), too, was intoxicated by Hegelianism. He went to Berlin and sought to prove in the dialectic the primacy of negative to positive. He ended a famous essay he contributed to a Hegelian periodical in 1841: 'Let us put our trust, therefore, in the eternal spirit, who shatters and destroys only because he is the unfathomable and eternally creative source of all that lives. The desire to destroy is itself a creative desire.'[34] He had visions of ecstatic conflagration: 'the whole of Europe, with St Petersburg, Paris and London, transformed into an enormous rubbish-heap'.[35] Herzen tells the story of Bakúnin travelling between Paris and Prague and coming across a revolt of German peasants, who were milling round the castle, making an uproar, not knowing what to do. Bakúnin got out of his coach, wasted no time in asking questions, formed them into ranks (he had been an artillery officer in Russia), and got the castle burning on all four sides. He then resumed his journey.[36] This was a superbly literal Heraclitan gesture. He quarrelled with Marx over the control of the First International. The successes of the Paris Commune in 1871 enraptured Bakúnin: 'He entered the group room with rapid strides...struck the table with his stick and cried: "Well, my friends, the Tuileries are in flames. I'll stand a punch all around!" '[37] In his last days in Italy, old and ill, in 1876, a friend played Beethoven for him. 'Everything will pass, and the world will perish, but the Ninth Symphony will remain.'[38] Perhaps this is an expression of the primacy of harmony; and romantic revolutionism only. 'Bakúnin differed from Marx as poetry differs from prose.'[39]

When Proudhon (1809–65) offered his 'Philosophy of Poverty' (*La Philosophie de la Misère*) to Marx for criticism, Marx thought this bourgeois socialism dangerous: 'To leave error unrefuted is to encourage intellectual immorality.'[40] He wrote a tremendous attack on Proudhon: the 'Poverty of Philosophy' (1847), which was the first exposition of Marxist philosophy and 'the bitterest attack delivered by one thinker upon another since the celebrated polemics of the Renaissance'.[41] It is also immensely funny. Marx was concerned to show that Proudhon did not understand the Hegelian dialectic. Proudhon saw it as struggle between good and evil, therefore he would formulate the problem thus: preserve the good side, eliminate the bad. But then, says Marx, the dialectical process would stop. 'What constitutes dialectical movement is the co-existence of two contradictory sides, their conflict and their fusion into a new category. The very formulation of the problem as one of eliminating the bad side cuts short the dialectic movement.'[42] This implies the primacy of contradiction. 'Genuine progress is constituted not by the triumph of one side and the defeat of the other, but by the duel itself which necessarily involves the destruction of both.'[43]

In Lenin's philosophical studies in Switzerland in the First World War, and in his 'Philosophical Notebooks' published in 1933, there are extracts from Hegel, Feuerbach, Lassalle on Heraclitus, and Aristotle.[44] He copied out a passage from Hegel's *Science of Logic*, put heavy strokes in the margin, and underlined the reference to contradiction as the source of all movement.[45] This is necessary to his materialism. 'Metaphysics' sees motion as imparted to matter by a push from the outside, which implies a first cause. Lenin asserts the self-movement of matter, that real contradictions are inherent in things: 'Dialectic in the proper sense is the study of contradiction in *the nature of things as such.*'[46] Hegelians and Marxists are not the only descendants of Machiavelli, and the doctrine of the primacy of contradiction, which is the metaphysical counterpart of the political doctrine of the struggle for power, can be detected in its crude, nihilistic form in the barbaric rhapsodies of the Fascists and Nazis. (They represent, perhaps, the approximation of the revolutionary Kantian and the passionate Machiavellian.) But in Marxism, the primacy of contradiction is consciously detected as a basic principle, and this illustrates at a metaphysical level the toughness and flexibility of Marxism.

Power is Antecedent to Law, Custom, and Justice

Machiavelli argued that the badness of human nature, the folly of the populace, and the tendency of societies to degenerate can in some degree be controlled or regulated by laws, which, once established, evoke the imitativeness of men, and endure.

> ...men never do good unless necessity drives them to it; but when they are free to choose and can do just as they please, confusion and disorder become everywhere rampant. Hence it is said that hunger and poverty make men industrious, and that laws make them good... when such good customs break down, legislation... becomes necessary.[47]

Here customs seem prior to laws, but customs and laws are not properly distinguished: 'just as for the maintenance of good customs laws are required, so if laws are to be observed, there is need of good customs.'[48] And they presuppose power:

> The chief foundations of all states... are good laws and good arms; and as there cannot be good laws where the state is not well armed, it

follows that where they are well armed they have good laws. I shall leave the laws out of the discussion and shall speak of the arms.[49]

The security of all states is based on good military discipline, and... where it does not exist, there can neither be good laws nor anything else that is good.[50]

Thus his account of the origin of the notion of justice is purely political. In the beginning, when men were few, they lived scattered; when they multiplied, to defend themselves better, they 'began to look about for a man stronger and more courageous than the rest, made him their head, and obeyed him'. And so men learned to distinguish the honest and good from the wicked, for the sight of someone injuring his benefactor evoked hatred and sympathy, since they saw that the same injuries might have been done to themselves. Hence laws and punishments developed. 'The notion of justice thus came into being.'[51] This is a rehash of Polybius, but it is also very Hobbesian: 'before the names of just, and unjust can have place, there must be some coercive power, to compel men... to the performance of their covenants'.[52] One may compare E. H. Carr's chapter on the foundations of law in *The Twenty Years' Crisis*. After a perfunctory account of naturalism as against 'realist' theory, Carr provides a synthesis that is a restatement of realist theory:

International law is a function of the political community of nations.
Law is a function of a given political order.
Behind all law there is this necessary political background. The ultimate authority of law derives from politics.
Any international moral order must rest on some hegemony of power.[53]

Similarly Hans J. Morgenthau, in *In Defense of the National Interest*, says: 'There is a profound and neglected truth hidden in Hobbes's extreme dictum that the state creates morality as well as law and that there is neither morality nor law outside the state.'[54] In *Dilemmas of Politics* he modifies this, under criticism, and recedes a little.[55] Reviewing him in *International Affairs*, I wrote that in the former book he had *endorsed* Hobbes's doctrine.[56] He replied that he did not *endorse* it: he called it an 'extreme dictum', that is, he puts the weight of his own self-exegesis on the word 'extreme' as against 'profound and neglected truth'.

It follows that the sophisticated Machiavellian may in a sense admit of the existence of moral values, but will see them as epiphenomenal. Morality is an epiphenomenon of security. It is not that it overrules power, as Grotius said, but that power permits the emergence even of morality. One can compare Karl Marx in the classic expression of the basic principle of historical materialism: 'It is not the consciousness of men that determines their existence, but, on the contrary, it is their social existence that determines their consciousness.'[57] If Britain has been able to be Grotian, it is only because of an ingrained sense of security, a lack of fear. She lacks a Continental frontier, and has never been invaded since England became a nation. Thus Chamberlain could say: 'It is for a great country to do what a small or a weak country cannot always afford to do—to show magnanimity.'[58] Rebecca West observes: '... negotiation is an art safely to be practised only in the years of plenty, when there is a surplus which can be comfortably haggled over by the parties involved. In gaunter times a country must lay down the conditions necessary for its own preservation, and annihilate those that will not concede them.'[59] Which recalls Thucydides: '... in peace and prosperity both states and individuals have gentler feelings, because men are not then forced to face conditions of dire necessity; but war, which robs men of the easy supply of their daily wants, is a rough schoolmaster, and creates in most people a temper that matches their condition.'[60] The existential truth of this seems to be the greatest difficulty that the Grotian interpretation of international politics faces, especially in the context of nuclear warfare, and it raises the question whether the Grotian can only save his principles by abandoning his traditional camp and beating a retreat to the neighbourhood of Gandhi.

Causal Complexity of Politics

The foundation of Machiavellian philosophy and its deepest insight is a *sense of proportion*. It corresponds to the Grotian apprehension of the moral complexity of politics. Do not bother your head, or anyway not mine, Machiavelli seems to say, about the problem of attributing moral responsibility in politics, but only consider the unfathomable complexity, the multiple causes, the cross-currents, accidents, unintended results, the ironies of politics: the swerves. Note, he says, how many lines of causation converge to produce a single result, and how a single act or event will radiate out to produce divergent results; how men intend one effect and produce the opposite; and how the same act, in different circumstances, will produce quite different effects. This is the special picture of political life one gets from reading Machiavelli himself and 'irony' is a category of philosophical Machiavellians. The word is not, I think, found in Machiavelli, but political irony is in fact what he very lovingly studied. Irony is a Machiavellian category while tragedy is a Grotian category. 'Tragedy' implies a standpoint outside the political drama, in which we experience, for example, admiration for Othello's nobility, pity for his weakness, and terror at Iago's wickedness. Translated into history: one may admire the aims of Athens or of the League of Nations, pity the defeat of Lord Cecil's ideals in the matter of Abyssinia,[61] and experience terror at the destruction of Melos, or at the enormities of Hitler and Stalin. Admiration for nobility, and terror at wickedness, imply a moral standpoint, while pity for weakness and suffering implies self-identification. Now, it is difficult to adopt a tragic standpoint about politics, because 'politics' implies a situation in which we are still involved, where we can still act and affect the outcome, and anyway where we do not *know* the outcome because the drama is unfinished. To become fully tragic, politics have to be dead politics, that is, history: the tragedy of Athens, and of the League of Nations.

Machiavelli

Irony is, so to speak, the factual skeleton of tragedy, stripped of its moral and transcendental clothing. In literature it is the warping of a statement by its context; a character means one thing by a statement but we know the context and outcome that he does not, and see it has a different meaning. As Banquo rides away to be murdered, as Macbeth has arranged, Macbeth says to him genially: 'Fail not our feast'—'My lord, I will not.'[62] This is Sophoclean irony and there are other kinds, more complex. Irony can be seen in politics when statesmen pursue ends that recoil upon them, and turn into their opposites. Hugh R. Wilson, in *Diplomat between Wars*, says that the policy of the USA was of 'overwhelming importance' to the League of Nations in the Manchurian crisis,[63] which makes ironic America's fear of commitment and involvement: however little she wanted to be committed she was certainly involved, and by refusing to commit herself at that time she made her involvement in the struggle with Japan all the more certain. It is equally ironical that Britain and France went to war in 1939 to restore the balance of power in Europe by destroying Nazi Germany, embraced the Soviet alliance for that purpose, and ended with Europe as badly unbalanced by Stalin's power as it had been by Hitler's.

In *The Irony of American History* Reinhold Niebuhr sees 'the necessity of using the threat of atomic destruction as an instrument for the preservation of peace... [as] a tragic element in our contemporary situation'.[64] It is not tragic, but ironic only; it is not tragic, because we are involved in it, we cannot be detached about it. Tragic vision has a movement, or rhythm: first an initial standpoint outside the drama, detachment; then a self-projection into the drama, identification; and lastly, the discovery of the universal relevance of the drama, the recognition of having been told a truth about all mankind, including ourselves. This is the catharsis, the self-recognition, which brings a deeper understanding of the human predicament. We admire and pity Oedipus or Othello, or Lord Cecil and the League of Nations men[65] because we identify ourselves with them and then recognize ourselves in them, but there is no such movement of tragic understanding in relation to our contemporary situation. The only emotion we can feel about the threat of atomic destruction as an instrument for peace is *self-pity*, and this is not a tragic emotion: it is notoriously the most unpurifying and impure of all emotions, the very opposite of self-recognition as part of universal humanity. Niebuhr, a Christian Machiavellian [see Appendix II], in his *Irony of American History* (1952) falsifies the relation of irony and tragedy and shows the Machiavellian's inability to understand the nature of tragedy.

If a connoisseur of the irony of political life is struck solemn by it, if he talks of tragic irony, then he is a 'wet' Machiavellian, a Christian. If he is fascinated by it, intellectually interested, he is a central Machiavellian, like the master himself. If he is amused by the irony of political life, he is an extreme Machiavellian, a cynic, a man who enjoys the sufferings and embarrassments of others. Just as Machiavellians do not understand the nature of tragedy, so Grotians are unable to understand the structure or texture of irony, which has several strands.

The first is that of mere accident. Thus Cesare Borgia made many precautions against Alexander VI's death: he exterminated his enemies so far as possible, won over the nobility of Rome, won over the College of Cardinals, and set about acquiring self-sufficient territorial power (which he had not completely done). He could have made the new pope, too, or vetoed an unsatisfactory pope. Machiavelli recalls: 'On the day that Julius II was elected, he told me that he had thought of everything that might occur at the death of his father, and had provided a remedy for all, except that he had never foreseen that, when the death did happen, he himself would be on the point to die.'[66] Also, this century, there was the chanciness of the vice-presidential nomination in the USA, when Truman was selected over Wallace in 1944;[67] and the accident of Eden's illness at the height of the Suez Crisis in 1956.

Machiavelli

Another strand of historical irony is multiple or cumulative causation of a single result. Thus there were many mistakes in Louis XII's policy in Italy: he destroyed the small powers; aggrandized a greater power, the papacy; and called in a foreign power, Spain. He did not settle in Italy, nor send colonies to Italy, and he weakened the Venetians. 'A given effect may be due to a plurality of causes', notes Machiavelli, 'such that, if any one be lacking, the effect will not ensue'.[68] Is this true? There were several causes of the First World War: South Slav nationalism; Austrian militarism; Russo-Austrian rivalry in the Balkans; the French desire to recover Alsace-Lorraine; and Anglo-German naval rivalry. Perhaps, without any one of these, it would not have happened.

A third strand is the single causation of opposite results, or paradox. Marxists like this notion: the bourgeoisie created simultaneously a single world economy and the extreme of international anarchy. The Seven Years War gave Canada to Britain, removed the urgency for the defence of the Thirteen Colonies, but also produced the scheme for a standing army there, and raised the constitutional issue of taxation that led to revolution and independence. Hitler's persecution of the Jews helped bring about the State of Israel, the ascendancy of realism and geopolitical thinking in the USA and Great Britain, and Soviet prowess in military research and development—none of which he intended.

A fourth strand of irony is self-frustration, or failure. Men intend one result and produce another. Thus, observes Machiavelli in *The Prince*, France, by invading Italy, has produced the greatness of the Church and of Spain there, and her ruin may be attributed to them.[69] Japan, too, by attempting to conquer China, did much to make China instead of herself the future Great Power of the Orient. [The Anglo-French intervention over Suez in 1956 is a superb example of this type of irony, as of several others. Designed to destroy Nasserite Arab nationalism, it enormously strengthened it. –Eds.]

A fifth strand in historical irony is that the same policy, in different circumstances, will produce different effects. [Martin Wight gave no examples of this, leaving a blank space in the notes. Yet we may again cite the ill-fated Suez affair, contrasting the effects of the interventions in Egypt of Gladstone in 1882 and Eden in 1956. –Eds.]

The sixth and last strand is that contrary policies, in different circumstances, can produce the same effects. This is discussed in an unintentionally amusing way in *The Discourses* (bk III), when Machiavelli discusses whether harsh methods or mild are the more efficacious. He lists examples where humanity, kindness, common decency, and generosity paid political dividends, including Fabricius' rejection of the offer to poison Pyrrhus.[70] But Hannibal obtained fame and victory by exactly opposite methods: cruelty, violence, rapine, and perfidy. This puzzles and fascinates Machiavelli: 'I conclude, therefore, that it does not matter much in what way a general behaves, provided his efficiency be so great that it quite makes up for how he behaves, whether it be in this way or that... in both there are defects and dangers unless they be corrected by outstanding efficiency.'[71] Two principles are embedded here, which form the core of Machiavelli's position.

The first principle is *virtù*. *Virtù* is technical virtuosity—'efficiency' in the above quotation—within the broad limits of loyalty to a state or leader. It is derived from the Latin *virtus*, the character becoming to a *vir*.[72] One mark of *virtù*, of political efficiency, is not to take the middle course. Repeatedly through *The Discourses* Machiavelli says: 'doubtless the middle course would be the best, were it possible to adopt it. As, however, I am convinced that this middle course is impracticable...' it is better either to commit yourself wholly to a prince or to make war openly upon him.[73] The Suez invasion is a good example of a bungled middle course. The Machiavellian judgement of it would be that that was all that was wrong with it. There is a Machiavellian bias in favour of extremism and ruthlessness, of firm, decisive action; whereas the Grotian bias is in favour of moderation.

Machiavelli

[During the Suez crisis, Eden consulted Montgomery who later recounted the occasion in a television interview. It went like this: Montgomery—'Prime Minister. What are you trying to do?' Eden—'Topple Nasser.' Montgomery—'Then you must go for Cairo. Forget the Canal and go for Cairo!' This admirably illustrates Machiavelli's advice. Eden's aim was Machiavellian, but his instincts, as befitted a Western liberal politician, were Grotian. The instincts of Montgomery were straightforwardly Machiavellian. –Eds.]

The second principle is *fortuna*. There are two ways of rising to be a prince, says Machiavelli, through ability, or through favour or luck (*per virtù o per fortuna*).[74] *Fortuna* expresses the idea that the causal complexity of politics is so great that it eludes complete calculation; only probabilities can be calculated. As Machiavelli says in *The Prince*: 'Never let any Government imagine that it can choose perfectly safe courses; rather let it expect to have to take very doubtful ones, because it is found in ordinary affairs that one never seeks to avoid one trouble without running into another.'[75]

And, again, in *The Discourses*:

> ...in all human affairs one notices, if one examines them closely, that it is impossible to remove one inconvenience without another emerging ...Hence in all discussions one should consider which alternative involves fewer inconveniences and should adopt this as the better course; for one never finds any issue that is clear cut and not open to question.[76]

In *The Prince* (ch. 25), Machiavelli says he is sometimes tempted, when considering the political revolutions of his time, to believe that human affairs are out of human control, guided only by God or chance: 'Nevertheless, not to extinguish our free choice, I think the truth is that fortune is the arbiter of one half of our actions, but that she still leaves us to direct the other half, or perhaps a little less.'[77] This expresses a universal experience of statecraft, though with a quaint quantitative estimate of the role of decision within the framework of necessity. Fortune is like a river in flood, destroying everything; but banks and barriers can be raised against it. As A. J. P. Taylor quotes Bismarck in his biography: 'Man cannot create the current of events. He can only float with it and steer.'; and again: 'A statesman cannot create anything himself. He must wait and listen until he hears the steps of God sounding through events; then leap up and grasp the hem of his garment.'[78] [There is a more recent German example: Hitler said, in a speech in Munich on 14 March 1936, 'I go with the certainty of a sleepwalker along the path laid out for me by Providence.'[79] Wight himself drew attention to this in his contribution 'Germany' in *The World in March 1939*, observing that it was 'perhaps the most terrifying sentence he ever uttered, expressing the menace of a resistless revolutionary tread that was itself one of the causes of demoralization in his adversaries'.[80] –Eds.] 'I believe', said Machiavelli in *The Prince*, 'that we are successful when our ways are suited to the times and circumstances, and unsuccessful when they are not'.[81] This idea of *fortuna* is reflected in Napoleon's comment, 'I want lucky marshals.' For Machiavelli the key to successful opportunism is to cultivate judgement of events; to be prepared, not expecting things always to be favourable; and to be bold, not shrinking from decisive action. [Wight also notes the passage at the close of ch. xxv of *The Prince* in which the submission of *fortuna* to those who seek to master her is likened to the success of *macho* courtship by young men. Here again Napoleon, a Corsican of Tuscan ancestry whose first language was Italian, and who was thus, in a sense, Machiavelli's compatriot of three centuries later, exemplifies what Machiavelli meant: his whole early career may be seen as the triumph of brilliant and daring opportunism carried out in the Revolutionary spirit of *'Toujours de l'audace!'* –Eds.]

So what is *fortuna*, the pagan goddess Τύχη, 'chance'? For Machiavelli it is the fortuitous, the incalculable, the accident in human affairs.

Machiavelli

Notes

1. Niccolò Machiavelli, *The Prince*, ch. VIII.
   [This and subsequent quotations from *The Prince* have been taken from Wight's notes. In the main they seem to have been freely adapted from the Everyman edition of 1908 (translation by W. K. Marriott, London, J.M. Dent) although sometimes the wording is clearly his own. Here we refer throughout, as does he, to the Everyman edition as well as to the Italian text as edited by L. A. Burd (*Il Principe*, Oxford, Clarendon Press, 1891). Thus, for this quotation, see Ev. p. 69, Burd p. 233.

   Note: Wight's 'political skill' is Machiavelli's *virtù*, a word he uses in several senses. Usually it denotes 'energy', 'drive', 'ability', or 'courage', but here it has overtones of 'moral virtue'; see Quentin Skinner and Russell Price, eds., *The Prince* (Cambridge: Cambridge University Press, 1988), p. 31n. –Eds.]
2. Machiavelli, *The Prince*, ch. XXI, Ev. p. 180, Burd pp. 342–3.
3. Ibid., ch. XXVI, Ev. p. 216, Burd p. 371.
4. Ibid., ch. XV, Ev. p. 121, Burd p. 283.
5. Francesco Guicciardini (1483–1540), Francesco Vettori (1474–1539), both historians and friends of Machiavelli.
6. Machiavelli, *The Discourses of Niccolò Machiavelli*, tr. Leslie J. Walker (London: Routledge & Kegan Paul, 1950), bk I, disc. 25, vol. I, p. 272.
7. Ibid., bk I, disc. 25, vol. I, p. 205.
8. Ibid., p. 206.
9. Ibid.
10. See Herbert Butterfield, *The Statecraft of Machiavelli* (London: G. Bell and Sons Ltd, 1940), pp. 28, 30, 71.
11. Henry St John Viscount Bolingbroke, *Letters on the Study and Use of History* (London: A. Millar, 1752), vol. I, p. 15; see also David Hume, 'An Inquiry Concerning Human Understanding', *Essays and Treatises* (Edinburgh: Bell and Bradfute, 1825), vol. II, sec. VIII, pp. 83–4; and Machiavelli, *The Discourses*, bk III, disc. 43, vol. I, p. 575.
12. Hugo Grotius, 'Prolegomena to the Law of War and Peace', *De Jure Belli ac Pacis Vol. II The Translation: On the Law of War and Peace*, tr. F. W. Kelsey (Oxford: Clarendon Press, 1925), nos. 42, 45, pp. 24, 26.

13 Greek original ascribed to Aristotle, *The Oxford Dictionary of Quotations*, 3rd edn. (London: Geoffrey Cumberlege; Oxford University Press, 1982), no. 12, p. 12.
14 E. H. Carr, *The Twenty Years' Crisis 1919–1939* (London: Macmillan & Co., 1939).
15 *The Prince*, ch. XVII, Ev. p. 134, Burd p. 292.
16 Ibid., ch. XVIII, Ev. p. 142, Burd p. 303.
17 *The Discourses*, bk I, disc. 58, vol. I, p. 341.
18 Ibid., p. 310.
19 James Burnham, *The Managerial Revolution* (London: Putnam, 1942), p. 271.
20 M. J. Oakeshott, 'Scientific Politics', *Cambridge Journal*, vol. 1, no. 6 (1948), p. 356.
21 *The Discourses*, bk I, disc. 37, vol. I, p. 295.
22 Thomas Hobbes, *Leviathan*, ed. Michael Oakeshott (Oxford: Basil Blackwell, 1946), pp. 63, 64.
23 *The Discourses*, bk I, disc. 40, vol. I, p. 309.
24 Hugo Grotius, *On the Law of War and Peace*, bk II, ch. I.ix, p. 177.
25 Ibid.
26 See John Stuart Mill, *Utilitarianism, Liberty, and Representative Government* (London: Dent, 1929), pp. 47–8.
27 Ian Fleming, *Casino Royale* (London: Pan, 1955), p. 145.
28 Quoted by Plato in *Cratylus* (402a) *The Oxford Dictionary of Quotations*, 3rd edn. (London: Geoffrey Cumberlege; Oxford University Press, 1982), no. 5, p. 246.
29 See Clement C. J. Webb, *A History of Philosophy* (London: Thornton Butterworth Ltd, 1937), pp. 16–17.
30 Benjamin Farrington, *Greek Science* (London: Penguin Books, 1949), vol. I, pp. 35ff.
31 Friedrich Hegel, *Science of Logic*, tr. W. H. Johnston and L. G. Struthers (London: George Allen and Unwin Ltd, 1929), vol. II, p. 67.
32 Edmund Wilson, *To the Finland Station* (London: Martin Secker and Warburg Ltd, 1941), p. 233.
33 See also Isaiah Berlin, *Karl Marx* (London: Thornton Butterworth Ltd, 1939), pp. 188–9.
34 Mikhail Bakúnin in Gustav A. Wetter, *Dialectical Materialism*, tr. Peter Heath (London: Routledge & Kegan Paul, 1958), pp. 335–6.
35 Wilson, *To the Finland Station*, p. 267.

36. Ibid.
37. Ibid., p. 281.
38. Ibid., p. 283.
39. Isaiah Berlin, *Karl Marx*, p. 105.
40. Karl Marx in Isaiah Berlin, *Karl Marx*, p. 113.
41. Ibid., p. 113; see also Wilson, *To the Finland Station*, p. 155.
42. Karl Marx, 'The Poverty of Philosophy', in Emile Burns, ed., *A Handbook of Marxism* (London: Victor Gollancz Ltd, 1935), p. 358.
43. Berlin, *Karl Marx*, p. 113.
44. See Wetter, *Dialectical Materialism*, p. 119.
45. Ibid., p. 335.
46. V. I. Lenin, 'Philosophical Notebooks' in Wetter, *Dialectical Materialism*, p. 146.
47. *The Discourses*, bk I, disc. 3, vol. I, p. 217.
48. Ibid., bk I, disc. 18, vol. I, p. 258.
49. *The Prince*, ch. XII, Ev. p. 97, Burd pp. 253–5.
50. *The Discourses*, bk III, disc. 31, vol. I, p. 551.
51. Ibid., bk I, disc. 2, vol. I, pp. 212–13.
52. Hobbes, *Leviathan*, p. 94.
53. Carr, *The Twenty Years' Crisis*, see pp. 228, 229, 231, and 213.
54. Hans J. Morgenthau, *In Defense of the National Interest* (New York: Alfred J. Knopf, 1951), p. 34.
55. Hans J. Morgenthau, *Dilemmas of Politics* (Chicago: University of Chicago Press, 1958), pp. 81–3.
56. Martin Wight, 'Philosophy and Politics', *International Affairs*, vol. 35, no. 2 (April 1959), pp. 199–200.
57. Marx, 'A Contribution to "the Critique of Political Economy"', 1859, in *A Handbook of Marxism*, p. 372; see also Wetter, *Dialectical Materialism*, p. 32.
58. Neville Chamberlain in the House of Commons, 22 February 1938, *Hansard's Parliamentary Debates*, vol. 332, col. 223.
59. Rebecca West, *Black Lamb and Grey Falcon* (New York: The Viking Press, 1944), p. 883.
60. Thucydides, *History of the Peleponnesian War*, tr. Charles Forster Smith (London: W. Heinemann Ltd, 1953), bk iii, ch. LXXXII, Loeb vol. ii, p. 143.

61 See F. P. Walters, *A History of the League of Nations* (London: RIIA and Oxford University Press, 1952), vol. II, pp. 684ff.
62 William Shakespeare, *Macbeth*, Act 3 Scene 1.
63 Hugh R. Wilson, *Diplomat Between Wars* (London: Longmans, Green & Co., 1941), p. 260.
64 Reinhold Niebuhr, *The Irony of American History* (London: Nisbet & Co. Ltd, 1952), preface pp. ix–x.
65 Lord Robert Cecil, 'The League is dead, Long live the United Nations'. At the last Assembly of the League in the Palais des Nations, Geneva, April 1946. See Walters, *A History of the League of Nations*, vol. II, p. 815.
66 *The Prince*, ch. VII, Ev. pp. 61–2, Burd pp. 226–7.
67 [See: Roy Jenkins, *Truman* (London: Collins, 1986), p. 62; Richard Lawrence Miller, *Truman: The Rise to Power* (New York: McGraw-Hill Book Co., 1986), pp. 383–4; and William E. Pemberton, *Harry S. Truman* (Boston: Twayne Publishers, 1989), pp. 33–4. –Eds.]
68 *The Discourses*, intro. IX, axiom VII, vol. I, p. 98.
69 *The Prince*, ch. III, Ev. p. 27, Burd p. 199.
70 See *The Discourses*, bk III, disc. 20, vol. I, p. 524.
71 Ibid., bk III, disc. 21, vol. I, pp. 525, 527.
72 [In English the idea is perhaps best expressed in Kipling's poem 'If—', with its clinching closing line. In its advice to a youth aspiring to be a Man, its worldly-wise counsel, and its advocating daring instead of caution, the poem exudes the Machiavellian spirit of *virtù*. –Eds.]
73 *The Discourses*, bk III, disc. 2, vol. I, pp. 464–5; see also bk II, disc. 23, p. 425, and vol. II, p. 129.
74 *The Prince*, ch. VII, Ev. p. 54, Burd p. 213. [Cf. Shakespeare's 'some are born great, some achieve greatness, and some have greatness thrust upon them' (*Twelfth Night*, Act 2 Scene 5). –Eds.]
75 *The Prince*, ch. XXI, Ev. p. 181, Burd pp. 344–5.
76 *The Discourses*, bk I, disc. 6, vol. I, p. 225.
77 *The Prince*, ch. XXV, Ev. p. 203, Burd p. 358.
78 A. J. P. Taylor, *Bismarck: The Man and Statesman* (London: Hamish Hamilton, 1955), pp. 70, 115.
79 Ian Kershaw, *Hitler* (London: Allen Lane, The Penguin Press, 1998), vol. I, p. 591.

Machiavelli

80 Martin Wight, 'Germany', in Arnold Toynbee and Frank T. Ashton-Gwatkin, eds., *The World in March 1939* (London: Oxford University Press, 1952), p. 347. The reference given is Hitler: *Speeches* (N. H. Baines, ed.) ii, 1307.

81 *The Prince*, ch. XXV, Ev. p. 205, Burd p. 360. See also *The Discourses*, bk III, disc. 9, vol. I, p. 496.

Chapter 2

Grotius

10 April 1583–28 August 1645

Life and Achievement

Grotius is famous for his precocity, erudition, and omnicompetence. He represented the glory of Baroque learning as Kant did the Enlightenment. Born at Delft during the Dutch Revolt, of a good family, he had at the age of fourteen brought out a new edition of Martianus Capella's *The Wedding of Philology and Mercury* (written between AD 410 and 439). This was a romantic fictionalized account of a system of education that provided the authentic medieval description of the liberal arts: grammar, rhetoric, dialectic, arithmetic, geometry, music, and astronomy.[1]

Grotius, when aged fifteen, travelled with Oldenbarnevelt on his mission to Henry IV in 1598, and Henry is reputed to have said of him, 'Behold the miracle of Holland.' He spent a year in France, and produced at the age of sixteen a Latin translation of Stevin's treatise on navigation by compass, displaying his good knowledge of mathematics. After this precocious start Grotius in time became a lawyer, jurist, poet, theologian, and politician.

He was Attorney-General (Advocaat-Fiscaal) of Holland and Zealand at twenty-four. When he was eighteen he wrote

Grotius

Adamus Exul, a tragedy in Latin verse, and a few years later *Christus Patiens*. As theologian he wrote commentaries on the Old and New Testaments and *On the Verity of the Christian Religion*. His biblical criticism is a lucid detached scientific exegesis showing a wide historical background. He had an ecumenical and irenic standpoint, transcending the Reformation, writing for 'the whole Christian world'. Several Christian persuasions contended for him (it is thought he died a Catholic) and he always advocated toleration. He was an ancestor of the World Council of Churches; he envisaged a council of the Churches not represented at the Council of Trent. When he visited England with the mission negotiating freedom of navigation and commerce in the Indian seas, he also tried to persuade James I to hold a general synod and bring about a union of all Reformed Churches. He became identified with Arminian liberal Calvinism.[2]

Grotius was not successful as a politician. In 1612 he became Pensionary (or Mayor) of Rotterdam, the second city of the Union. But Grotius was an intellectual in politics and could not handle men—nor survive the Dutch revolution of 1618. It was fought over the independence of the smaller provinces against Holland; the war with Spain as against peace with Spain; the Calvinists fighting the Arminians, and Maurice fighting Oldenbarnevelt. Grotius and Oldenbarnevelt were arrested and tried for treason; the latter was beheaded, Grotius imprisoned for life. He was kept in Loevestein Castle from 1619 to 1621 with his wife, children, and books. He wrote several books there, among them *Introduction to the Jurisprudence of Holland* and, aided by his wife, escaped in 1621 in a chest of books, while questioning 'whether it is permissible to use ruse or deceit in war'![3]

He fled to Paris, where he lived from 1621 to 1631 receiving a pension from the French government, which was later discontinued by Richelieu. In 1632 he went to Germany but returned to Paris as Swedish ambassador in 1635. He was thus the representative of France's chief ally, and negotiated the alliance between them. He was competent, but disillusioned. He was recalled to Sweden and died at Rostock in 1645. 'By undertaking many things I have accomplished little', he said of himself.[4] But he is the acknowledged father of International Law. *De Jure Praedae* (*The Law of Prize*), written during the winter of 1604–5, and unknown until rediscovered in 1864 and published in 1868, briefed the Dutch East India Company in its dispute with the Portuguese. *Mare Liberum* was one of its chapters and the only one published (in 1609). It was particularly relevant to the controversy shortly afterwards between the English and the Dutch over fishing rights (Selden's *Mare Clausum* of 1618, published in 1635, put the English case). It was also relevant to the Spanish designs against the Dutch in the Eastern seas. His *De Jure Belli ac Pacis* (1625), written in Paris and dedicated to Louis XIII, was an immediate success. 'It supplied...the protestant nations... with...a rational theory of international relations emancipated from theology.'[5] It became the textbook of the new Europe of Westphalia. The book was put on the Papal Index, not for any doctrine that it enunciated but for the petty reason that it did not refer to the popes by their proper Roman Catholic titles. This probably promoted its sales. In 1899 when Leo XIII applied for an invitation to the Hague Peace Conference he was refused, among other reasons, because Grotius was still banned. The ban was lifted two years later in 1901.

Ambiguity and Inaccessibility

One of the main difficulties in studying Grotius is his ambiguity, and this stems not least from his inaccessibility. *De Jure Belli ac Pacis* is a very difficult book. It is systematic in an obsolete way, a legal encyclopaedia, including much that is not international law and buttressed with ancient learning and classical quotations. Grotius avoided contemporary political examples so as not to give offence and because ancient ones were deemed better.⁶ It is difficult to find clear doctrines and principles in it; it can appear self-contradictory and confused, but it also displays richness and tension. Lauterpacht has commented:

> We cannot even consider him as what is usually described as a 'Grotian' who has accomplished a workable synthesis of natural law and state practice. The fact seems to be that on most subjects which he discusses in his treatise it is impossible to say what is Grotius's view of the legal position. He will tell us, often with regard to the same question, what is the law of nature, the law of nations, divine law, Mosaic law, the law of the Gospel, Roman law, the law of charity, the obligations of honour, or considerations of utility. But we often look in vain for a statement as to what is *the* law governing the matter... The fact is that we are often at a loss as to the true meaning which he attaches to the law of nature.⁷

One consequence of this ambiguity is that Grotius can be posthumously all things to all men; he is interpretable in various ways. Lauterpacht draws him in the image of Lauterpacht: he attributes to Grotius 'pacifism', 'the idea of peace', and 'the tradition of idealism and progress'.⁸ In contrast see Walter Schiffer in *The Legal Community of Mankind*:

> He obviously did not believe that some time in the future men would become so reasonable that they would generally arrive at uniform judgments with regard to the justice or injustice of the causes of wars... He did not expect that generally the law of nations would constantly improve until it was identical with natural law... Grotius neither expected nor suggested any fundamental changes in the conditions on which his legal theory was based.⁹

In a word, he did *not* believe in progress.¹⁰

Richness and Complexity

Such ambiguity is not due just to methodological confusion, but to a richness and complexity that reflects international politics themselves. There is a moral complexity in the question of Allied area bombing of Germany in the Second World War, or in the attempted distinction between the tactical and strategic use of atomic weapons. Does the numerical increase in the number of combatants or fighting men who are killed with one nuclear bomb alter the quality of the attack? Is the marginal destruction of non-combatants morally decisive, for instance in destroying railway junctions [or dams –Eds.]? What proportion of non-combatants may be destroyed without exceeding the bounds of necessity? Has the distinction between combatants and non-combatants become obsolete? Is the effect of the use of certain weapons upon the future morally decisive—the effect not so much on posterity, in tactical use only, but on the long-term physical geography of the locality attacked, making it a desert? Has the moral quality of the act been altered if it is done as reprisal or retaliation—the declaration of 'no first use' being seen as a moral justification? Does the moral quality of tactical use depend entirely on the pragmatic validity of the distinction from strategic use: that is, on success in avoiding a general nuclear war; or on restricting destruction to no-man's-lands (Koreas, Germanys, Middle Easts) and avoiding the destructions of the Great Powers? [Written 1959].

This is the maze in which we are lost. Grotius reflects more accurately this morally multidimensional character of our experience than, arguably, any other writer on the subject. (It is true, he was seeking to establish legal, not moral rules, but he is throughout concerned with both and does not always succeed in distinguishing them.) He reproduces an endless dialectic of the real and ideal, the actual and permissible, with all its tensions and facets, hesitations, and qualifications. To simplify crudely: if you are apt to think the moral problems of international politics are simple, you are a natural, instinctive Kantian; if you think they are non-existent, bogus, or delusory, you are a natural Machiavellian; and if you are apt to think them infinitely complex, bewildering, and perplexing, you are probably a natural Grotian.

Grotius

Reconciler: The Middle Way

Another aspect of the Grotian genius is the golden mean, or Aristotelian moderation. He was a reconciler and synthesizer; *De Veritate Religionis Christianae* (1627) offered a programme for the reunion of Christendom: 'Grotius suggested that the views of all Christianity might be reconciled, if a common basis of piety were stressed, and doctrinal differences minimized; on the basis of scriptural evidence, he set forth a series of propositions common to all Christianity.'[11] The monstrous barbarity of the Thirty Years War had led many to believe that all arms should be forbidden to a Christian. Grotius tells us that this idea had earlier been expressed by his countryman Erasmus, perhaps

> on the principle that to straighten a bent stick one must bend it strongly the other way. But this attempt to force too much to an opposite extreme often does more harm than good, inasmuch as exaggeration, so readily apparent, detracts from the authority of a more reasonably advanced truth. A remedy must therefore be found for both schools of extremists—for those that believe that in war nothing is lawful and for those for whom all things are lawful in war.[12]

This moderation is shown also in Grotius' quotation from Gellius on disobedience to unjust orders: 'The middle view therefore seems the best and safest, that some commands are to be obeyed, and some other commands not.'[13]

Restrain Evil: Lessen Suffering

It is plain that Grotius was deeply sensitive to human suffering, and equally did not imagine it could ever disappear. There is a famous account in the 'Prolegomena' to *On the Law of War and Peace* of Grotius' motive in writing:

> ... there were many and weighty considerations impelling me to write a treatise on the subject of [the law of war]. I observed everywhere in Christendom a lawlessness in warfare of which even barbarous

nations would be ashamed. Nations would rush to arms on the slightest pretext or even without cause at all. And arms once taken up, there would be an end to all respect for law, whether human or divine, as though a fury had been let loose with general licence for all manner of crime.[14]

But it is clear that he did not imagine war could be abolished. His aim was, by distinguishing the just from the unjust, to canalize war and restrain its brutality. He repudiated the idea of world government:

> Nor should any one be influenced by the arguments of Dante, by which he strives to prove that such a right belongs to the Emperor because that is advantageous for the human race. The advantages which it brings are in fact offset by its disadvantages. For as a ship may attain to such a size that it cannot be steered, so also the number of inhabitants and the distance between places may be so great as not to tolerate a single government.[15]

He imagined a static condition of affairs, both in the continuation of a half-anarchical international society, and in the consistency of good and evil, happiness and suffering. This view has been echoed since, notably by Burke:

> We must soften into a credulity below the milkiness of infancy, to think all men virtuous. We must be tainted with a malignity truly diabolical, to believe all the world to be equally wicked and corrupt. Men are in publick life as in private, some good, some evil. The elevation of the one, and the depression of the other, are the first objects of all true policy.[16]

And Nehru later observed:

> Gandhi said on one occasion that it was his supreme ambition to wipe every tear from every eye. That was an ambition beyond even his power to realise, for many millions of eyes have shed tears in India, in Asia, and in the rest of the world; and perhaps it may never be possible to stop, completely, this unending flow of human sorrow. But it is certainly possible for us to lessen human want and misery and suffering; and what are politics and all our arguments worth if they do not have this aim in view?[17]

Natural Law

Grotius identified various aspects of natural law. The first is man's sociability: '...among the traits characteristic of man is an impelling desire for society, that is, for the social life—not of any and every sort, but peaceful, and organized according to the measure of his intelligence, with those who are of his own kind; this social trend the Stoics called "sociableness."'[18] Behind this sociability run certain fundamental principles, which guide human life.

This maintenance of the social order...which is consonant with human intelligence, is the source of law properly so called...[19]

...the law of nature...proceeding as it does from the essential traits implanted in man...[20]

For the very nature of man, which even if we had no lack of anything would lead us into the mutual relations of society, is the mother of the law of nature. But the mother of municipal law is that obligation which arises from mutual consent; and since this obligation derives its force from the law of nature, nature may be considered, so to say, the great-grandmother of municipal law.[21]

There are various examples of this natural law: property rights—abstaining from that which is another's and restoring possessions to their owner; reparation—making good a loss incurred through our own fault; and punishment—inflicting penalties according to deserts ('Prolegomena' 8). There is also a principle of distributive justice: the 'rational allotment to each man, or to each social group, of those things which are properly theirs'—giving preference to a relative rather than a stranger, the poor man rather than the well-to-do, a wise man rather than a fool, 'as the conduct of each or the nature of the thing suggests'.[22] Keeping promises is another principle of natural law—*Pacta sunt servanda*: '...it is a rule of the law of nature to abide by pacts (for it was necessary that among men there be some method of obligating themselves to one another, and no other natural method can be imagined).'[23] This is the source of municipal law.

The law of nature is not concerned only with justice and its enforcement, but also with actions exemplifying other virtues, such as self-mastery, bravery, and prudence, which are not merely honourable, but even obligatory when constrained by regard for others.[24] Thus self-defence is allowed by natural law but not if it involves the death of a man useful to the state, such as the king. This seems to be a statement of what Grotius thinks natural law to be—'the law of nature, in so far as it has the force of a law, holds in view not only the dictates of expletive justice ... but also actions exemplifying other virtues'.[25]

It may be necessary to guard against the notion of natural law as a kind of super-morality, a statement of the highest ethic of political life; as a suit that trumps all other suits in the card-game of political argument. It is concerned with the fundamental principles of human social life as they can be rationally deduced, and this is a different enterprise from exploring the highest ethic. Take, for example, the principles of marriage. Grotius says that polygamy, concubinage, and divorce are permissible by the law of nature, though forbidden by the Gospel. He says, with unusual irritation for him (not naming certain Puritans, no doubt):

It is amazing to see how ... [some people] labour in the effort to prove that things which are forbidden by the Gospel are not permissible by the law of nature ... These things in fact are of such a nature that reason itself declares that it is morally better to abstain from them, but they are not such that wickedness would be manifest in them without divine law ... Pertinent is the saying of Justin: 'To live according to nature is the problem of him who has not yet become a believer.'[26]

Thus natural law is not necessarily *Christian* theory at all.

On the other hand, consider the principles of slavery: liberty is attributed to men by nature; by nature no one is a slave, slavery is contrary to nature. (By contrast, elsewhere Grotius quotes Aristotle's *Politics*: 'Aristotle said that some men are by nature slaves, that is, are suited to slavery, so there are some peoples so constituted that they understand better how to be ruled than to rule.')[27] However, says Grotius, it is not a right of man never to be enslaved; it is not in conflict with natural justice that slavery should have its origin in a human act.[28] There is a form of voluntary subjection; complete slavery in exchange for certainty of lifelong support.[29] Liberty depends also on the law of nations: 'According to the law of nations all persons captured in a war that is public become slaves.'[30] There is a qualified argument here that children can be born into slavery, that it has hereditary status. However, slaves may flee, if a master is unjust.[31]

> ...just as the law of nations...permits many things which are forbidden by the law of nature, so it forbids certain things which are permissible by the law of nature. If you take account only of the law of nature, in [circumstances where] it is permissible to kill a person, it makes no difference whether you kill him by the sword or by poison [although it is nobler to give him the chance to defend himself].[32]

Nevertheless the law of nations has long forbidden poison. 'Agreement upon this matter arose from a consideration of the common advantage, in order that the dangers of war...might not be too widely extended.' (Would this apply to poison gas too?)

Grotius also saw natural law as corresponding with the principles of utility: 'The law of nature...has the reinforcement of expediency; for the Author of nature willed that as individuals we should be weak, and should lack many things needed in order to live properly, to the end that we might be the more constrained to cultivate the social life.'[33] Utility or expediency is the occasion of municipal law. It is as if Grotius says to posterity: 'You may think of natural law in terms of utility or expediency if you like.'[34] Would Bentham have agreed?

Grotius made a famous declaration that the fundamental principles of human social life are valid irrespective of being willed by God or any other supernatural authority: 'What we have been saying would have a degree of validity even if we should concede that which cannot be conceded without the utmost wickedness, that there is no God, or that the affairs of men are of no concern to Him.'[35] But Grotius does believe in God, and if natural law proceeds from the essential traits of human nature, it was God who arranged such traits to be there.[36] He argues that law is not founded on expediency alone: no state is so powerful that it may not need the help of others sometimes, either for commerce or defence; the most powerful states seek alliances 'which are quite devoid of significance according to the point of view of those who confine law within the boundaries of states. Most true is the saying, that all things are uncertain the moment men depart from law.'[37] That is, the principle of utility presupposes natural law.

We come to know natural law by reason. Natural law concerns the fundamental principles of *human* social life, not of animal social life, for humans alone have reason and speech. Reason is that 'knowledge which prompts [man] to similar actions under similar conditions', the 'faculty of knowing and of acting in accordance with general principles', the 'power of discrimination which enables him to decide what things are agreeable or harmful (as to both things present and things to come) . . .'[38]

Grotius saw natural law as being rational, that is, wholly open to exploration by reason and reducible to a systematic form. Natural law is based on the nature of human beings, not, like other laws, on their will, nor directly on the will of God;[39] but it covers matters resulting from human will. '. . . outside of the law of nature, the binding force of law comes from the will of him who makes the law.'[40] It is unchanging: 'The law of nature, again, is unchangeable—even in the sense that it cannot be changed by God.' He quotes Aristotle: 'Some things are thought of as bad the moment they are named', their badness is intrinsic, a property. Acts enjoined by the law of nature can change, when the thing concerned has changed:

. . . some things belong to the law of nature not through a simple relation but as a result of . . . circumstances. Thus the use of things in common was in accordance with the law of nature so long as ownership by individuals was not introduced; and the right to use force in obtaining one's own existed before laws were promulgated.[41]

Thus it seems there is a natural law with a variable content.

Natural law is self-evident:

> I have made it my concern to refer the proofs of things touching the law of nature to certain fundamental conceptions which are beyond question, so that no one can deny them without doing violence to himself. For the principles of that law, if only you pay strict heed to them, are in themselves manifest and clear, almost as evident as are those things which we perceive by the external senses.[42]

It also resembles mathematics: 'With all truthfulness I aver that, just as mathematicians treat their figures as abstracted from bodies, so in treating law I have withdrawn my mind from every particular fact.'[43] Thus it is unfair to think, he says, that in his writing he has current international controversies in mind. In the law of nature one must distinguish between what is evident and what is not; between general principles such as: live honourably, do not seize another's possessions; and inferences: marriage excludes adultery, vengeance satisfied with inflicting pain is wicked. 'Here we have almost the same thing as in mathematics, where there are certain primary notions, or notions akin to those that are primary, certain proofs which are at once recognized and admitted, and certain others which are true indeed but not evident to all.'[44] The law of nature is unchangeable even by God, on the analogy of mathematics: 'Just as even God, then, cannot cause that two times two should not make four [this being a contradiction], so He cannot cause that that which is intrinsically evil be not evil.'[45]

Grotius also believed natural law is reducible to a system, 'codifiable', and potentially scientific: '. . . the principles of the law of nature, since they are always the same, can easily be brought into a systematic form; but the elements of positive law, since they often undergo change and are different in different places, are outside the domain of systematic treatment.'[46] Proofs of natural law can be *a priori* or *a posteriori*. 'Proof *a priori* consists in demonstrating the necessary agreement or disagreement of anything with a rational and social nature.'[47] Proof *a posteriori* is when you conclude that *probably* a matter has been considered natural law among all nations, or among the most civilized. (Note the qualification on higher European standards.)[48] To prove its existence *a posteriori*, he uses evidence of philosophers, historians, poets, and orators, with discrimination. History supplies both the illustrations and the judgements, by which the law of nature is supported.[49]

> ... when many at different times, and in different places, affirm the same thing as certain, that ought to be referred to a universal cause.

> ... an effect that is universal demands a universal cause; and the cause of such an opinion can hardly be anything else than the feeling which is called the common sense of mankind.[50]

This universal cause must be either a correct deduction from the principles of nature, which points to the law of nature, or a common consent among mankind, which points to the law of nations.[51]

Natural law is contrasted with *Jus Gentium* (the law of nations). '[W]hatever cannot be deduced from certain principles by a sure process of reasoning, ... must have its origin in the free will of man.'[52] *Jus Gentium* also arises from utility: having 'in view the advantage, not of particular states, but of the great society of states'. It has no immediate sanction: '... law, even though without a sanction, is not entirely void of effect. For justice brings peace of conscience, while injustice causes torments and anguish.'[53] It is not foolish to obey the laws of your country; nor for a nation to observe laws common to all:

> For just as the national, who violates the law of his country in order to obtain an immediate advantage, breaks down that by which the advantages of himself and his posterity are ... assured, so the state which transgresses the laws of nature and of nations cuts away also the bulwarks which safeguard its own future peace. Even if no advantage were

to be contemplated from the keeping of the law, it would be a mark of wisdom, not of folly, to allow ourselves to be drawn towards that to which we feel that our nature leads.[54]

Thus its sanctions are utility and morals in the modern language of legal theory. Grotius' sanctions are expressed in his dedication to *Mare Liberum*: 'God who reserves to himself the ultimate decision, slow, hidden, inevitable, has nevertheless delegated two judges for the cognizance of human affairs, whom the most fortunate of guilty men cannot escape—his own conscience, and the judgement of the society to which he belongs.'[55] Here, shorn of all technicalities, is the Grotian theory of justice between nations, based in part upon the law of nature, in part upon the voluntary law, i.e. the moral standard of right conduct in international affairs.[56]

But Grotius argues that law is not only command.[57] He rejects a voluntarist theory of law; law has a wider nature and function than command. For Hooker, law is: 'any kind of rule or canon, whereby actions are framed'; for Aquinas: 'Law is a rule or measure of action in virtue of which one is led to perform certain actions and restrained from the performance of others';[58] and for Locke: 'The state of Nature has a law of Nature to govern it, which obliges every one, and reason, which is that law, teaches all mankind who will but consult it....'[59] Grotius' famous definition is that: 'The law of nature is a dictate of right reason, which points out that an act, according as it is or is not in conformity with rational nature, has in it a quality of moral baseness or moral necessity; and that, in consequence, such an act is either forbidden or enjoined by the author of nature, God.'[60] The law of nature indicates that an act has moral qualities. The roof of natural law is open to the sky of morality, just as the whole of the front of a building is open to the law of nations.

It is important to distinguish all this from Kant. Kant too has 'Reason', 'Nature', 'Laws of Nature' in his vocabulary, but Kant stands at the further end of the natural law discussion, which by his time is scarcely recognizable. D'Entrèves includes Kant among 'the greatest natural law theorists'[61] because he argued that jurisprudence cannot be based on empirical or positivist principles alone: a universal criterion of right and wrong, just and unjust 'may remain entirely hidden even from the practical Jurist until he abandon his empirical principles for a time, and search in the pure Reason for the sources of such judgments, in order to lay a real foundation for actual positive Legislations'.[62]

Several changes in the argument may be noted: 'Nature' has become dynamized, divinized, become purposeful, equated with Providence or Fate; it is the immanent significance of the movement of human affairs. Meanwhile the 'Law of Nature' has become physicized (following Hobbes and Newton), by a contrary development. It is to do with the regularities of inanimate nature, and the starry heavens—the 'Natural Law of [man's] wants' only, not the realm of ends and morality.[63] And 'Natural Law' has become individualistic and passed over into 'Natural Rights'. Kant's idealism is akin to a natural right doctrine, denying the sociality of man and positing the being of an individual as the first and highest thing.[64] The norms of human social behaviour, which is the law of nature for Grotius, can be discovered by the empirical study of human nature and they are not isolated from factual existence. But for Kant they are so isolated, laid down by the action of the constructive human mind.[65] 'Reason' has also become inflated and divinized. It is no longer just the faculty of drawing conclusions from premises, but now a 'legislative' faculty, 'pure spontaneity'; 'it manifests its highest function in distinguishing the sensible and intelligible worlds from one another and so in marking out limits for understanding itself.'[66] Thus reason provides *a priori* principles, and mostly Kant regards reasoning as an *a priori* activity, forming its concepts in isolation from experience, and producing moral law without reference to experience.[67] Reason transcends understanding.

It is the change in the meaning of 'Nature' that took place that is the most important. Natural law in the Grotian sense is replaced by progress in the Kantian sense. The natural law doctrine offered a static or stable order as the groundwork of history and society; progress substituted a dynamic order. Historically, one replaced the other; people ceased to believe in Grotian natural law and found themselves believing in progress, passing from one to the other across the bridge of natural rights. Contemporaries have not yet found a new alternative. Do we go back to natural law, resurrect progress, or go forward to nihilism?

Prescription

Before proceeding we must examine those aspects of natural law connected with political effects. Morgenthau said that natural law 'has ... always been a political ideology and predominantly an ideology of the status quo'.[68] It is also, he said, the ideology of imperialism.[69] D'Entrèves describes the radicalism of natural law in its natural rights form, as in 'Jefferson's radical assertion, that any form of government which proves destructive of the "inalienable rights" of man should be altered or abolished'.[70]

Perhaps the accounts of D'Entrèves and Morgenthau describe two phases of the decline of natural law. Yet classic natural law, in its Grotian form, presupposing a static and timeless moral order, tends to encourage stability (or stagnation) in politics. It upholds 'stability' as a political norm or value as against 'progress', 'moving forward', or 'change'. In Kennan's broadcast of 27 October 1959 concerning atomic weapons development and East–West relations over Berlin, the keyword was 'stability', as if the situation was sliding downhill and an enormous effort were needed to shore it up.[71]

The natural law doctrine in the sphere of international theoretical jurisprudence has its natural offspring in the doctrine of prescription in practical law. This is the opposite of 'revolutionary presumption'—the belief in only a provisional right of existing political forms and powers. Prescription asserts a presumption in favour of existing political forms. This is Burke's position: if an institution has lasted a long time, it has acquired merits, proved its virtues, been tested, and become venerable. It is the Englishman's 'sullen resistance of innovation' and 'unalterable perseverance in the wisdom of prejudice'.[72] It goes naturally with a backward-looking view:

> A spirit of innovation is generally the result of a selfish temper, and confined views. People will not look forward to posterity, who never look backward to their ancestors... Always acting as if in the presence of canonized forefathers, the spirit of freedom, leading in itself to misrule and excess, is tempered with an awful gravity.[73]

Contrast the Kantian assumption that we must strive from present and past imperfections to a better world, or Bentham's belief that old institutions were not venerable, but vested interests: 'The wisdom of our ancestors is the infantile foolishness of the cradle of the race.'

Grotius discusses prescription under its Roman civil law term: 'usucaption'—the acquisition of a right to property by uninterrupted and undisputed possession for a prescribed term. '...time...in its own nature has no effective force; nothing is done by time, though everything is done in time.'[74] Usucaption was introduced by municipal law. If its principle is not valid internationally, then 'a very serious inconvenience clearly follows, in that contests about kingdoms and the boundaries of kingdoms never come to an end with lapse of time. Such a condition... not only tends to disturb the minds of many and to occasion wars, but is also contrary to the common sense of nations.'[75] He concludes that lapse of time and non-possession and silence lead to the abandonment of right. The lapse of time must be time 'exceeding the memory of man', such memory being normally less than a century, or three generations. This is probably the law of nations by consent.[76] It seems to be a principle of international law today. Prescription in international law is defined as 'the acquisition of sovereignty over a territory through continuous and undisturbed exercise of sovereignty over it during such a period as is necessary to create under the influence of historical development the general conviction that the present condition of things is in conformity with international order.'[77] For the Kantian this does not wash; a hundred years' unright, usurpation, does not make a right. Dante, wanting to revive the Roman Empire (a backward-looking revolutionary), asserts that prescription cannot annul a right, which expires only with the end of time itself.[78]

The principle of prescription also leads to the doctrine of precedents. The Kantian argues that one should not be bound by an old precedent but create a new one. Thus: 'For Milton, the fact that it is unprecedented for a Protestant State to cut off the head of its king counts *in favour* of doing it. The true ideologist always prefers creating a shining new precedent to being tied by stale old precedents.'[79]

Political Variety: Multiformity versus Uniformity

A doctrine of prescription tends to sanction a wide variety of political conditions. If the criterion of validity is conformity to some pattern, like Kant's republicanism or Stalin's 'people's democracies', then political uniformity will tend to follow. But if the criterion of validity is simply long-continuance or duration, then political variety will tend to establish itself, since all development, political as well as biological, seems to move from the simple to the complex, the homogeneous to the heterogeneous. Grotius, as a prescriptionist, advocated multiformity. He expressly rejected the opinion that everywhere and without exception sovereignty resides in the people. A people can legally surrender its right to govern and:

submit itself to some one person, or to several persons, in such a way as plainly to transfer to him the legal right to govern, retaining no vestige of that right for itself...

Just as, in fact, there are many ways of living, one being better than another, and out of so many ways of living each is free to select that which he prefers, so also a people can select the form of government which it wishes; and the extent of its legal right in the matter is not to be measured by the superior excellence of this or that form of government, in regard to which different men hold different views, but by its free choice.[80]

Sometimes, says Grotius, a monarchy or dictatorship is necessary for the safety and welfare of the state (e.g. Augustus Caesar). He holds, too, that it is not universally true that all government is constituted for the benefit of the governed though that is mostly true, and he also states that unjust kings cannot be removed: there is no right of revolution.[81]

Grotius' reluctance to champion political liberty against absolutist monarchy has worried some commentators who have sought such explanations as that *De Jure Belli ac Pacis* was dedicated to Louis XIII in 1625 (as mentioned above, p. 31),[82] but his position here does seem consonant with the rest of his outlook. It is prophetic of the European *Ancien Régime* introduced by the Treaty of Westphalia in 1648. This brought neither Catholic uniformity (the Lutherans and Calvinists were validated), nor political uniformity: it accommodated absolute monarchies, limited monarchies (Britain); elective monarchies (Poland); aristocratic republics (Venice, Genoa, Hansa), and federal democracies (Switzerland, Holland, and eventually the United States as hymned by Burke). The French Revolution, assaulting this as it crumbled, started the pendulum swinging. It first swung towards the Rights of Man and popular sovereignty, and then back to the Holy Alliance and legitimacy. Nevertheless, the nineteenth century, the age of the Concert, saw perhaps the maximum political variety when Turkey was admitted to the family of nations. The *Ancien Régime* had been a Christian family, although divided; in 1856 the principle of cultural exclusion was abandoned and the principle of political exclusion was not yet successfully established.

The First World War pushed the pendulum again: the League of Nations Covenant (Article 1) refers to 'any fully self-governing State, Dominion or Colony', and Wilson meant this to be a democratic qualification for membership; but the Charter (Article 4) speaks of 'all other peace-loving States'. The general assumption about political legitimacy today [late 1950s –Eds.] is that it is democratic: this is Kantian. There is, for example, a bland British assumption that the newly emerging countries of the Commonwealth might take a long time before they become adept in working parliamentary government. But perhaps Ghana, Ceylon [Sri Lanka], and Malaya are not going in that direction at all, but working out a new kind of political form in accordance with their own traditions, wherein wigs, maces, and lords-of-appeal-in-ordinary will play but a small part. Grotius did not conceive of an outlaw state; the 'society of the human race' embraced all. One can find reasons in him to guess that he would have favoured the diplomatic recognition of Communist China (though the principles of diplomatic recognition were a problem for the future), and would not have favoured the withdrawal of ambassadors from Franco's Spain, although if Communist China was to be ostracized as a branded aggressor he would have had sympathy with the particular cause of ostracism. [This refers to the General Assembly's condemnation in February 1951 of Chinese intervention in Korea. –Eds.]

This question of political uniformity as against multiformity reflects a question of moral philosophy. Are there many ways of achieving the good life or only one way? Are there many roads to heaven, or only one? Is goodness simple, badness manifold? In *The Republic* Plato states the principle of the *unity of virtue*: 'on this point of vantage to which we have climbed... What I see is that, whereas there is only one form of excellence, imperfection exists in innumerable shapes.'[83] This is repeated in Aristotle's *Ethics*: 'error is multiform... whereas success is possible in one way only'.[84]

We need not trouble to sort out this unexpected accord between the two philosophers, whom one might expect to find on opposite sides in such an issue. They illustrate one moral standpoint—believing in the *unity of virtue*. It is echoed by Tolstoy in *Anna Karenina*: 'Happy families are all alike; every unhappy family is unhappy in its own way.'[85] Tolstoy was a Platonist; it is not an empirical observation, but an assertion by one whose philosophy or temperament leads him to see more clearly the similarities in happy families and the dissimilarities in unhappy ones. Are happy countries all alike, and unhappy ones each unhappy in its own way? The opposite principle would be the *variety of virtue*, perhaps: *dilige, et fac quod vis* ('Love, and do what thou wilt').[86] Kantians assert a unity of political virtue, Grotians a variety.

Beyond Natural Law: Hierarchy of Moral Life

Natural law is not enough; beyond it is the hierarchy of moral life. It is sometimes thought that the doctrine of natural law (and its revival today) means 'an assertion that law is a part of ethics'.[87] This is true so far as it goes, but it does not mean that all political ethics are comprised in natural law, whatever that is agreed to be. If natural law resembles a house open to the sky, then the moral realm exists up above where the roof might be. Just as natural law lies beyond positive law, so morals lie beyond natural law, and there is a hierarchy of moral laws and values. Natural law consists of the fundamental principles of human social life, but these do not comprise all the principles of the good life. Natural law is the measure of conduct a man is entitled to require from others; it is not a final measure of duty by which he ought to regulate his own conduct. '... the rules of love are broader than the rules of law.'[88] The rich creditor who squeezes a needy debtor to the last penny may have law on his side, but not morals; and conversely, a debt incurred, not in strict justice, but by principles of generosity, gratitude, pity, or charity, cannot be enforced—either in the law-courts or by war:

He who confers a kindness has no right to demand gratitude.[89]

... what accords with a strict interpretation of right is not always, or in all respects, permitted. Often, in fact, love for our neighbour prevents us from pressing our right to the utmost limit.[90]

[We are] bound by the laws of Christ beyond the limit of obligation imposed by the law of nature.[91]

Cicero [Grotius says] draws the boundary line between justice and a sense of reverence (*verecundia*) in this way, [holding] that it is the function of justice not to do violence to men, [and] that of the sense of reverence not to offend them.[92]

...we desire...to restrict the unrestrained licence of war to that which is permitted by nature, or to the choice of the better among the things permitted.[93]

Here the hierarchy of moral laws and values is made explicit. He quotes Seneca's *Trojan Women*, where Agamemnon says: What law permits, the sense of shame forbids. '... the sense of shame [says Grotius] signifies not so much a regard for men and reputation as a regard for what is just and good, or at any rate for that which is more just and better.'[94]

Wherever there are statements of a kind that are, so to speak, open to the moral sky, statements of political description or obligation that are indefinite, implying not only that something is left unsaid, but also that this something is in the moral dimension, they are likely to illustrate a Grotian mode of thought. Nehru in his opening speech at a symposium on 'Problems and Prospects of Democracy in Asian Countries' (New Delhi, December 1958) said that political democracy is not enough, economic democracy is necessary, but also that economic democracy is not enough, because individual freedom is needed too: 'Democracy is something deeper than a political form of government... It is a manner of thinking, a manner of action, a manner of behaviour to your neighbour, a manner of behaviour to your adversary.'[95]

Grotius

Grotius is concerned, first of all, with the tension between natural law (roughly moral law) and the law of nations (volitional law, or positive international law). Crudely, he says that natural law forbids or restrains while the law of nations sanctions or permits. A famous example is his emphasis on the distinction between the just and the unjust war. Only the just war is legal and a belligerent engaged in a just war may inflict punishment on his enemy, and the enemy (the unjust belligerent) is not entitled to defend himself;[96] but he then admits that in practice the distinction is negligible: once war is in being, it must be conducted according to rules of war without regard to causes or the justice of it. The unjust party has the protection of the laws of war[97] because it is always difficult and dangerous for third parties to determine the justice of a war between two Powers:

> Furthermore, even in a lawful war, from external indications it can hardly be adequately known what is the just limit of self-defence, of recovering what is one's own, or of inflicting punishments; in consequence it has seemed altogether preferable to leave decisions in regard to such matters to the scruples of the belligerents rather than to have recourse to the judgements of others.[98]

Grotius tempers the law of nature by a realistic acceptance of political practice, but he equally tempers or condemns political practice by a realistic assertion of moral principle. Chapter 10 of book III of *The Law of War and Peace* begins with a discussion on how 'a sense of honour may be said to forbid what the law permits':

> I must retrace my steps, and must deprive those who wage war of nearly all the privileges which I seemed to grant, yet did not grant to them. For when I first set out to explain this part of the law of nations I bore witness that many things are said to be 'lawful' or 'permissible' for the reason that they are done with impunity, in part also because coactive tribunals [The original text uses the expression *judicia coactiva*. Possibly 'enforceable judgements' conveys more accurately the intention of the author.—Lauterpacht][99] lend to them their authority; things which, nevertheless, either deviate from the rule of right (whether this

51

has its basis in law strictly so called, or in the admonitions of other virtues), or at any rate may be omitted on higher grounds and with greater praise among good men.[100]

This introduces the Grotian doctrine of *temperamenta* (proper measure, moderation). It is not a formal doctrine, but the idea of such restraint runs through much of book III where Grotius discusses moderation with regard to the conduct and consequences of warfare under the following heads: the right of killing in a lawful war; devastation and similar matters; captured property; prisoners of war; acquiring sovereignty; and those things which by the law of nations do not have the right of postliminy (restoration of persons and things to their *ante bellum* status or condition).[101]

The dialectical quality of Grotius' thought or system (if 'dialectical' can be used to describe his perpetual qualifying, counterbalancing, and interweaving of opposite principles) seems to be his outstanding quality and the one that has assured his fame and influence. Grotius is a figure of the European 'Establishment', a highly respectable culture-uncle, like Aristotle. The cynic might say it is because he showed how governments can have their moral cake and eat it, but the contrary argument is equally true: he reminds governments, while eating their cakes according to state-practice and the law of nations, that there are moral principles, permanently valid, which they should acknowledge, and this, too, Western governments like to remember. The West by tradition is morally amphibious, living half in the world of natural law, half in *raison d'état*; but the Establishment in Britain, in the USA less, even in France, is Grotian by tendency. As the authors of a notable history of International Law have observed:

The reluctance among human beings to press home to the full conclusions justified by logic has been so common as to become systematic. It has tempered obligations, reduced rights, protected the indefensible, and mollified harshness. Grotius went to the Law of Nature to find in it principles which should overrule the crude and at times inequitable enactments of positive law. He called these principles *temperamenta*.[102]

Individual Moral Responsibility

For Grotius the moral quality in politics depends on the individual. There is an apparent paradox in the Kantian mode of thought, with its positing of the individual as the first and highest thing, atomizing society with its emphasis on individual duty, in that it tends in the upshot to subordinate the individual to society. Rousseau's doctrine of the General Will is the most celebrated theoretical mechanism for breaking the individual before the juggernaut of society. This compares with Kant on the subordination of the private ends of men and women to a 'different and far nobler end' for which the world exists (see below, p. 68). But the Grotian mode of thought with its premise of the individual's sociability and responsibility to the judgement of society tends in the upshot to make the individual conscience the engine, the animating impulse of politics. In Grotius himself individualism is explicit: international law today is a law creating rights and duties for states, not individuals, and Grotius does not make a system of international law in this sense. His rules bind peoples indeed, but more particularly their rulers. The law of war binds the individual conscience[103] so that subjects who believe the cause of a war is unjust ought not to serve.[104] He states here the full principle of conscientious objection. But more generally, any emphasis on the moral content of politics will be an emphasis on the individual decision in politics. Law (roughly) is in the sphere of society, morals in that of the individual,[105] and the Grotian tends to moralize law, to assert that law is morally binding. If the motives of love, charity, shame, reverence, or honour are to temper the political conflict, then it must be in so far as these direct the individual conscience, because the masses (the Grotian will say) do not feel these impulses.

There are examples of an individual moral decision that sets the moral tone of society. When Fox became Foreign Secretary after Pitt's death in January 1806, a Frenchman came to him with a scheme for assassinating Napoleon. Fox had the man detained and reported the overture to Talleyrand, who sent a courteous acknowledgement and professions of peacefulness. (Would this have happened if the issue had been put to a popular vote?) Was this an echo of Fabricius and Pyrrhus? Fox after all was educated on the classics, not international relations. Pyrrhus of Epirus invaded southern Italy in 279 BC and was opposed by the consul Fabricius. A traitor came from Pyrrhus' camp to the Roman, offering, if rewarded, to poison Pyrrhus. Fabricius sent him back to the king 'with the somewhat ostentatious rectitude of that day's rustic nobility'.[106] There is a Grotian comment by Cicero: 'And yet, if the mere show of expediency and the popular conception of it are all we want, this one deserter would have put an end to that wasting war and to a formidable foe of our supremacy; but it would have been a lasting shame and disgrace to us to have overcome not by valour but by crime.'[107]

Another example is that of Churchill, Stalin, and the German General Staff. At the Tehran Conference, in November 1943, Stalin said that the German General Staff must be liquidated—50,000 officers and technicians were to be rounded up and shot. Churchill replied: 'The British Parliament and public will never tolerate mass executions.' Stalin insisted, perhaps only in mischief, and pursued the subject. Churchill, deeply angered, retorted, 'I would rather be taken out into the garden here and now and be shot myself than sully my own and my country's honour by such infamy.' F. D. Roosevelt suggested a compromise proposal—that they shoot only 49,000. By this he hoped, no doubt, 'to reduce the whole matter to ridicule' but Elliott Roosevelt intervened to agree with Stalin, saying the US Army would agree. Churchill left the room and went next door, where Stalin and Molotov came to re-call him.[108]

The Grotian interpretation of such incidents would be that the moral sense, or honour, of a key individual made a decision for the whole community. One can contrast the experience of popular judgement on such issues: for example in the Khaki election of December 1918 with the 'Hang the Kaiser' campaign[109] [and in the public lynching of Mussolini, which also incensed Churchill –Eds.].

The principle of individual moral responsibility, especially for politicians, presupposes another theoretical position: Plato's argument that the *just man is prior to the just state*. Justice in the individual is self-discipline, 'an internal order of the soul', the harmony of elements in the soul.[110] This is implicit in Grotius, and explicit in Jowett's remark to Belloc: 'You cannot have a Republic without Republicans.'[111] It contrasts with the Kantian position in *Perpetual Peace*, that even a race of devils could attempt to form a true republic provided they followed intelligently the progress of nature.[112] Here the good state is prior to good men; it comes into being by a *coup d'état* or mechanism of nature, and moulds its citizens to itself.

Notes

1 E. R. Curtius, *European Literature and the Latin Middle Ages*, tr. W. R. Trusk (New York: Pantheon Books, 1953), pp. 37–8.
2 See R. W. Lee, 'Hugo Grotius: Annual Lecture on a Master Mind', Henriette Hertz Trust of the British Academy in *Proceedings of the British Academy, 1930*, (London: Humphrey Milford), pp. 6, 7, 15–17.
3 Ibid., pp. 32–6.
4 W. S. M. Knight, *The Life and Works of Hugo Grotius* (London: Sweet and Maxwell Ltd, 1925), p. 289.
5 Lee, Hugo Grotius, p. 57.
6 See Hugo Grotius, 'Prolegomena to the Law of War and Peace', *De Jure Belli ac Pacis Libri Tres Vol. II: The Translation: On the Law of War and Peace*, tr. F. W. Kelsey (Oxford: Clarendon Press, 1925), nos. 46, 58, pp. 26, 29–30.
7 H. Lauterpacht, 'The Grotian Tradition in International Law', *British Year Book of International Law*, vol. XXIII (1946), pp. 5, 7.

8   H. Lauterpacht, 'The Grotian Tradition in International Law', pp. 46, 48.
9   Walter Schiffer, *The Legal Community of Mankind* (New York: Columbia University Press, 1954), pp. 47–8.
10 See also John Westlake, *The Collected Papers of John Westlake on Public International Law*, ed. L. Oppenheim (Cambridge: University Press, 1914), pp. 49–50; and A. P. D'Entrèves, *Natural Law* (London: Hutchinson's University Library, 1951), p. 54.
11 Carl J. Friedrich, *The Age of the Baroque* (New York: Harper and Brothers, 1952), p. 94.
12 Hugo Grotius, *The Law of War and Peace, Selections from De Jure Belli ac Pacis 1625*, tr. W. S. M. Knight (London: Peace Book Co., 1939), pp. 35–6.
13 Grotius, *On The Law of War and Peace*, tr. Kelsey, bk II, ch. XXVI, p. 588.
14 Grotius, 'Prolegomena', *The Law of War and Peace*, tr. Knight, no. 28, p. 35; Grotius, *On The Law of War and Peace*, tr. Kelsey, p. 20.
15 Grotius, *On the Law of War and Peace*, tr. Kelsey, bk II, ch. XXII, no. 13, p. 552.
16 Edmund Burke, 'Thoughts on the Cause of These Present Discontents', *The Works of the Right Hon. Edmund Burke* (London: Samuel Holdsworth, 1842), vol. I, p. 134.
17 Jawaharlal Nehru, *Visit to America* (New York: John Day, 1950), p. 121. Address to University of California, 31 October 1949.
18 Grotius, 'Prolegomena', *On the Law of War and Peace*, tr. Kelsey, no. 6, p. 11.
19 Ibid., no. 8, p. 12.
20 Ibid., no. 12, p. 14.
21 Ibid., no. 16, p. 15.
22 Ibid., no. 10, p. 13.
23 Ibid., no. 15, p. 14; see also John Locke, *Of Civil Government* (London: J.M. Dent, 1924), bk II, ch. II, pp. 119–20.
24 Grotius, *On the Law of War and Peace*, tr. Kelsey, bk II, ch. I.ix, p. 176.
25 Ibid.
26 Ibid., bk I, ch. II.vi, p. 61.
27 Ibid., bk I, ch. III.viii, p. 105.
28 Ibid., bk II, ch. XXII.xi, p. 551; and bk III, ch. VII.i, pp. 690–1.

29 See Ibid., bk II, ch. V.xxvii, p. 255; and bk I, ch. III.viii, p. 103.
30 Ibid., bk III, ch. VII.i, p. 690; see also ch. X.ii, p. 718; and ch. XIV.i and ii, pp. 761–2.
31 Ibid., bk II, ch. V.xxix, pp. 256–7; and bk III, ch. VII.ii, p. 691.
32 Ibid., bk III, ch. IV.xv, pp. 651–2.
33 Grotius, 'Prolegomena', *On the Law of War and Peace*, tr. Kelsey, no. 16, p. 13.
34 Westlake, *Collected Papers*, pp. 44–5.
35 Grotius, 'Prolegomena', *On the Law of War and Peace*, tr. Kelsey, no. 11, p. 13, quoted by A. P. D'Entrèves, *Natural Law*, p. 52.
36 Grotius, 'Prolegomena', *On the Law of War and Peace*, tr. Kelsey, no. 12, p. 14.
37 Ibid., no. 22, p. 17.
38 Ibid., no. 7, p. 12; and no. 9, p. 13.
39 Grotius, *On the Law of War and Peace*, tr. Kelsey, bk I, ch. I.x, pp. 38–9.
40 Ibid., bk I, ch. I.xvi, p. 48.
41 Ibid., bk I, ch. I.x, p. 40; and Aristotle, *The Nicomachean Ethics*, tr. H. Rackham (London: William Heinemann Ltd, 1947), bk II, vi, 18, p. 97.
42 Grotius, 'Prolegomena', *On the Law of War and Peace*, tr. Kelsey, no. 39, p. 23.
43 Ibid., no. 58, p. 30.
44 Grotius, *On the Law of War and Peace*, tr. Kelsey, bk II, ch. XX.xliii, p. 507.
45 Ibid., bk I, ch. I.x, p. 40.
46 Grotius, 'Prolegomena', *On the Law of War and Peace*, tr. Kelsey, no. 30, p. 21.
47 Grotius, *On the Law of War and Peace*, tr. Kelsey, bk I, ch. I.xii, p. 42.
48 Ibid., see bk III, ch. IV.xvi, p. 653.
49 Grotius, 'Prolegomena', *On the Law of War and Peace*, tr. Kelsey, no. 46, p. 26.
50 Ibid., no. 40, p. 23; Grotius, *On the Law of War and Peace*, tr. Kelsey, bk I, ch. I.xii, p. 42.
51 Ibid., no. 40, pp. 23–4.
52 Ibid., p. 24.

53 Ibid., no. 17, p. 15; and no. 20, p. 16.
54 Ibid., no. 18, p. 16.
55 Hugo Grotius, *Mare Liberum*, p. 2, quoted by Lee, *Hugo Grotius*, p. 55.
56 See Lee, 'Hugo Grotius', p. 55.
57 See D'Entrèves, *Natural Law*, p. 71.
58 Ibid., pp. 76–7.
59 John Locke, *Of Civil Government* (London: J.M. Dent, 1924), ch. II.6, p. 119.
60 Grotius, *On the Law of War and Peace*, tr. Kelsey, bk I, ch. I.x, pp. 38–9.
61 D'Entrèves, *Natural Law*, p. 115.
62 I. Kant, *The Philosophy of Law*, tr. W. Hastie (Edinburgh: T. & T. Clark, 1887), p. 44.
63 I. Kant, 'Metaphysical Foundations of Morals', *The Philosophy of Kant*, ed. C. J. Friedrich (New York: The Modern Library, 1949), pp. 186–7.
64 See Leo Strauss, *Natural Right and History* (Chicago: University of Chicago Press, 1953), p. 279.
65 See John Wild, *Plato's Modern Enemies and the Theory of Natural Law* (Chicago: University of Chicago Press, 1953), p. 176.
66 I. Kant, *The Moral Law*, tr. H. J. Paton (London: Hutchinson University Library, 1947), p. 120.
67 See A. D. Lindsay, *Kant* (London: Oxford University Press, 1936), pp. 286–7.
68 Hans J. Morgenthau, *Dilemmas of Politics* (Chicago: University of Chicago Press, 1958), p. 380.
69 Hans J. Morgenthau, *Politics among Nations* (New York: Alfred Knopf, 1954), pp. 84–6.
70 D'Entrèves, *Natural Law*, p. 58.
71 George F. Kennan, 'Russia, the Atom and the West, 1959', *Listener*, LXII (29 October 1959), pp. 711–13.
72 John Morley, *Burke* (London: Macmillan & Co. Ltd, 1897), p. 314.
73 Edmund Burke, 'Reflections on the Revolution in France', *The Works of the Right Honourable Edmund Burke* (London: Samuel Holdsworth, 1842), vol. I, pp. 393–4.
74 Grotius, *On the Law of War and Peace*, tr. Kelsey, bk II, ch. IV.i, p. 220.

75 Ibid.
76 Ibid., bk II, ch. IV.vi, p. 223; and ch. IV.ix, p. 226.
77 L. Oppenheim, *International Law*, ed. H. Lauterpacht (London: Longmans Green & Co. Ltd, 1955), 8th edn., vol. I, para. 242, p. 576.
78 Dante, *Monarchy and Three Political Letters*, tr. Donald Nicholl (London: Weidenfeld and Nicolson, 1954), p. 104.
79 J. W. N. Watkins, 'Milton's Vision of a Reformed England', *Listener*, LXI (22 January 1959), p. 169.
80 Grotius, *On the Law of War and Peace*, tr. Kelsey, bk I, ch. III.viii, pp. 103, 104.
81 Ibid., pp. 105, 109–10, 111.
82 See A. J. Carlyle, *Political Liberty* (London: Frank Cass & Co., 1963), p. 95.
83 Plato, *The Republic of Plato*, tr. F. M. Cornford (Oxford: Clarendon Press, 1941), bk IV, 445, ch. XV, p. 142.
84 Aristotle, *The Nicomachean Ethics*, bk II, ch. vi. 14, p. 95.
85 Leo Tolstoy, *Anna Karenina*, tr. C. Garnett (London: The Modern Library, 1936), p. 3.
86 St Augustine, 'Ten Homilies on the First Epistle General of St. John', *Augustine: Later Works*, tr. John Burnaby (London: SCM Press Ltd, 1955), vol. VIII, p. 316.
87 D'Entrèves, *Natural Law*, p. 116.
88 Grotius, *On the Law of War and Peace*, tr. Kelsey, bk III, ch. XIII.iv, p. 759. See also John Westlake, *The Collected Papers on Public International Law* (Cambridge: Cambridge University Press, 1914), p. 45.
89 Grotius, *On the Law of War and Peace*, tr. Kelsey, bk II, ch. XXII.xvi, p. 556.
90 Ibid., bk III, ch. I.iv, p. 601.
91 Ibid., bk I, ch. II.vi, p. 61.
92 Ibid., bk III, ch. X.i, p. 717.
93 Ibid., bk III, ch. XII.viii, p. 754.
94 Ibid., bk III, ch. X.i, p. 716; see also Grotius on moral justice and injustice; *justicia interna* and *interna injusticia*, in Ibid., tr. Kelsey, bk III, ch. XI.ii, p. 723; and ch. X.iii, pp. 718–19.

95 Jawaharlal Nehru, quoted in Hugh Tinker's review of 'Future of Asian Democracy', *International Affairs*, vol. 35, no. 4 (October 1959), p. 458.
96 Grotius, *On the Law of War and Peace*, tr. Kelsey, bk II, ch. I.xviii, p. 185.
97 Ibid., bk III, ch. IV.iii, pp. 643–4; and ch. VI.ii, p. 664.
98 Ibid., bk III, ch. IV.iv, p. 644.
99 H. Lauterpacht, 'The Grotian Tradition in International Law', *The British Year Book of International Law*, vol. XXIII (1946), p. 6.
100 Grotius, *On the Law of War and Peace*, tr. Kelsey, bk III, ch. X.i, p. 716.
101 See ibid., chs. XI–XVI, pp. 722–82.
102 Sir Geoffrey Butler and Simon Maccoby, *The Development of International Law* (London: Longmans, Green & Co. Ltd, 1928), p. 193.
103 Lee, 'Hugo Grotius', p. 55.
104 Grotius, *On the Law of War and Peace*, tr. Kelsey, bk II, ch. XXVI.iii, pp. 587–8.
105 See D'Entrèves, *Natural Law*, pp. 85ff.
106 Tenney Frank, 'Pyrrhus' in *The Cambridge Ancient History* (Cambridge: University Press, 1928), vol. VII, ch. XX, p. 650.
107 Cicero, *De Officiis*, tr. Walter Miller (London: William Heinemann Ltd, 1947), p. 361.
108 Winston S. Churchill, *The Second World War vol. V, Closing the Ring* (London: Cassell & Co. Ltd., 1952), p. 330; see also Hans J. Morgenthau, *Politics among Nations* (New York: Alfred Knopf, 1954), p. 214.
109 [This is the popular cry that went up in Britain in 1918, fanned by the jingoist press like Horatio Bottomley's *John Bull*. Lloyd George and other leading figures were secretly relieved when the Dutch refused to hand him over. –Eds.]
110 Plato, *The Republic of Plato*, pp. 136–9; see also D'Entrèves, *Natural Law*, pp. 90ff.

111 Dr Benjamin Jowett in Hilaire Belloc, *The Cruise of the 'Nona'* (London: Constable & Co., 1925), p. 56.
112 Kant, 'Perpetual Peace', first supplement, *Kant's Principles of Politics*, tr. and ed. W. Hastie (Edinburgh: T. & T. Clark, 1891), pp. 111, 112. The quotation is given on p. 79 below.

Chapter 3

Kant

22 April 1724–12 February 1804

Life and Influence

Kant was the greatest of modern philosophers, whose influence can be seen in Goethe and Schiller, in Beethoven, and in English philosophy. In systematic philosophy he is comparable only to Plato, Aristotle, and Aquinas. His greatest disciple was Hegel, who played Aristotle to his Plato (as Hegel's greatest disciple was Marx). Kant has probably had more books written about him— to praise, explain, or refute him—than any philosopher except Plato, and this is an index of his influence.[1] In the nineteenth century he came to be regarded as the inventor and patentee of morality or duty. He was the chief glory of the Enlightenment, and chief philosophical architect to the Revolution—a wizened, scrupulous, exact, punctual man, 5 feet high.

Kant was appointed Professor of Logic and Metaphysics at Königsberg in 1770 (a date to remember along with 1776). He refused better posts (at Erlangen, Jena, and Halle). He gave 26 to 28 hours of lectures a week as *magister*, and two hours a day as professor, one on Saturday. His lectures were extremely impressive but largely inaudible. He never left Königsberg,

Kant

except occasionally for a holiday in the Lithuanian forest, but Königsberg—a cultural frontier post, and the least provincial of Prussian cities—was a good base for studying peoples, geography, and international relations. From 1758 until 1762 it was under Russian occupation, and at this time Kant gave lessons in mathematics to Russian officers.

He achieved international fame before his death, and was a brilliant and fascinating talker at meals—about anything but philosophy. He never married. Schopenhauer said that all great philosophers had died unmarried—pointing to Heraclitus, Democritus, Plato, Zeno, Descartes, Hobbes, Spinoza, Locke, Hume, and Leibnitz along with Kant. (To Schopenhauer's list we might add Wittgenstein, Broad, Moore, Santayana, and Samuel Alexander, but we should also need to consider such important contrary cases as Socrates, Aristotle, Hegel, Marx, and Bertrand Russell.) Kant, however, enjoyed warm friendships, most notably with Joseph Green, an English merchant, and we may picture him sleeping in Green's chair of an afternoon. He kept a regular routine, being awakened at 5 a.m. with the cry 'It is time!' He ate only once a day, between 1 and 4 p.m. 'He suffered from ill-health but had an iron will and self-control. He attached the greatest importance to living as long as possible and, as Jachmann mentions, "for many years he had the Königsberg police authorities supply him with the monthly list of deaths, in order to calculate therefrom his probable expectation of life"'.[2] His life was a triumph of mind over body. Heine gave the classic description of Kant in *Religion and Philosophy in Germany*.[3]

Kant's political sympathies were with liberalism, as illustrated by the beginnings of his acquaintance with Green. He was keenly interested in geography and current politics, and supported the American and French Revolutions, despite his belief that rebellion was wrong. The liberalism with which his sympathies lay, however, was of a curious Prussian form. He was a Prussian civil servant and the greatest subject of Frederick the Great, whom he praised in his 1784 essay, 'What is Enlightenment?'.

Kant

When rebuked and censured by Frederick William II in 1794 for undermining Christianity, Kant submitted, and promised not to lecture in public on the subject of religion.[4]

Was Kant a Revolutionary?

What are the grounds for the picture of Kant as a revolutionary? His intellectual development can be seen as governed first by Newton, then by Hume, and then by Rousseau. In his first or Newtonian phase, Kant was a scientist: his early works (before Herschel) were on the rings of Saturn and on evolutionary doctrine, and his desire was to make philosophy a science, or to find the philosophy of science. Hume initiated Kant's sceptical and speculative phase. Hume, he wrote, 'first interrupted my dogmatic slumbers'; he had 'critical reason', something more than common sense; he discredited the idea of causation or causality as a 'bastard of the imagination', showing that no necessary connection can be demonstrated or intuited between one existence and another; he abolished metaphysics.[5] Kant sought to generalize what Hume had taught, and developed his 'critical' philosophy in his great works *Critique of Pure Reason* (1781 and 1788), *Critique of Practical Reason* (1788), and *Critique of Judgement* (1789–93).

The *Critique of Pure Reason* seeks to establish the limits of reason by executing a Copernican revolution in metaphysics. Copernicus could not make satisfactory progress by supposing that the sun revolved around the spectator and so tried the experiment of supposing that the spectator revolved around the sun. In metaphysics it had hitherto been assumed that our knowledge must conform to objects; Kant instead asks us to see if we have more success by assuming that objects must conform to our knowledge.[6] 'All previous metaphysics had started with the object of knowledge; Kant asks about the judgment regarding such objects.'[7] Like Copernicus, Kant suggests that explanation of certain elements in our knowledge is to be found in ourselves, in what the mind contributes.[8] The *Critique of Pure Reason* attempts to revolutionize metaphysics 'in accordance with the example set by the geometers and physicists'.[9]

Our experience, according to Kant, is divided into two, separate, incommunicable realms. One is the realm of the phenomenal—the realm of necessity, of appearances, of sense, of brute facts, or of nature: of this alone do we have knowledge. The other is the realm of the noumenal—the realm of freedom of thought, of ideals and morals, God, freedom of the will, and immortality: of this realm (what Kant calls the kingdom of ends) we have only moral experience. In traditional philosophy—in Plato, Aristotle, and Christian scholasticism—these two realms were organically united in a hierarchy of manifestations of rational nature, politics, ethics, and metaphysics, all of which we could apprehend.

Two things followed from this separation. On the one hand, the phenomenal world is open to the exploration of reason, which is authorized and stimulated to chart this realm of necessity. There is philosophical warrant for the scientific and technological advances that have transformed the world, including the world of international relations, since Kant's day. On the other hand, the realm of freedom, the kingdom of ends, is closed to knowledge, beyond cognitive reach: all we have of it is moral experience. 'I have therefore found it necessary', Kant wrote, 'to deny *knowledge*' [i.e. of God, freedom, and immortality] 'in order to make room for *faith*'.[10] Or to quote Kant's famous sentence: 'Two things fill the mind with ever new and increasing admiration and awe, the oftener and the more steadily we reflect on them: *the starry heavens above and the moral law within.*'[11]

There are two sides to Kant, one critical and destructive, the other positive and constructive. The destructive side, as we have seen, involved the demolition of traditional metaphysics, a virtual declaration that metaphysics was impossible. God, freedom, and immortality, in Kant's view, are beyond the reach of knowledge, beyond the capability of proof or disproof. This was Kant 'the smasher of everything' (Moses Mendelssohn),

Kant

'the arch destroyer in the realm of thought' (Heine), the philosopher who passed sentence of death on deism and claims to the knowledge of God. If today we assume that the traditional proofs of the existence of God and the immortality of the soul are debunked, this is because of Kant.

The Categorical Imperative: Duty

On the other hand, Kant has a positive and constructive side. It has often been pointed out how, having made a clean sweep of metaphysics, Kant hastened to put Humpty-Dumpty together again in a slightly different, damaged way: he denied knowledge to make room for faith. But his positive side was no less revolutionary than his negative one. His critical, analytical genius was balanced by the most acutely developed *moral* consciousness of any philosopher, a feeling of moral passion and a concept of duty set out in the idea of the categorical imperative. Kant's hymn to duty in the *Critique of Practical Reason* is a lapse into poetry, like an elephant breaking into a rumba:

Duty! Thou sublime and mighty name [*Pflicht, du erhabener grosser Name*] that dost embrace nothing charming or insinuating, but requirest submission, and yet seekest not to move the will by threatening aught that would arouse natural aversion or terror, but merely holdest forth a law which of itself finds entrance into the mind, and yet gains reluctant reverence (though not always obedience), a law before which all inclinations are dumb, even though they secretly counter-work it; what origin is there worthy of thee, and where is to be found the root of thy noble descent which proudly rejects all kindred with the inclinations; a root to be derived from which is the indispensable condition of the only worth which men can give themselves?[12]

Kant's *Fundamental Principles of the Metaphysics of Morals* (1785) begins with the assertion that the only purely good thing that can be conceived in the world is a good will. A good will is not good because of what it does or what it aims at, but simply by virtue of the volition, the purity of its dedication to duty. A good will is not a means to happiness but a good in itself: happiness is a degraded objective: 'the existence of world order has a different and far nobler end for which . . . reason is properly intended. Therefore this end must be regarded as the supreme condition to which the private ends of man must yield for the most part.'[13] Moreover, good will is present when conduct springs not from fear or inclination, not from benevolence or affection, but from consciousness of duty. This is the categorical imperative. A. D. Lindsay writes:

> A certain Dr. Collenbusch once wrote a letter to Kant, in which he said: 'Dr. Kant's morality is a morality quite pure from all love, and this makes me ask, "What is the difference between the morality of the devil and the morality of Dr. Kant?"' When we read certain parts of Kant's ethical writings, we can feel a certain sympathy with Dr. Collenbusch.[14]

The end of man must be something universal and inclusive:

> In regard to happiness, the will of all has not one and the same object, but everyone has his own object (his private welfare), which may accidentally accord with the purposes of others which are equally selfish, but it is far from sufficing for a law; because the occasional exceptions which one is permitted to make are endless, and cannot be definitely embraced in one universal rule. The resulting harmony would be like that described in a satirical poem about a married couple bent on going to ruin, 'Oh marvellous harmony, what he wishes she wishes too'; or like what is said of the pledge of Francis I to the Emperor Charles V, 'What my brother Charles wants, that I want also.' (namely Milan).[15]

As Khrushchev would say: 'What my friend President Eisenhower wants, that I want also' (namely West Berlin). What then does the categorical imperative command us to do? First, to act only on a principle which you can will should become a general universal law. 'We must be *able to will* that a maxim of our action should be a general law.'[16] Second: 'So act

Kant

as to treat humanity, whether in thine own person or in that of any other, in every case as an end as well, and never as means only.'[17] Now, this conception of duty is blank (not negative, but empty: like a blank cheque).

It leaves us to construct the whole fabric of Right out of the elementary idea of the Will and of Justice; out of such conceptions as that of the inalienable freedom of the will, and such abstract commands as 'Be just to all mankind'. Now these conceptions and 'categorical imperatives' are clearly, in themselves, an absolute blank. It is only by experience, and the practical instinct born of experience, that they win any definite content. Every thoughtful reader of Kant's ethical writings has probably felt the failure of Kant's attempt to deduce the specific duties of practical conduct from the abstract idea of Duty.[18]

Kant's ethics give rules, not for our actions, but for principles on which we should act. It prescribes principles, but leaves the application of the principles to individual moral judgement in a given situation.[19] The conception of duty also tends to be subjective:

Having proved in his youth that we know nothing about God, old Kant was beginning to suspect that he himself might be God: 'God is not a being outside me, but merely a thought in me. God is the morally practical self-legislative reason... God can be sought only in us... There is a Being in me which... inwardly directs me... and I, as man, am myself this Being.'[20]

This is subjective; and it is also egotistical, infallible, and ruthless.

My conviction is not *logical*, but *moral* certainty; and since it rests on subjective grounds (of the moral sentiment), I must not even say, '*It is* morally certain that there is a God, etc.'... In other words, belief in a God and in another world is so interwoven with my moral sentiment that as there is little danger of my losing the latter, there is equally little cause for fear that the former can ever be taken from me.[21]

The conception of duty tends to break loose, expand, and migrate. Moral experience is manifested in the creative energy of the will; willing to do its duty, willing that the principle of its action should become a universal law. Moral reason is thus creative, or 'constructive'.[22] Rousseau, in *Savoyard Vicar*, proclaimed: 'O Conscience! Conscience! thou divine instinct... thou infallible judge of good and evil...'[23] Kant echoes this: 'Duty! Thou sublime and mighty name'; as does Fichte's hymn to the will: 'Sublime and Living Will! named by no name, compassed by no thought! I may well raise my soul to Thee, for Thou and I are not divided. Thy voice sounds within me, mine resounds in Thee.'[24]

Kant's conception of the moral law was revolutionary, because it was divorced from metaphysics. Moral experience and moral action were traditionally like a tram, following the rails of a metaphysical universe where God, the starry heavens above, history, society, and the individual were all parts of a rationally coherent whole. Kant's moral experience, since he has torn up the rails, is a jeep, a land-rover, a tractor, moving where it will; its principle of motion is within itself, not outside; it is inner-directed, not other-directed. Moral experience is manifested in the creative energy of the will;[25] and sometimes the jeep or land-rover seems more like an armoured car.[26]

What is the responsibility of a thinker or teacher for the consequences of his teaching? When we disapprove the teacher, we belabour him with the effects he has produced and condemn Marx by Stalin. What was the different and far nobler end for which the world's existence was intended? Here the importance of Rousseau is apparent. Rousseau was the third influence on Kant, greater than Newton's or Hume's (see p. 65 above). Kant's study was furnished with Spartan simplicity, there was no decoration; the only portrait was of Jean-Jacques Rousseau; the only breach of Kant's punctuality and routine was when he missed his walk to read *Émile*. There are great differences between Kant and Rousseau: Kant's regularity and puritanical restraint contrast with Rousseau's wayward, undisciplined self-indulgence and sentimental exhibitionism. Kant was celibate, whereas Rousseau was licentious; Kant stayed in Königsberg with a single job, whilst Rousseau was a nomadic wanderer and had nine different occupations in his life-time. Kant was Hume's disciple; Rousseau became Hume's enemy; and Kant had a packing-paper style while Rousseau was an angelic and melodious writer.[27]

Kant called Rousseau the 'Newton of the moral world'. Rousseau taught him to respect human nature, not to despise the masses in pursuit of knowledge, but to believe in humanity;[28] and a conception of humanity runs through Kant's later, political writings, especially those on international relations. The influence of Rousseau on domestic politics, and on the relations of governments and peoples, detonated in the French Revolution; his influence on international politics detonated in Kant. The Kantian revolution was the counterpart in German philosophy of the French Revolution, and possibly it is the counterpart, too, in international theory.

The Kantian Type of International Theory: Revolutionary Presumption

There are several characteristics of the Kantian type of international theory. First, there is the revolutionary presumption: that is, the presumption that the present political state is not perfect and ought to be improved; therefore it has only provisional moral validity. Kant's political doctrine, as distinct from his international doctrine, is ambiguous and perhaps inconsistent.[29] He seems to have a static conception of society and the law, and as a Prussian civil servant he severely denies the right of rebellion; yet he is a professed republican, and in *Perpetual Peace* wrote of a republic as the one constitution embodying freedom and equality: 'the only constitution which is derived from the idea of an original contract upon which all rightful legislation of a nation must be based';[30] and as mentioned earlier he supported the American and French Revolutions. At the end of 'Rechtslehre', the first part of *Metaphysics of Morals* (1797), is a passage suggesting a different doctrine: the forms of the state are a dead letter; the spirit of the original contract imposes an obligation on the constituent power to bring the form of government into harmony with its idea. A gradual and unbroken series of changes must be made to bring the government into accord with the only rightful constitution, namely the republican: 'This is the final goal of all public Right; the condition under which alone Right can be said to have an absolute and peremptory existence. Till this is reached, Civil Society can be credited only with a provisional and private Right.'[31]

Whatever Kant's doctrine of domestic politics, the revolutionary presumption in international politics is perfectly clear: international society as it exists at present must be renovated, revolutionized.

> The natural state of Nations as well as of individual men is a state which it is a duty to pass out of, in order to enter into a legal state. Until this transition occurs, all the Rights of Nations . . . are merely *provisory*.[32]

> Now, as a matter of fact, the morally practical Reason utters within us its irrevocable Veto: *'There shall be no War . . .'* We must *act* on the supposition that Perpetual Peace is possible. We must work for what may perhaps not be realised.[33]

The states, linked by commerce and the need for mutual intervention, 'are beginning to arrange for a great future political Body, such as the world has never yet seen. Although this political Body may as yet exist only in a rough outline, nevertheless a feeling begins, as it were, to stir in all its members, each of which has a common interest in the maintenance of the whole.'[34] Nobody had ever written about international politics like this before.

Federation of Republican States

The federation of republican states is the final goal of international relations, and *Perpetual Peace* is an imaginary draft treaty

Kant

to bring this about.[35] One can compare this with Wilson's Fourteen Points; there are six preliminary articles:

1. Kant calls for the abdication of revisionist claims; all causes of future war must be removed by a peace treaty, and there should be no mental reservations about claims for the future.
2. There must be a guarantee of integrity and independence of all states. This is echoed by Wilson's: 'Peoples and provinces are not to be bartered about from sovereignty to sovereignty as if they were mere chattels or pawns in a game...'
3. There must be disarmament and the abolition of standing armies.
4. There must be preventative economic sanctions and limitations on economic sovereignty; national debt is not to be contracted for foreign policy purposes.
5. He calls for non-intervention.
6. He requires that the rules of warfare be observed; there should be limitations on the methods of war; and no modes of hostility that would make mutual confidence impossible after war, such as assassination, spying, or internal subversion.[36]

A second supplement entitled 'Secret Article for Perpetual Peace' calls for freedom of information and of public opinion. The state will allow philosophers 'publicly and freely [to] talk about the general maxims of warfare and of the establishment of peace'. There will be no philosopher kings, because power corrupts the free judgement of reason: as a class philosophers are by their nature incapable of plotting and lobbying.[37] This ideal of a federation of republican states, of free self-determining national democracies, was developed with more fervent rhetoric but less intellectual analysis by Mazzini, and it is the framework of the Bandung philosophy of international politics.

Kant

Cosmopolitanism

Another characteristic of Kantian international theory is its cosmopolitanism. An alternative way of dissolving international relations is not by hoping for uniformity and harmony between states, but by dissolving them into component human beings. Cosmopolitanism is thus an alternative to internationalism. Kant's *Perpetual Peace* lays down (in the Third Definitive Article) the 'rights of men as citizens of the world in a cosmopolitical system'—a right of peaceful international intercourse and travel by individuals. 'The limited right of world citizenship is intended to express the bond uniting all individual members of the human race.'[38]

Whenever there is the hope that peoples will throw down the artificial barriers dividing them, then 'nation shall speak peace unto nation' (as the BBC motto says), rather than government shall negotiate with government. 'Hands-across-the-frontiers' and 'workers-of-the-world-unite' are expressions of this cosmopolitanism. The desire for weighted votes in the General Assembly proportionate to population goes the same way, as it seeks to revolutionize international society by demolishing the fiction of state equality.

But what is the end of cosmopolitanism? Either it is world anarchy, in the technical sense; the withering away of all states and the human race living happily in peace without governmental institutions; or it is a world state. (Marxism promises the second as a prelude to the first.) Kant describes a world state, the Universal Republic, as a positive ideal that states are unlikely to submit to, and he sees a federation of states as a negative substitute.[39] Such a federation is definitely preferable to a universal monarchy established by one state conquering all the rest; this remedy would be worse than the disease, a 'soulless despotism' leading to anarchy, like the Roman Empire did.[40]

In 1784, in the *Idea of a Universal History from a Cosmopolitical Point of View*, after making the point referred to above, that by their growing fear of war and consciousness of interdependence states were feeling their way towards a great universal political body, Kant concluded: 'And this may well inspire the hope that after many political revolutions and transformations, the highest purpose of Nature will be at last realised in the establishment of a universal *Cosmopolitical Institution*, in the bosom of which all the original capacities and endowments of the human species will be unfolded and developed.'[41] A decade later, in *The Relation of Theory to Practice in International Law* (1793), he said:

> For my part... I trust to a theory which is based upon the principle of Right as determining what the relations between men and states, *ought to be*; and which lays down to these earthly gods the maxim that they ought so to proceed in their disputes that such a universal International State [*ein solcher allgemeiner Völkerstaat*] may be introduced thereby, and to assume it therefore as not only possible in practice but such as may yet be presented in reality.[42]

In practice, of course, cosmopolitanism has come nearest to fulfilment in a revolutionary great power that is the embryo of a world state, offering its potential citizenship and liberation to the inhabitants of other states; for example, in revolutionary France, or Soviet Russia. This course of development is nourished by an older theoretical stream than Kant; it is the philosophy of imperial mission or vocation expressed in Dante.

Harmony of Interests

Kant believed that international society can be renovated because national politics are intrinsically reconcilable. This harmony of interests (as it is usually called) was one of the most widespread conceptions among eighteenth century thinkers, and can be seen in Bernard de Mandeville, Adam Smith, Malthus, and Voltaire's *Candide*. It is also in Morellet, where the law of self-love in the moral sphere corresponds to the law of gravitation in the physical sphere, and in Hegel's 'cunning of reason', and Burke's 'divine tactic'. As Kant observed: 'Individual men, and even whole nations, little think, while they are pursuing their own purposes—each in his own way and often one in direct opposition to another—that they are advancing unconsciously under the guidance of a Purpose of Nature which is unknown to them, and that they are toiling for the realisation of an End which, even if it were known to them, might be regarded as of little importance.'[43]

Conflicting interests are reconcilable because there is a tendency in history to reconcile; the doctrine of harmony of interests is, in the end, a doctrine about history, a doctrine of progress. Every political philosophy presupposes a philosophy of history, as well as a doctrine of human nature, and conversely, belief in progress leads to the type of international theory I am calling Kantian. Progress can be conceived or imagined in several ways; the difficulty with all of them is that the doctrine of progress is a doctrine about human relationships, not government and the governed, or state and state, but men classified temporally, chronologically, generation and generation; and like all doctrines of human relationships, it misses questions of justice, common understanding, and purpose.

A crude doctrine of progress is the belief in mere process as good. Even more crude and simple is what is often referred to as the escalator conception; but this is wrong, because on the escalator, though those at the top are higher than those at the bottom, all are alive together and all are rising together. The escalator conception of progress is more like the fireman's ladder, lengthening steadily outwards and upwards, and the poor devils cranking the windlasses at the bottom of the ladder are the generations of the dead, and the new generations are seen with unbroken regularity on the new rungs of the ladder appearing steadily at the top. The latest is always the best, intrinsically, as in the manufacture of television sets. This was the view of Victorian Englishmen such as Macaulay and Herbert Spencer; it is the crude application of the Marxist dialectic of history; and it is the

Kant

crude popular view today, as expounded in the popular press with its slogans 'we believe in tomorrow' or 'forward with the people'. The later is the better, and the earlier lived and suffered for the sake of the later; successive generations are steps to the ultimate achievement of life, and only in the last stage does mankind reach fulfilment.[44] Ivan Karamazov's cry pleaded against the injustice of this idea of progress:

> ...not justice in some remote infinite time and space, but here on earth, and that I could see myself... Surely I haven't suffered, simply that I, my crimes and my sufferings, may manure the soil of the future harmony for somebody else...
>
> If all must suffer to pay for the eternal harmony, what have children to do with it, tell me, please?... Why should they, too, furnish material to enrich the soil for the harmony of the future?... While there is still time... I renounce the higher harmony altogether. It's not worth the tears of that one tortured child who beat itself on the breast with its little fist and prayed in its stinking outhouse... those tears must be atoned for, or there can be no harmony... If the sufferings of children go to swell the sum of sufferings which was necessary to pay for truth, then I protest that the truth is not worth such a price... too high a price is asked for harmony... And so I hasten to give back my entrance ticket... It's not God that I don't accept... only I most respectfully return Him the ticket.[45]

Any philosophy of history that sees meaning revealed at a given date is implicitly unjust to the generations preceding that date. The more sophisticated and satisfying conception of progress is that of organic development, where the connection between generations is not merely successive and mechanical, but organic, as in the stages of a person's growth.

Doctrine of Progress

Kant's doctrine of progress has two levels; on one level it is progress guaranteed by nature (nature being a substitute for providence). Eternal peace is guaranteed by nature, for reason presents peace to us as a duty, and nature wills that we should do our duty. '. . . the nature of things. . . compels movement in a direction even against the will of man.' *Fata volentem ducunt, nolentem trahunt.* ('. . . she does it herself whether we be willing or not.')[46] This conception of nature is elaborated by Kant (in what Hastie calls 'The Principle of Progress') in an essay of 1792.[47] In *Perpetual Peace* nature is represented as working through the commercial spirit, which cannot coexist with war, and sooner or later controls every nation. 'In this way Nature guarantees the conditions of Perpetual Peace by the mechanism involved in our human inclinations themselves.'[48] This doctrine is exactly that of Cobden and the Manchester School, and of all who believe in peace through the growing economic interdependence of powers.

The second level of Kant's doctrine of progress is an argument from desperation: what use is it to magnify the glory and wisdom of creation in the domain of nature, if human history affords constant objections to that glory and wisdom? 'The spectacle of History if thus viewed would compel us to turn away our eyes from it against our will; and the despair of ever finding a perfect rational Purpose in its movement, would reduce us to hope for it, if at all, only in another world [*indem wir verzweifeln*].'[49]

In 'The Principle of Progress' he writes:

In presence of the saddening spectacle, not merely of the evils which oppress the human race from natural causes, but still more of those which men inflict on each other, the heart is still gladdened by the prospect that it may become better in the future, and that this will be accomplished in part by our unselfish benevolence, even after we have been long in the grave and have ceased to be able to reap the fruits which we ourselves have sown.[50]

In *Perpetual Peace* the argument from desperation comes in a discussion of the disagreement between morals and politics; it seems like a flying leap beyond the furthest point of reasoned argument:

. . . the process of creation, by which such a brood of corrupt beings has been put upon the earth, can apparently be justified by no theodicy or theory of Providence, if we assume that it never will be better, nor can be better, with the human race... We shall thus be inevitably driven to a position of despair in consequence of such reasonings, if we do not admit that the pure principles of right and justice have objective reality and that they can be realised in fact (...*zu solchen verzweifelten Folgerungen werden wir unvermeidlich hingetrieben*...).[51]

There is a necessary conjunction, so to speak, between a belief in progress and pessimism about man.

... many have asserted that the realisation of a true Republic would be like a State formed by angels, because men with their selfish inclinations are incapable of carrying out a constitution of so sublime a form... [but the] problem of the institution of a state... would not be insoluble even for a race of devils, assuming only that they have intelligence... For it does not turn directly upon the moral improvement of men, but only upon the mechanism of nature.[52]

There is a certain parallel here with Kant's doctrine about God. He demolished the traditional arguments of natural theology for the existence of God and proved that God was unknowable, but he certainly believed in God; and at the end of the *Critique of Pure Reason* he puts forward a doctrine of the 'As if': we must view experience *as if* the sum of appearances 'had a single, highest, and all-sufficient ground beyond itself, namely, a self-subsistent, original, creative reason'.[53] It is not unfair to compare this with the argument from desperation.

It is of course not a good argument for a theory of international politics that we shall be driven to despair if we do not accept it; yet it is neither a contemptible nor a dishonourable one. Optimism has several kinds, and foundations of varying depths. There is the superficial or shallow optimism of some member of the 'smart young set' who says 'Don't talk about another international crisis!', either because it would interfere with holiday plans or because he or she is emotionally incapable of facing any but the reassuring segments of experience. There is also naive optimism, based on an inadequate intellectual grasp of the situation, as of the old lady who said 'the Powers will intervene'. But the optimism grounded in despair, of the person who has looked into the abyss, but who says, 'No, looking down makes me giddy: I can only go on climbing if I look upwards', merits respect. Kant is among the supreme philosophers because he is universal; he has seen everything human, the precipices as well as the heights, and his system takes account of them all, *except* of a future that does not go as he expected it would (even though he was cautious about the possibility of prophecy or historical prediction).[54]

The weakness of the argument from desperation is that if the future produces massive evidence against optimism, one may be driven to despair, and knocked off the ladder. Degenerate children of Kant have said: 'Our side must win, because if we lose, history will have lost its meaning' (Marc Bloch's fellow-officers, Walther Rathenau, Goebbels, the Red Army).[55] In today's circumstances [1959 –Eds.], it might be said, to be intellectually strong and morally secure, one needs an optimism that will say: 'Even if there is a full thermo-nuclear war, history will not have lost its meaning', but such a position of philosophical self-mastery might not be called optimism, and certainly would not be Kantian.

Perfectibility of Man

Along with a harmony of interests, and progress, another characteristic of Kant's international theory is the perfectibility of man. Kant asserted this, with due caution. He postulates a teleology, a doctrine of final causes,[56] and the first proposition of his 'Universal History' is: 'All the capacities implanted in a Creature by nature, are destined to unfold themselves, completely and conformably to their End, in the course of time.'[57] Man's natural capacities are directed towards the use of his reason, and could only be completely developed in the species, not in the individual.[58] One can compare Dante, in *Monarchy*:[59] The specific

Kant

capacity of man is his intellectual potentiality, and universal peace is the best condition for fulfilling this. '. . . as in human nature there is always a living respect for Right and Duty, I neither can nor will regard it as so sunk in evil that the practical moral Reason could ultimately fail to triumph over this evil, even after many of its attempts have failed.'[60] But he was cautious, and the belief is qualified: 'Out of such crooked material as man is made of, nothing can be hammered quite straight.'[61] There is a vein of pessimism in Kant: 'Schopenhauer's unpleasant conclusion that of all conceivable worlds this is the worst, is one of the speculations for which Kant may be held ultimately responsible.'[62] Is it the mark of a great philosopher that diametrically different schools of thought can claim descent with equal cogency? Kant is claimed by the idealists such as Hegel, as well as by Schopenhauer; Aquinas and the Whigs as well as Hegel claim descent from Aristotle; and Plato can be seen as the father of both mystical quietism and Communism.

Eradication of Suffering and Sin

It would falsify the Kantian school, the school of moral passion, to suggest that the belief in progress is its deepest element. Our own experience, or the observation of others, will suggest that there is a deeper root in the passionate desire to abolish suffering and sin. This underlies Isaiah Berlin's words:

One belief, more than any other, is responsible for the slaughter of individuals on the altars of the great historical ideals . . . This is the belief that somewhere, in the past, or in the future, in divine revelation, or in the mind of an individual thinker, in the pronouncements of history or science, or in the simple heart of an uncorrupted good man, there is a final solution.[63]

The passion to abolish suffering and sin cannot really be found in Kant; he was a puritan, concerned positively with duty; 'suffering'

Kant

and 'sin' are words that appear little, if at all, in his writings. He did not grapple with 'the problem of evil'. He agreed with the Stoic about pain: 'Good and evil . . . are properly referred to actions, not to the sensations of the person . . . pain did not in the least diminish the worth of his [viz. the Stoic's] person, but only that of his condition.'[64] But there are children of Kant who experience this passion much more acutely. Lenin 'was particularly great' [said Gorki] 'precisely because . . . of his burning faith that suffering was not an essential and unavoidable part of life, but an abomination that people ought [to] and could sweep away'.[65] It has been said of Beatrice Webb that, like Shaw, she did not 'love the poor' [but] she wanted to abolish them. 'Gandhi said on one occasion that it was his supreme ambition to wipe every tear from every eye';[66] this recalls the Book of Revelation: 'and God shall wipe all tears from their eyes'.[67]

Sin and suffering are mysteriously conjoined; perhaps even causally connected, although not all suffering is due to sin nor is all sin the cause of suffering. They are twin aspects of what moral theologians call the problem of evil; that is, how to account for the radical discords in the cosmos, for nature red in tooth and claw, and man's inhumanity to man. Now, man's inhumanity to man arouses different reactions in different natures: sorrow or indignation, sympathy or anger, a sense of suffering or sin; and this corresponds not always, but roughly, with the distinction made elsewhere between evolutionary and revolutionary Kantians. Evolutionary Kantians tend to work on the assumption that suffering is the principal cause of sin, and if suffering is eradicated, if conditions are improved, the inherent tendency towards the improvement of human nature will be liberated and sin will wither away.

Revolutionary Kantians tend to hold the assumption that sin is the principal cause of suffering and to give priority to the eradication of sin. First, they must 'draw the sword of Gideon and smite the Amalekite'; 'strangle the last king in the entrails of the last priest'; 'expropriate the expropriators'; 'liquidate the imperialists and warmongers'. In discussing the Kantians, two pairs of antitheses are seen to emerge: internationalism as against cosmopolitanism, and the evolutionary (indirect) as against the revolutionary (direct) approach. This can be illustrated in the following way.

Diagram of Kantians

	Evolutionary Kantians	Revolutionary Kantians
Motive	Eradicate suffering	Eradicate sin
Method	Evolutionary Indirect Soft Utopians	Revolutionary Direct Hard Utopians
Internationalism	*Wilson* Nehru Democratic Socialism	*Mazzini*
Cosmopolitanism	*Cobden* UNESCO	Doctrinal Imperialism Jacobinism Communism

Kant's Universality

What is worth noting for students of great philosophers like Kant and Plato is their comprehensiveness and universality; they cover everything from the origin of the human species to the end of all things. And also, those who come to read them should not be deterred by the difficulties of technical language, the 'fishbones' in their works.

Kant

Notes

1. See also W. Hastie (quoting De Quincey) in Immanuel Kant, *Kant's Principles of Politics*, tr. and ed. W. Hastie (Edinburgh: T. & T. Clark, 1891), pp. viii–ix.
2. Willibald Klinke, *Kant for Everyman*, tr. Michael Bullock (London: Routledge & Kegan Paul, 1952), pp. 41–3, 49–50.
3. Heinrich Heine, *Religion and Philosophy in Germany*, tr. John Snodgrass (London: Trübner & Co., 1882), pp. 108–9.
4. Klinke, *Kant for Everyman*, pp. 68–9.
5. Immanuel Kant, 'Prolegomena' in *The Philosophy of Kant*, ed. Carl J. Friedrich (New York: The Modern Library, 1949), pp. 43, 45.
6. See Kant, *Immanuel Kant's Critique of Pure Reason*, tr. Norman Kemp Smith (London: Macmillan & Co. Ltd, 1933), preface to 2nd edn., p. 22.
7. Carl J. Friedrich, 'Introduction' to Kant, *The Philosophy of Kant*, p. xxvi.
8. A. D. Lindsay, *Kant* (Oxford: Oxford University Press, 1936), pp. 50–1.
9. Kant, *Critique of Pure Reason*, preface to 2nd edn., p. 25.
10. Ibid., p. 29.
11. Kant, *Critique of Practical Reason*, tr. T. K. Abbott (London: Longmans, Green & Co., 1948), p. 260.
12. Ibid., p. 180.
13. Kant, 'Metaphysical Foundations of Morals', *The Philosophy of Kant*, p. 143.
14. Lindsay, *Kant*, p. 191.
15. Kant, *Critique of Practical Reason*, p. 116; see also Kant, *The Philosophy of Kant*, pp. 219–20.
16. Kant, *The Philosophy of Kant*, p. 172.
17. Lindsay, *Kant*, p. 175.
18. C. E. Vaughan, *Studies in the History of Political Philosophy* (Manchester: Manchester University Press, 1925), vol. II, pp. 81–2; see also p. 90.
19. Lindsay, *Kant*, p. 189.
20. Étienne Gilson, quoting from T. N. Greene, *Kant Selections*, in *The Unity of Philosophical Experience* (London: Sheed & Ward, 1938), pp. 243–4.
21. Kant, *Critique of Pure Reason*, p. 650.

22 Lindsay, *Kant*, p. 182.
23 J. J. Rousseau, *Profession of Faith of a Savoyard Vicar*, tr. O. Schreiner (New York: Peter Eckler, 1889), p. 64.
24 Etienne Gilson, quoting from T. N. Greene, *Kant Selections*; and Fichte, *The Vocation of Man*, in *The Unity of Philosophical Experience*, pp. 237, 246.
25 C. E. Vaughan, *Studies in the History of Political Philosophy*, vol. II, p. 67.
26 See Santayana's criticism of Kant in George Santayana, *Egotism in German Philosophy* (London: J.M. Dent & Sons, 1939), pp. 49–51; and a Kantian's repudiation thereof in Friedrich's 'Introduction' to Kant, *The Philosophy of Kant*, p. xii.
27 Ernst Cassirer, *Rousseau, Kant, Goethe*, tr. J. Gutmann et al. (Princeton: Princeton University Press, 1945), pp. 1–3.
28 Ibid., pp. 1–2.
29 See Vaughan, *Studies in the History of Political Philosophy*, vol. II, pp. 64–93.
30 Kant, 'First Definitive Article', *The Philosophy of Kant*, p. 437.
31 Kant, 'Rechtslehre', quoted in Vaughan, *Studies in the History of Political Philosophy*, vol. II, p. 83.
32 Kant, *The Philosophy of Law. An Exposition of the Fundamental Principles of Jurisprudence as the Science of Right by Immanuel Kant*, tr. W. Hastie (Edinburgh: T. & T. Clark, 1887), p. 224.
33 See ibid., conclusion, pp. 229–30.
34 Kant, 'Idea of a Universal History from a Cosmopolitical Point of View' in *Kant's Principles of Politics*, p. 24.
35 Woodrow Wilson's 'Four Principles Speech', 11 February 1918, in H. W. V. Temperley, *A History of the Peace Conference of Paris* (London: Henry Frowde and Hodder & Stoughton, 1920), vol. I, esp. p. 439.
36 Kant, *Perpetual Peace*, ed. Lewis White Beck (Indianapolis: Bobbs Merrill Co. Inc., 1957), pp. 3–7; see also the six proposals in Wilson's Fourteen Points, 'Address to Congress', 8 January 1918, in H. W. V. Temperley, *A History of the Peace Conference of Paris*, vol. I, pp. 433–5.
37 Kant, *Perpetual Peace*, end of Second Supplement, a Secret Article for Perpetual Peace, pp. 33–4.
38 Walter Schiffer, *The Legal Community of Mankind* (New York: Columbia University Press, 1954), p. 112.

Kant

39 Kant, 'Perpetual Peace', *The Philosophy of Kant*, p. 445.
40 Ibid., p. 454.
41 Kant, 'Universal History', *Principles of Politics*, pp. 24–5; see also p. 20.
42 Kant, 'The Principle of Progress' in *Principles of Politics*, pp. 75–6; see also Ibid., p. 72; and Kant, *Immanuel Kant Kleinere Schriften zur Geschichtsphilosophie Ethik und Politik*, Sonderausgabe Nr. 8 *Theorie und Praxis*, ed. Karl Vorländer (Leipzig: Felix Meiner, 1913), Band 47.I, p. 113.
43 Kant, 'Universal History' in *Principles of Politics*, p. 4.
44 M. C. D'Arcy, SJ, *The Sense of History* (London: Faber & Faber, 1959), p. 119.
45 Fyodor Dostoevsky, *The Brothers Karamazov*, tr. Constance Garnett (London: William Heinemann, 1915), pp. 256–8.
46 Kant, 'The Principle of Progress' in *Principles of Politics*, p. 76; and 'Perpetual Peace' in *Principles of Politics*, p. 111.
47 Kant, 'On the Proverbial Saying: "All very well in theory, but no good in practice," ' (1793). *Über den Gemeinspruch: Das mag in der Theorie richtig sein, taugt aber nicht für die Praxis* in *Kleinere Schriften zur Geschichtsphilosophie*, pp. 67–113.
48 Kant, 'Perpetual Peace' *Principles of Politics*, p. 115.
49 Kant, 'Universal History', ninth proposition, p. 28; see also Kant, *Kleinere Schriften*, p. 20; and Kant, *The Philosophy of Kant*, p. 130.
50 Kant, 'Principle of Progress', *Principles of Politics*, p. 69; see also Kant, *Kleinere Schriften*, p. 109.
51 Kant, 'Perpetual Peace', in *Principles of Politics*, appendix, p. 136; see also Kant, *Kleinere Schriften*, p. 162.
52 Kant, 'Perpetual Peace', in *Principles of Politics*, first supplement, pp. 111, 112.
53 Kant, *Critique of Pure Reason*, p. 551; see also Lindsay, *Kant*, pp. 160–1.
54 Kant, 'Universal History', in *Principles of Politics*, p. 27; and 'Perpetual Peace', first supplement, p. 115.
55 Marc Bloch, *Metier d'Historien, Apologie pour l'histoire* (Paris: Colin, 1949), p. x; Marc Bloch, *The Historian's Craft*, tr. Peter Putnam (Manchester: Manchester University Press, 1967), p. 6; H. Kessler, *Walther Rathenau: His Life and Work* (London: Gerald Howe Ltd, 1929), pp. 279–80, 367; Goebbels, speech in the

Berliner Sportpalast, 3 October 1943 (*Völkischer Beobachter*, 4 October 1943); Evgany Krieger, of November 1941, *From Moscow to the Prussian Frontier* (London: Hutchinson, 1945), p. 8.
56 J. B. Bury, *The Idea of Progress* (New York: Dover, 1932), p. 244.
57 Kant, 'Universal History', in *Principles of Politics*, p. 5.
58 Ibid., pp. 6–7.
59 Dante, *Monarchy*, tr. Donald Nicholl (London: Weidenfeld & Nicolson, 1954), pp. 7–9.
60 Kant, 'Principle of Progress', in *Principles of Politics*, p. 76; see also Kant, *Kleinere Schriften*, p. 12.
61 Kant, 'Universal History', in *Principles of Politics*, sixth proposition, p. 15; see also Kant, *Kleinere Schriften*, p. 12.
62 Bury, *The Idea of Progress*, p. 250.
63 Isaiah Berlin, *Two Concepts of Liberty* (Oxford: Clarendon Press, 1958), p. 52.
64 Kant, *Critique of Practical Reason*, p. 151.
65 Gorki quoted in Edmund Wilson, *To the Finland Station* (London: Martin Secker & Warburg Ltd, 1941), pp. 450–1.
66 Jawaharlal Nehru, *Visit to America* (New York: John Day, 1950), p. 121.
67 *Revelation* vii:17 (King James version), an echo of *Isaiah* xxv:8.

Chapter 4

Mazzini

22 June 1805–10 March 1872

Bibliographical Inaccessibility

Of the four international thinkers discussed here, Guiseppe Mazzini is probably the most inaccessible. It is a double inaccessibility: first, it is bibliographical. The national edition of his writings passed its 100th volume in the 1950s. The more manageable six-volume *Life and Writings*[1] in English, first published in 1870, was apparently supervised by Mazzini, and he seems to have written for it the autobiographical thread that links together the various articles that are reprinted there. But this is a confusing edition to use, its arrangement being wholly inconsequential: vols. 1, 3, and 5 are 'Autobiographical and Political'; 2, 4, and 6 are 'Critical and Literary'. The order of the pieces is not chronological; some of the most important material, such as the decrees of the Roman Republic, is tucked away in appendices, and it contains no index. There is a volume on Mazzini in the Cassell's 'Living Thoughts Library',[2] which Silone was asked to do and that came out in 1939, but this series is one of the most shockingly unscholarly ever sponsored by a reputable publisher; the extracts are published without references to the works of the author concerned, and without the date of writing. Obviously Silone was the right choice for the Mazzini volume, but the volume is perhaps less interesting for the study of Mazzini than for the study of Silone himself. He was haphazard in selecting the extracts, and he inserted some obscure and unimportant passages for their value as ammunition against Mussolini. He enlisted Mazzini in the current political struggle, in fact, just as Mazzini in his day had enlisted his great predecessors, Dante (1265–1321), Sarpi (1552–1623), and Foscolo (1778–1827), and Mazzini himself would certainly not have disapproved. Perhaps the most useful compendium for Mazzini study is the Everyman Library volume that contains *The Duties of Man*[3] and other writings.

A 'Victorian'

But second, the more serious inaccessibility of Mazzini is one of style, mode of expression, and spirit. Wherever he is opened on any two pages, all his main ideas, broad simple themes, are indefinitely repeated with a richness of verbiage. One finds high generalities about duty, humanity, sacrifice, providence, improvement; it is much like Ruskin or George Eliot, and this poses, I think, the problem of historical understanding. In what context, against what background, should Mazzini be seen? His orotunding is the rhetoric of Italian literary romanticism but we may get a cross-bearing if we remember to what an extent Mazzini was a Victorian—a Victorian in every sense except that he was not a British subject. He first came to London in the year of the Queen's accession, 1837, when he was thirty-two and for the remaining thirty-four years of his life he lived in London, except for infrequent excursions back to Italy, only one of which lasted more than twelve months.

He not only lived in London, as did so many revolutionaries, but unlike them, he became a part of English life, differing from Herzen, Bakúnin, Lassalle, Kossuth, and notably Marx, in making his friends in English literary and liberal-radical circles. His affairs became a matter of British domestic politics, as when the post office opened his correspondence in 1844; he was discussed in the House of Commons; and there were correspondences about him in *The Times*. Swinburne dedicated 'Songs before Sunrise' to him; he became a British institution—he would undoubtedly have been asked to do the Reith lectures—and in later life he wrote almost as easily in English as in Italian. In this sense, he belongs to the world of Carlyle and Ruskin, the Brownings, the Mills, Jowett, Toynbee (the social reformer and economist), Panizzi and the Rossettis,[4] and Swinburne (and it might be interesting to work out the affinity with the political and social creed of Ruskin especially, in some detail).

Mazzini's career, of course, has a brilliant zenith or central tableau; for about three months, from March to June 1849, he stands in the full blaze of European history: as dictator of the Roman Republic. Out of modesty he refused the title of dictator, which the Roman Assembly would have elected him to; he preferred to be a triumvir, but the other two did not count, and he had sole power. The acts of the Roman Republic were promulgated under the heading 'God and the People', and a great banner bearing these words, '*Dio e Popolo*', floated above the Vatican.[5] This was the most famous of Mazzini's many slogans, 'these principle-involving and eternal words',[6] words that summed up a philosophy both of history and of international politics.

Mazzini and Religion

Mazzini was an essentially religious person, both as a man and as a thinker; he was profoundly and entirely a religious type. He said it was impossible to keep religion out of politics: 'It is there "in all questions of the franchise, of the condition of the masses, of nationality"—all intimately linked with the religious thought of the time, all part of God's providential scheme for man.'[7]

He was an ex-Catholic, but a reluctant one, who had been brought up a Catholic with a mother-fixation. At an early age he ceased to believe, but he knew just what he had ceased to believe, and why, and all his life he remained within the ambience of Catholicism. He respected it as a religion, and he protected it when he was dictator. Unlike all the other revolutionaries of his time he thought religion was important, or rather essential, and he had an intellectual grasp of it; he was not theologically illiterate. The most important thing he ceased to believe in was the divinity of Christ, but in a sense his life was animated by a personal devotion to Christ as the supreme moral revolutionary. He was steeped in the New Testament, and he used it in controversy with powerful effect; he was fighting political Catholicism, so to speak, from the inside, and this was why Catholics regarded him as so dangerous. Generally he was an Italian literary romantic; sociologically a Victorian; but more precisely and intellectually he really belongs to the liberal Catholicism of the early nineteenth century, though out on the left wing.[8]

God in Politics: Providence and Progress

For Mazzini God in politics meant, in effect, three things: providence, progress, and duty. Mazzini's conception of God was quite traditional, he was neither pantheist nor immanentist. God was an objective transcendent spiritual being who presided over human affairs. 'He who can deny God either in the face of a starlight night, when standing beside the tomb of those dearest to him, or in the presence of martyrdom, is either greatly unhappy or greatly guilty.'[9] God's will would in due course be done on earth as it was in heaven—a favourite text with Mazzini. 'If there be not a governing Mind, supreme over every human mind, what shall preserve us from the dominion of our fellow-men, whenever they are stronger than ourselves?'[10]

It is in his theory of progress that Mazzini becomes distinctive and heretical and interesting: God's providence is manifested on earth in the law of progress. 'There was no Fall';[11] God has steadily led man upwards towards the 'angelification' of the individual, and the establishment of God's kingdom on earth. The criterion of progress was a moral one. Mazzini demolished the theological structure of the Christian economy of salvation, and repudiated the doctrines of the Fall, redemption, and grace. He left the moral structure standing with a kind of accentuated beauty; with the doctrines of self-dedication, moral virtue, self-sacrifice, and expiation. Since he saw progress as moral progress, he was repeatedly asserting, against the utilitarians and Marxists, the priority of ideas, ideals, and the moral factor, over material factors, and economic betterment. He saw this as both a logical and a practical priority. For him, a living faith came before a living wage; being good came before doing good, let alone doing well.

Little it matters to me that Italy, a territory of so many square leagues, eats its corn and cabbages cheaper; little I care for Rome, if a great European initiative is not to issue from it. What I do care for is that Italy shall be great and good, moral and virtuous, that she comes to fulfil a mission in the world.[12]

A law of progress implies that Mazzini, like Hegel and Marx, had his own historical escalator, but it was not the Hegelian escalator. He detested Hegel and disliked professors as a class; he saw them as desiccated, analytical, positivist, and destructive of ideals and of moral fervour. He especially disliked German professors and German philosophy. 'He blamed the appointment of Germans at Oxford; he was very angry that Hegel was taught at the University of Naples. "One fine day", he wrote, "we will sweep out all that stuff." '[13] Mazzini's escalator is a pre-Hegelian model derived from Herder and especially Vico, who were formative influences in his student days, but Mazzini's conception of progress really derives from sources older than Vico. It is an authentic reappearance, a bubbling up again, of one of the most venerable European beliefs, the Joachite heresy.

Joachim of Flora (*c*.1145–1202) was a Calabrian abbot. He modified the traditional and orthodox division of history into before and after the incarnation by developing a triple scheme: the age of the Father, before incarnation; the age of the Son, since incarnation; and the age of the Holy Spirit, which was about to begin. It would be an age of great spiritual intensification, purity, and fulfilment, when politics and family life would wither away and the earth would become a single vast convent with the human race transformed into monks, bound together in worship and love. This triple scheme has cropped up regularly ever since in utopian and revolutionist thinking. In Turgot and Comte, Hegel and Marx, and in Schelling, in the idea of Moscow as the Third Rome, and in the Third Reich, there is the mystical messianic significance of the third phase. It is unclear whether the Joachite influence on Mazzini was direct. In later life one finds him reading Joachim, but, characteristically, for Joachim the personal mystic rather than for his philosophy of history.[14] Probably this way of life and thought was first mediated through Lessing's *Die Erziehung des Menschengeschlechts* ('The Education of the Human Race'). Joachism is implicit in his attitude to Christianity:

'I am not a Christian,' he wrote to an English friend, 'I belong to what I believe to be a still purer and higher Faith; but its time has not yet come; and until that day the Christian manifestation remains the most sacred revelation of the ever-onward progressing spirit of mankind.'[15]

Christianity was the religion of the second age; the third age will be characterized by the collective life of humanity.

Revolution is then for us a work of education, a religious mission... As there exists no church save one hostile to the Spirit of Truth, and degenerated from its first institution, *we* are now the Militant Church of Precursors to the temple which shall be rebuilt, invoking *the kingdom of God, upon earth as it is in heaven*. We are the Church of Precursors until the virtuous who feel the necessity of a true and living faith, as the unifier of all human efforts, and inspirer of all human faculties, having assembled in council, having interrogated progress, having explored the evils, and decreed the remedies for our state, shall lay the first stone of the UNIVERSAL CHURCH of Humanity. And then only, the world being conquered by his teaching, Jesus will be able to repeat to the Father with an ineffable smile: 'I have manifested thy name unto the men which thou gavest me out of the world; thine they were, and thou gavest them me; and they have kept thy word' (John xvii, 6).[16]

The Joachism becomes explicit in the often-repeated idea of the Third Rome. In one of his stirring Manifestos (1844), Mazzini declared:

Bend the knee and worship: there beats the heart of Italy: there in eternal solemnity lies Rome. There juts out the capital of the Christian world...Those recumbent worlds await a third world, vaster and more sublime than themselves, rising out of the mighty ruins...This is the Trinity of History, of which the Word is in Rome. Tyrants and false prophets may delay the incarnation of the Word; none can prevent it. Many cities have perished from the earth, all can perish, but Rome, by the design of Providence discerned by the peoples, is eternal. Rome of the Caesars which unified much of Europe by Action, gave way to Rome of the Popes which by Thought unified Europe and America. Now Rome of the People will supplant the other two, to unify, by the faith of Thought and Action, Europe, America and the rest of the world...This will happen when you Italians understand that the life of a nation is Religion.[17]

Here is the Third Rome: Rome the moral centre of the coming age of collective Humanity.[18] Sometimes he exhorted others besides Italians to comply with the Trinity of History; for example, he told the German nationalists that their country had had two big moments: they invaded the Roman Empire 'to protest in the name of human liberty' against its materialism, and rejuvenated it; and 'Centuries later, with the applause of half the world, you raised another protest through the ringing voice of

Luther. Consider those two mighty manifestations of German nationality and find in them the duty to say a third great thing: "That conquest by might does not make right..."'[19]

But Germany was saying her third great thing with blood and iron, through Bismarck.

God in Politics: Duty

If progress was what God decreed for men, duty was what men owed to God. The strong belief in providence, the vigorous historical confidence (as is usual in Islam, Calvinism, and Communism), for Mazzini also intensifies, organizes, and disciplines the will and sharpens an imperative doctrine of ethics.

> World history slowly evolves from the continuous interplay of two forces: the activity of individuals and the design of Providence. The word that defines the first is liberty. The word that defines the second is progress. Time and space are ours. We can retard or accelerate progress. We cannot prevent it.
>
> Progress is the law of God. That law will be carried out, whatever we do. But its progressive fulfilment does not relieve us of responsibility for our acts or even reduce the amount of our responsibility. The sins and mistakes of one generation serve as lessons to succeeding generations; but the generation that sins or errs deserves blame or punishment, and punishment it will suffer, either here on earth or elsewhere.[20]

Mazzini is the great nineteenth-century apostle of duty. His chief work is *The Duties of Man*, which he meant as a counterblast to Paine's *Rights of Man*. He was out of sympathy with the incessant claim for rights and would have been still more so today. Logically and morally, duties were prior to rights: 'the individual has no rights except as a consequence of duties fulfilled'.[21] Historically it is true, the demand for rights had preceded a clarification of duties, but its power was only destructive and individualistic; it was a mark of the passing age of individualism that had culminated in the French Revolution. Mazzini wrote:

The theory of Rights may suffice to arouse men to overthrow the obstacles placed in their path by tyranny, but it is impotent where the object in view is to create a noble and powerful harmony between the various elements of which the Nation is composed. With the theory of happiness as the primary aim of existence, we shall only produce egotists who will carry the old passions and desires into the new order of things, and introduce corruption into it a few months after.

We have therefore to seek a Principle of Education superior to any such theory, and capable of guiding mankind onwards towards their own improvement, of teaching them constancy and self-sacrifice, and of uniting them with their fellow-men, without making them dependent either on the *idea* of a single man or the *force* of the majority.

This principle is DUTY.[22]

And again:

The doctrine of Rights puts an end to sacrifice, and cancels martyrdom from the world: in every theory of individual rights, interests become the governing and motive power, and martyrdom an absurdity, for what interest can endure beyond the tomb? Yet, how often has martyrdom been the initiation of progress, the baptism of a world![23]

So the law of progress has as its correlative and counterpart a law of personal moral responsibility. Mazzini is not here confusing two senses of the word law, sliding unawares from sociological law to moral law; his use of the word antedates that distinction and he was singularly uninterested in sociological laws. Law for him was much what it was for Hooker: law is what God ordains; He ordains progress for mankind as a whole; He ordains moral freedom and moral responsibility for men individually. Nor, it seems, was there any Kantian influence on Mazzini's doctrine of duty; he did read some Kant, but was not influenced by him. Just as his 'law' was pre-Comte and pre-Buckle, pre-Turgot and pre-Condorcet, so his 'duty' was pre-Kant; though a question may be raised about this (see below, pp. 109, 112 and n. 77). There is a double criterion of duty in politics: the objective and the subjective; not only a clear conscience but also an instructed conscience is necessary to know the needs of the situation: 'In order...to know the Law of God, you must interrogate not only *your own* conscience, but also the conscience and consent of Humanity. In order to know your own duties you must interrogate the present wants of Humanity.'[24] At the same time the criterion of political action is the intention, not the consequences. He fulminated against the justification of tyrants and dictators (like Louis Napoleon) by the argument that they produce good results, or provide social benefits like security or welfare. The moral flaw in the creed of Caesarism or Bonapartism is the 'energetic, over-bearing, assertion of self' by the conqueror. 'To anyone who asks: "Why should I believe in you?" he invariably answers: "Because I believe in myself." '[25] In a review of Louis Napoleon's life of Julius Caesar, Mazzini says:

Genius by itself does not constitute title to sovereignty. The purpose alone is sovereign...

A deep and persistent confusing of two essentially different things lies at the bottom of Caesarism. The agent is inevitably confused with the objective results of his career, even the remote and incidental results. The instrument is confused with the law that should control the agent's action. The man is mistaken for God...

There was an ancient heresy that worshipped Judas; for, so it was argued, had it not been for Judas there would have been no crucifixion and therefore no redemption. Caesarism is an application to history of just such a heresy. No! We cannot confuse the acts of the free responsible creature with the objective workings of providential laws. Curses upon Judas, and glory be to God, who allows no Judas to change humanity's destinies! That we raise that twin war cry is a vital condition to human living, if the achievement of those destinies is not to be too long postponed.[26]

His Political and Social Theory

Mazzini's political and social theory was that of a democratic socialist. He was represented by delegates at the formation of the First International in London in 1864, and Marx's inaugural address contained some moralistic and reformist sentiments which represented, from Marx's point of view, a tactical compromise to satisfy Mazzini and his 'detestable bourgeois patriotism', as Bakúnin put it.[27] Young Italy, Mazzini's revolutionary organization, was a middle-class movement, and on the whole Mazzini was not interested in an anti-feudal revolution on the rural estates of Italy at the same time as the anti-Austrian national revolution.[28] He was essentially a man of 1848, out of touch with the harsher world of Cavour, Bismarck, and Marx in the 1860s, when he lost the labouring masses in the Italian towns to the Marxist International, and the middle-class to the Cavourian policy of unification through Piedmont.[29]

Two points about Mazzini's general political theory deserve to be made in an introduction to his international theory. First, one of his key words was republic or republicanism, and it is used almost mystically. Sometimes it means a purified, sanctified democracy; sometimes something more like theocracy. These quotations come from Bolton King's *Life*: ' "Sovereignty is not in I nor we [*sic*] but God." "There is no sovereignty of right in any one; sovereignty is in the aim." A government was legitimate in proportion as it stood for righteousness. "There is no sovereignty in the individual or society, except in so far as either conforms itself to the divine plan and law." '[30] As Bolton King says, this is the fourteenth-century doctrine of dominion founded on grace, whose most celebrated exponent was John Wycliffe (*c*.1320–1384).[31] So Mazzini was a political Platonist: he believed in government by the virtuous, attaching intense importance to education. 'It is for republics to make republicans, not republicans republics.'[32]

The second point is to do with his use of the word association. By association he meant the right and duty of men to combine together in order to pursue the aims of moral improvement. A state or nation is an association in matters common to all its citizens; there ought to be innumerable lesser associations (in Austrian-dominated Italy of course there were not). Association is the security for progress, the instrument of progress, a right 'as sacred as Religion itself, which is the association of souls'.[33]

Of any international theorist there are two fundamental, central, questions to be asked, which intersect with one another. The first is, how does he strike the balance, weigh the scales, between the sovereign state and international society; between the loyalties, rights, and duties connected with the nation and those transcending it? What is the relation between the City of Cecrops and the City of Zeus? The second is, how does he strike the balance, weigh the scales, between power and morality? What casuistry of morals in politics does he offer us? To both these questions Mazzini gave a distinctive answer.

Nationalism and Internationalism

There are two ways of striking the balance between the state and international society. One is to subordinate the state completely to a world society of individuals: this is cosmopolitanism. The other is to subordinate international society to a single state: this is imperialism, probably ideological imperialism. Both of these Mazzini repudiated. He experienced these two tendencies when he started his revolutionary life in the Carbonari. The Carbonari were a secret society that developed out of Freemasonry in Naples under French rule, and became an Italy-wide organization of liberal malcontents against the Austrian restoration. [They originally met in the huts of coal-dealers and the term was adopted in memory of these first conspirators for Italian independence.] After the revolutions of 1820 (Naples) and 1821 (Piedmont) the headquarters of the Carbonari moved to Paris, and the organization spread in France and Spain. Mazzini said later:

The Carbonari ... naturally endeavoured to extend their work into all lands, and admitted men of every nation into their ranks. But it was a *cosmopolitan* association, in the philosophical sense of the word. It recognised only the *human race* and *individuals*; and it regarded its members simply as individuals. In their *Ventes* [meetings] neither altar nor banner was raised in the name of the Fatherland. When once initiated, the Pole, the Russian, the German, all became *Carbonari* and nothing more. Idolatrously worshipping the doctrines of the French Revolution, they went not a step beyond. Their aim was the conquest for each and all men of what they termed their *rights*, rights of liberty and equality, nothing more. They regarded every *collective* idea, and consequently the national idea, as useless, or—if judged by its results in the past—as dangerous.[34]

For Mazzini, the individual fulfils himself in the nation, the nation fulfils itself in humanity, and cosmopolitanism left out the essential middle link:

> For us the starting-point is Country; the object or aim is Collective Humanity. For those who call themselves cosmopolitans, the *aim* may be Humanity; but the starting-point is Individual Man. This distinction is vital: it is almost identical with the distinction which separates the believers in association from those who recognise no other instrument of action than unlimited liberty.[35]

But a cosmopolitan association, an association of individuals, is incapable of affecting international society unless it brings its weight to bear on some member of international society, that is, some state. If it does not do this, it bombinates in a void. As Mazzini himself said; 'Before we speak of putting a lever in motion, we must not only possess a lever, but a definite object upon which to exert its power.'[36]

The Carbonari did in fact come to depend on one state: they came to look to France for salvation, to look to the great revolutionary nation to resume its European revolutionary task. They became a potential instrument of French foreign policy: Louis Philippe was too cautious to use it, Louis Napoleon used the remnants of it, and in the end the surviving Carbonari supported the unification of Italy by Piedmont backed by France. This to Mazzini was the ultimate betrayal: 'Not having a *principle* upon which to found it [their bond of unity], they set themselves to seek it in a *man*—a *prince*. This was the ruin of Carbonarism.'[37] Mazzini was consistently anti-French; France had been corrupted by the Revolution, and Europe needed to be freed from her political and literary dominance. This was a fully developed and reasoned antagonism, even before Napoleon III arrived to incarnate all that Mazzini distrusted in France.

Nationality

Mazzini is famous as a prophet of nationalism but 'humanity' is his keyword, not 'nationality'. 'Your first duties, first not as to time, but as to importance—because unless you understand these, you can only imperfectly fulfil the rest—your first duties are towards Humanity.'[38]

But you cannot do your duty to humanity without associating first in nations; nationality is the most important expression of the principle of association. 'Even as a wise overseer of labour distributes the various branches of employment according to the different capacities of the workmen, he [God] divided Humanity into distinct groups or nuclei upon the face of the earth, thus creating the germ of Nationalities.' This 'division of European labour' is essential to the progress of Europe, and, through it, of the world.[39] Humanity is an army, and nations are regiments, each with its special task in the common operation.[40]

Among the various marks or indices of nationality there are natural frontiers, or geographical boundaries. Providence has traced the outlines of the nations on the map of Europe but England and France are the only countries whose boundaries correspond to the design. Italy has her 'sublime, irrefutable boundary marks', and Spain and Portugal ought to form a single country, as should Scandinavia.[41] Another mark of nationality is language and culture: in Italy, for example, the writings of Dante (in the vernacular) are the bearer of Italian nationality. Self-determination is important too; in Switzerland and Alsace it overrides the linguistic test, for 'Nationalities can be founded only for and upon and by the people.'[42]

So much is commonplace, and if it were only that, Mazzini would simply be the prophet of the Versailles Settlement. However, he went further: he identified also a moral purpose as one of the marks of nationality. For him, nationalism, like everything political, is to be judged and justified by its purpose, intention, or moral aim. 'In questions of nationality, as in every other question, the end alone is sovereign.'[43] 'There is therefore no true country without an uniform Right. There is no true country where the uniformity of that Right is violated by the existence of castes, privilege, and inequality.'[44] Here Mazzini is going deeper than the contemporary doctrine of national self-determination, and would probably have found himself in agreement with Elie Kedourie's critique of Arab nationalism. In a sense, he even foresaw that international society might be gatecrashed by nationalist impostors; that nationalist societies without a moral aim might force their way to membership of international society. This, in the deepest sense, was what he believed about Cavourian Italy and it was on these grounds that he condemned Irish nationalism. Irish nationalism did not have 'any distinct principle of life... derived from native peculiarities, and contrasting radically with English wants and wishes', but above all it did not claim any 'high special function' in the interests of humanity.[45] (He did not link up with Gladstone over the latter's approach to Ireland.) Mazzini's doctrine was a doctrine of *Collective Vocation*: 'Each people will have its mission and that mission will constitute its test of nationality.'[46] He was fanciful and unsuccessful in describing the various national missions, suggesting that England's is 'industry and colonies'; Russia's, the civilizing of Asia; Poland's, 'the Slav initiative' (whatever that means); that of Germany is thought; of France, action; and of Italy, thought and action united.

A national vocation he loved to dream of, and hope for, was that of Italy's revolutionary leadership. The myth of the revolutionary hegemony of a special nation was part of the stock-in-trade of nineteenth-century revolutionary nationalism: the myth of the nation-messiah. (Fichte claimed primacy for Germany, Guizot for France, Mickievicz and Cieszkowski for Poland, Hirzel for Switzerland, and Gioberti besides Mazzini for Italy.)[47] Mazzini claimed a primacy for Italy that differed from all the others in its shyness, inclusiveness, and humility. It was a primacy of service, duty, self-sacrifice, and initiative, and of course it flowed naturally from and was congruous with the doctrine of the Trinity of History, of Rome the Third Rome. In a fine critical essay, written in 1838, on Paolo Sarpi,[48] Mazzini suddenly bursts into italics:

There are Italians who believe that Italy could not, without abandoning the part assigned to her by Providence in the civilisation of Europe, formally throw off her unifying character; that she is bound to exist such as she is, till the moment when, throwing off her old formula of unity, she can substitute for it a new one; and that perhaps she is at this hour maturing in her bosom the germs of a religious transformation which will reveal itself with a political revolution, and whose European results will be of the highest importance.[49]

The doctrine of national vocation is essentially traditional: 'Your country is the sign of the mission God has given you to fulfil towards humanity.'[50] Its unconscious sources are the Old Testament: 'Are ye not as children of the Ethiopians unto me, O children of Israel? saith the Lord. Have not I brought up Israel out of the land of Egypt? and the Philistines from Caphtor, and the Syrians from Kir?'[51] and the Virgilian: *'Ego poscor Olympo.'* ('It is I who am summoned of Heaven.')[52]

The Revolutionary Situation

The doctrine of nationality was derived immediately from and testified to a revolutionary situation; the situation of international society demanded revolution. The international arrangements of Europe were unjust and immoral, and no arguments of right or international law could be based on them. Evil governments, by their greed and conquests, had disfigured the divine design, and instead of the natural divisions based on the spontaneous innate tendencies of peoples there were arbitrary divisions.[53]

The compulsory conjunction of different races, utterly devoid of that unity of faith and moral aim in which true nationality consists, does not in fact constitute a nation. The division of Europe, sanctioned in the treaties of 1815, by the excess of power given to some states, produced a consequent weakness in others, and placed them in the necessity of leaning upon some one of the great powers, no matter upon what terms, for support; while the germs of internal dissension that division had implanted in the heart of every people had created an insurmountable barrier to the normal and secure development of liberty.

To reconstruct the map of Europe, then, in accordance with the special mission assigned to each people by their geographical, ethnographical, and historical conditions, was the first step necessary for all.[54]

What was true of Europe in general was especially true of Italy; in the territory traced by the finger of providence to form Italy there were seven states, seven members of international society, one of which was the Habsburg Empire, and the other six its satellites. (It is interesting to note that the Austrian ascendancy was maintained by means similar to those of the Stalinist Russian ascendancy in eastern Europe, such as forced confessions, brainwashings, torture, floggings, and the absence of a free press or the rule of law.) For Mazzini, none of these members of international society on Italian soil had any right to exist: 'The *autonomy* of the separate states into which Italy is at present divided, is an historic error. These states have not arisen by the effort of their own peculiar and spontaneous vitality, but have been formed by the *bon plaisir* of foreign or domestic tyranny.'[55]

Indeed, of all the oppressed nations, Italy alone had a double servitude: 'I find that among all nationalities we Italians alone have the double obstacle—perhaps I should call it the twin privilege—of the Hapsburg Empire and the Papacy.'[56] Both of which, in Mazzini's view, ought to be abolished. In negative terms, Mazzini's aim was the abolition of the Habsburg and Ottoman Empires, and also the Russian Empire in Poland and Lithuania. In practice his aim was the situation of 1918.

Because there was a revolutionary situation, and international arrangements had no moral basis, it followed that the doctrine of non-intervention was not valid.

It has to be observed of this principle of Non-interference, that the very terms in which it is put forth, necessarily presuppose something, take something for granted. When it is said that the true principle of the mutual relations of nations is the principle of Non-intervention, a state of things is presupposed in which all the due conditions of Nationality have been attended to. It is between certain things called *Nations* that the principle of Non-intervention is to hold; the principle of Non-intervention is not to take effect except on the supposition that the parties concerned are distinct Nations...

If half of England were attached to France and the other half to Denmark, would not the governments of France and Denmark find themselves entangled together by the strong tendency of the severed halves of England to reunite themselves; and would it be fair to set up any abstract doctrine of Non-intervention as a reason why the two masses of Englishmen whom Nature had destined to form one, should turn their backs to each other, take no concern in each other's affairs, and prove false to their dearest instincts? And is not this a fair description of certain parts of that diplomatic dismemberment of Europe, falsely called a Political System, in perpetuation of which the doctrine of Non-intervention is jesuitically invoked?...

A nation is a more permanent thing than a system of rule, and ought to be guaranteed by higher maxims of inviolability. Destroy the system of rule in Russia, Spain, or England, and Russia, Spain, and England will still remain as much realities as before—facts engraven, so to speak, on the solid substance of the globe; destroy the system of rule centralized at Vienna, and there remains nothing at all in nature answering to the name of Austria. The charters by which Italy and Hungary exist separately are more ancient and more sacred than that which has handed them over to one and the same master.[57]

And he pointed out, what was already a diplomatic commonplace, that the principle of non-intervention meant, in practice, that the Holy Alliance intervened to put down free movements against corrupt despots, while Britain and France in the name of non-intervention acquiesced, and this to Mazzini was a degrading moral torpor: 'The absolute non-intervention doctrine in politics appears to me to be what indifference is in matters of religion—viz. a disguised atheism—the negative, without the vitality of a denial, of all belief, of all general principles, of every mission of nations on behalf of humanity.'[58] Why should it be lawful for the Czar to intervene to crush Hungary, he says: 'but not at all lawful for the free English people to drag that interfering Czar back... [?] ...the same theory which proclaims Non-interference as the first law of international politics, must include, as a secondary law, the right of interference to make good all prior infractions of the law of Non-interference.'[59]

Mazzini is arguing that what we would call ideological considerations, and what he would call moral considerations, must override international law. It is wrong for despots to intervene against national liberation movements, and wrong for free governments not to intervene against despotic interventions; his life was dedicated, of course, to organizing revolutionary international intervention against despotic governments. He emphasized a principle, which in his day played only a marginal and corrective part in international law, but that fifty years after his death began to assume equal importance with the principle of non-intervention; this was the principle of mutual involvement.

It begins to be felt that if on any spot of the world, even within the limits of an independent nation, some glaring wrong should be done... then other nations are not absolved from all concern in the matter simply because there may interpose between them and the scene of the wrong, seas, tracts of continent, and traditional diplomatic courtesies.[60]

But in his tract on non-intervention, which is probably his most powerful piece of political writing, he is addressing the English and does not want to seem to advocate general revolutionary interventionism, so he ends on a note of statesmanlike empiricism:

> [A] new method of international procedure will at length be evolved, the exact character of which we cannot foresee, but which will be equally distinct, it is believed, from a wretched neutrality on the one hand, and from a boisterous military activity on the other.
>
> Meanwhile this result is not to be arrived at by shutting our eyes or our hearts to what is actually going on, but by allowing each case of contemporary international wrong to produce its full impression upon us, and to stimulate us to some course of action immediately and specially appropriate. The theory of international polity can be perfected in no other way than by dealing sincerely and thoroughly with individual cases as they successively arise.[61]

Revolutionary Methods

Revolutionary means were necessary to deal with the revolutionary situation. He thought like a member of a resistance movement in an occupied country; the war was a holy war, a crusade, and national insurrection was the instrument of revolution.[62] His own conspiracies, like the Savoy raid of 1834, had a comic-opera character.[63] Like all international revolutionaries, he distrusted diplomacy and this was his central disagreement with Cavour. Simple principles, honest faith, popular initiative, were worth more [in Mazzini's eyes] than [Cavour's] 'Machiavellism', the paralysing diplomatic calculus, playing for the support of a French ally who could not be trusted; and the cession [by Cavour to France] of Savoy and Nice and Garibaldi's triumphs in Sicily and Naples seemed to confirm Mazzini's view.[64] A conspirator himself, he was a credulous attributor of conspiracies to his enemies. He was often misinformed, especially about Napoleon's policy, and having a lurid imagination he was eminently suspicious of despotic power politics, and of international Fascist-type deals—'the European *coup d'état*'. After Napoleon deserted

Piedmont and made the Armistice of Villafranca, Mazzini believed that France and Russia were going to partition Europe and make a triple alliance with Austria.[65] He feared the cooperation of 'the Czar of the West and the Czar of the North'.[66]

Humanity

For Mazzini humanity was more important than nationality: the greater included the less. 'And so long as you are ready to die for Humanity, the Life of your Country will be immortal' is the last sentence of his chapter on 'Duties towards Your Country' in *The Duties of Man*.[67] 'Nationality and humanity are therefore equally sacred. To forget humanity is to suppress the *aim* of our labours; to cancel the nation is to suppress the instrument by which to achieve the aim.'[68]

Freed and fulfilled nationalities would form a regenerated international society. When an international theorist talks like this there are two supplementary questions to be asked: 'What are the limits of his international society?' and 'How does he expect his regenerated international society to work?'. Mazzini's answer to the first question is striking because it is so traditional. He talks continually about humanity, but because of his passionate concentration on the sufferings of the cradle of European civilization in Italy, his international vision is limited to Europe and his international society to Christendom, both Western and Eastern. He did not even fit the Americas in, unlike Cobden. And when he demands the destruction of the Ottoman Empire, he is thinking of Turkey in Europe, the historic iniquitous buttress or shore of the Habsburgs, the co-oppressor of the Balkan Slavs; of Turkey-in-Asia he knows nothing. (The only Asiatic people he mentions, incidentally, as deserving national freedom, are the Circassians.) Asia was destined to be 'an appendix of Europe', to be colonized and civilized by Russia and England; Mazzini was a colonialist.[69]

And how did he expect the regenerated international society to work? The answer is in another of his famous slogans: 'The Holy Alliance of the Peoples'. 'We are bound to oppose the league of princes by a Holy Alliance of the peoples...We believe...in the Holy Alliance of the Peoples as being the vastest formula of association possible in our epoch.'[70] The old balance of power between greedy and fearful princes will be replaced by a new balance of power between sister nations, each, he says: 'performing its special mission, according to its special capacity, perform[ing] its part in the general work, and promot[ing] the progressive advance and prosperity of humanity.'[71] Italy would be the conductor of this fraternal orchestra, and in Rome, instead of the Papacy, would sit the general council of the nations, to 'declare the conception of the general mission of the peoples'.[72] (All that Rome has actually got today is the International Food and Agriculture Organization.) He evokes Isaiah's vision of the righteous harmony of the nations:

> In that day shall there be a highway out of Egypt to Assyria, and the Assyrian shall come into Egypt, and the Egyptian into Assyria, and the Egyptians shall serve with the Assyrians. In that day shall Israel be the third with Egypt and with Assyria, even a blessing in the midst of the land: Whom the Lord of hosts shall bless, saying, Blessed be Egypt my people, and Assyria the work of my hands, and Israel mine inheritance.[73]

'The Europe of the peoples will be One; avoiding alike the anarchy of absolute independence and the centralisation of conquest.'[74] That is how, in principle, Mazzini strikes a balance between the state and international society, and answers the first fundamental question of an international theorist.

Power and Morality

The second great question to be asked of the international theorist, how can one strike a balance between power and morality, is much more straightforward for Mazzini. Of all the great international thinkers, he is the most uncompromising moralist; of all of them, he says most resoundingly and satisfactorily, *Fiat justitia et ruat coelum*. (Let justice be done though the heavens fall.) He is always sharply asserting the sovereign primacy of the ideal over fact; right over might and duty over rights; principle over interest, and intention over consequence; and he believes that if men will seek first the kingdom of humanity, all these things will be added unto them. Here he is exhorting the 'Working Men of England' in 1855 in a letter about the Crimean War:

You must cancel the divorce now existing between what one *thinks* and what one *does*. And you must bid every man to *do*, to act according to his soul's creed, to make himself a living gospel, to stand up, and say, 'This is my faith; I will live in it, and, if wanted, I will die for it.' England is now proclaiming liberty at home and upholding tyranny abroad;—blessing with one hand our Italian martyrs of liberty, and grasping with the other the hand of their hangman, Austria;—muttering the watchword of progressive civilization, and trying to prop the rotten edifice of 1815; applauding Kossuth, and discountenancing Hungary;—sympathizing with Poland, and sacrificing her to Austria. This must cease, or you will never conquer; you have no *right* to conquer.

This question of *right* seems never to arise before the mind of your countrymen. It is the *true* question. I hear daily, chaotic, endless discussions about Lord Raglan's inefficiency;—about absurd, unjust methods of promotions in the army; ignorance or culpable neglect of your commissariat; want of energy in the rulers; military blunders, etc.; all real but secondary causes of your failure. Not a single known English voice has said hitherto to his countrymen:

Friends, the course you pursue is utterly wrong; the policy of your war is absolutely immoral; how can you hope for victory? [This was unfair to some public figures, notably John Bright who denounced the Crimean War as 'a crime'.—M. W.]

Right is the offspring of duty—duty fulfilled. What high duty are you now trying to fulfil towards Europe?[75]

Mazzini

In a letter to Cavour of June 1858 he trounces him and his supporters, after Orsini's attempt on Napoleon had obliged Cavour to introduce a Conspiracy Bill in Piedmont:

I have long known you [he begins] more solicitous for the Piedmontese monarchy than for our common country, a materialist worshipper of the event more than of any sacred and eternal principle, a man of an ingenious rather than a powerful mind... Partisans of opportunity, you have no right to invoke principles; worshippers of the *fait accompli*, you may not assume the garb of priest of morality. Your science lives in the phenomenal world, in the event of the day—you have no ideal. Your alliances are not with the free, but with the strong; they rest not on notions of right and wrong, but on notions of immediate material utility... Between you and me there is no difference but this one: I say, holy is every war against the foreigner, and I reverence him that tries it, even though he succumb; you say, holy is every war that succeeds, and you insult the fallen.[76]

Mazzini strikes no balance between moral man and immoral society. In this perennial argument, he fixes one of the great polar positions: like no other modern writer he asserts, in coherent and noble language, the indivisibility of moral standards:

Ask yourselves, as to every act you commit within the circle of family or country: *If what I now do were done by and for all men, would it be* beneficial or injurious to Humanity? and if your conscience tell you it would be injurious, desist: desist, even though it seem that an immediate advantage to your country or family would be the result.

And since the law is one; since it governs alike the two aspects, internal and external, of the life of each being; the two modes—personal and relative—subjective and objective—of every existence,—we hold the same creed with regard to each people, and the individuals of which it is composed, that we hold with regard to humanity, and the nations of which it is composed.[77]

It is true that it is easier for a revolutionary to adopt this position than for a conservative, and it is true that Mazzini did not explore the problem systematically (he probably did not understand its complexities); but he was not only a political theorist; he was also, in a feverish and unsuccessful way, a politician, and he *practised* his moral creed. In 'Rules for the Conduct of Guerrilla Bands', which he wrote in 1832, he declared himself at the beginning on those same moral problems that worried the non-Communist part of the French Resistance Movement:

> The political mission of the bands is to constitute the armed apostolate of the insurrection. Every band should be a living programme of the morality of the party. The most rigorous discipline is at once a duty and a necessity among them. It is a sacred duty towards their country, and a necessity for the bands themselves, which could not long exist if their conduct were such as to deprive them of the sympathy of the people... Guerrilla bands are the precursors of the nation, and endeavour to rouse the nation to insurrection. They have no right to substitute themselves for the nation... The right of compelling expiation, or executing justice upon those guilty in the past, belongs to the nation alone. The bands may not usurp this right. The vengeance of the country must not be entrusted to individuals, be they whom they may.[78]

Mazzini's political quality is best seen in his government of the Roman Republic; it was one of those rare moments in history—like Trotsky's position at Brest-Litovsk—when the ordinary rules of politics are suspended. Mazzini knew from the outset that the Republic was doomed and in consequence he was liberated from the necessity of calculation and compromise. Since there was nothing but the worst to be expected, he could act the best; since the heavens were bound to collapse, justice might be done. It was not regular statesmanship, but it was a masterpiece of the political art. (His biographers incidentally quote Palmerston as having described Mazzini's diplomatic despatches as 'models of reasoning and argument'[79] but I have not confirmed this in a Palmerstonian source.) Mazzini was wounded by the calumnies of the European press who claimed that he conducted a reign of terror in Rome, which was grotesquely untrue, and he wrote a fine open letter to Tocqueville, who as foreign minister had made this accusation in the French Assembly, in which he defended the conduct of the Republic.[80] In fact, the Roman Republic of 1849 was quite out of this world; it was the counterpart and opposite of the 1871 Paris Commune. 'Here in Rome [Mazzini told the Assembly] we may not be moral mediocrities.'[81] Mazzini moved among the Romans like a beloved father; when they dragged the confessional-boxes out of the churches to build barricades in the streets, Mazzini published a decree reminding them that from these confessionals had gone forth 'words of consolation to the aged mothers of those who are fighting for the Republic'[82] and the mob, bursting into tears, immediately bundled the confessionals back into the churches. When a number of the French besiegers were captured they were at once unconditionally released, the wounded were tenderly nursed, and they were then fêted in the streets and shown around St Peter's and returned to the French army.[83] 'A monster gift of cigars was sent to the enemy's quarters, wrapped in handbills that appealed to republican fraternity.'[84] When at length the Roman Assembly decided to cease resistance, Mazzini resigned, saying in Churchillian words that he 'had been elected a Triumvir to defend, and not to destroy the Republic';[85] and after the French had occupied the city, he remained there publicly for a week, walking the streets, to disprove that anybody wished to injure or assassinate him, and proving incidentally that the French dared not arrest him.

Mazzini is famous as a revolutionary, as the prophet of nationalism. After the Genoa Conference in 1921, there was a Mazzini Memorial meeting in London, with Lloyd George, George Bernard Shaw, and R. W. Seton-Watson as speakers. Lloyd George, then prime minister, made the chief speech on the theme, 'How *right* Mazzini was.' Was he? He was essentially the man of 1848 (one of his friends said that his watch had stopped in 1848), and he did not really understand what happened afterwards, or what Cavour was doing. If Cavourian Italy did not fulfil his dream, still less did the Italy of Crispi and Giolitti, of the Tripolitan War and *sacro egoismo*, still less the Italy of Fascism.

In 1919 it seemed that Mazzini's vision had come true on a wider stage, but the Versailles Settlement, like 1848, was one of those transient spring days in the history of liberal bliss. Mazzini had not foreseen the corruption of nationalism, nor his whole system of revolutionary interventionism being taken over by a new breed of despots beside whom Nicholas I of Russia was a Christian gentleman and Louis Napoleon a clumsy quack.

A Traditionalist Revolutionary

What is perhaps most interesting in Mazzini is his traditionalism; he is backward-looking even more than forward-looking. One can see this in his Catholic frame of thinking, his Trinity of History; the belief in Italy's mission, and intellectual dependence on Dante; the European limits of his international society, and the echo of the Conciliar Movement (1409–49) in his dream of replacing the papacy by a general council of the nations: in all this he does not foreshadow the future, but summarizes and orchestrates the past. He was, arguably, the last great Western international thinker before Marx and President Wilson. And, in a sense, the Roman Republic of 1849 was less the overture of the Risorgimento than the last flicker of the Roman city-state, the sequel to Rienzi in the fourteenth century, and Arnold of Brescia in the twelfth. Of the two kinds of prophet, the forecaster or the interpreter (foresight or insight), he fits into neither class. He was an apostle, 'apostolato' was one of his favourite words; the apostolate of insurrection, of republicanism, of the nation; an apostle, a political saint, a virginal type, less like Burke or Marx than like Savonarola. Immersed though he was in his own age, he did not fully understand it; and if he has lasting value or interest, it is not because he was an interpreter of his times, or because he wrenched and pummelled history into new channels, but because he drew his spiritual strength from timeless sources.

Notes

1. Joseph Mazzini, *Life and Writings of Joseph Mazzini* (London: Smith, Elder, & Co., 1890), 6 vols.
2. Ignazio Silone, *Mazzini* (London: Cassell & Co., Ltd, 1939). [The most recent scholarly biography is *Mazzini* by D. Mack Smith (New Haven and London: Yale University Press, 1994) –Eds.]
3. Joseph Mazzini, *The Duties of Man and other Essays* (London: J.M. Dent & Sons, 1912).
4. Antonio Genesio Maria Panizzi (1797–1879), forced to leave Italy 1822, professor of Italian, University College, London, and from 1856 principal librarian, British Museum. Gabriele Pasquale Rossetti (1783–1854), escaped to England 1824, became professor of Italian, King's College, London; Dante Gabriel (1828–82), his son, the painter and poet.
5. Mazzini, *Life and Writings*, vol. V, p. 296.
6. Ibid.
7. Bolton King, *The Life of Mazzini* (London: J.M. Dent & Sons Ltd, 1912), p. 223.
8. He refers to Lamennais, as 'the sole priest of the Epoch' (Mazzini, *Life and Writings*, vol. III, p. 87); see also his 'The Duties of Man' (vol. IV). Rossini and Manzoni *quâ* Jansenist represent this tradition as does the puritan Catholic, Ricasoli. [Mazzini's long article on Lamennais is found in *Life and Writings*, vol. VI, pp. 1–31. –Eds.]
9. Mazzini, 'The Duties of Man', *Life and Writings*, vol. IV, p. 232.
10. Ibid., vol. IV, p. 244.
11. King, *The Life of Mazzini*, p. 232. See also Mazzini, 'The Duties of Man', *Life and Writings*, vol. IV, p. 300.
12. King, *The Life of Mazzini*, p. 191.
13. Ibid., p. 275.
14. See ibid., p. 197.
15. Ibid., p. 230.
16. 'On the Encyclica of Pope Pius IX (Thoughts addressed to the Priests of Italy). Given [by the Pope] at Portici, 8 December 1849'. Mazzini, *Life and Writings*, vol. V, pp. 361–2.
17. Quoted in Cecil J. S. Sprigge, *The Development of Modern Italy* (London: Duckworth, 1943), pp. 33–4.

18 See Mazzini, *Life and Writings*, vol. V, p. 164.
19 Silone, *Mazzini*, p. 97.
20 Ibid., p. 86.
21 Mazzini, 'Autobiographical Notes', *Life and Writings*, vol. III, p. 6.
22 Mazzini, 'The Duties of Man', vol. IV, p. 223.
23 Mazzini, 'Faith and the Future', vol. III, p. 118.
24 Mazzini, 'The Duties of Man', vol. IV, p. 256.
25 Silone, *Mazzini*, p. 85.
26 Ibid., pp. 84, 86, 87–8.
27 See King, *The Life of Mazzini*, p. 283; and Silone, *Mazzini*, pp. 27–8.
28 See Silone, *Mazzini*, p. 31.
29 Ibid., p. 28.
30 King, *The Life of Mazzini*, p. 275; see also Mazzini, 'The Duties of Man', *Life and Writings*, vol. IV, p. 308.
31 R. W. Carlyle and A. J. Carlyle, *A History of Mediaeval Political Theory in the West* (Edinburgh and London: William Blackwood & Sons Ltd, 1950), vol. VI, p. 60.
32 King, *The Life of Mazzini*, p. 278.
33 Mazzini, 'The Duties of Man', *Life and Writings*, vol. IV, p. 326.
34 Ibid., vol. III, p. 6.
35 Ibid., pp. 7–8.
36 Ibid., p. 7.
37 Ibid., vol. I, p. 71; and Silone, *Mazzini*, p. 42.
38 Mazzini, 'The Duties of Man', *Life and Writings*, vol. IV, p. 258.
39 Ibid., p. 275; and King, *The Life of Mazzini*, p. 297.
40 See Mazzini, 'The Duties of Man', *Life and Writings*, vol. IV, p. 277.
41 Ibid., p. 275; and King, *The Life of Mazzini*, pp. 299, 308. [See also D. Mack Smith, *Mazzini*, pp. 155–7. –Eds.]
42 King, *The Life of Mazzini*, p. 300.
43 Ibid.
44 Mazzini, 'The Duties of Man', *Life and Writings*, vol. IV, p. 278.
45 King, *The Life of Mazzini*, p. 107.
46 Silone, *Mazzini*, p. 55.
47 Ibid., pp. 18–19.
48 [Fra Paolo Sarpi (1552–1623), theologian and author of a history of the Council of Trent. –Eds.]
49 Mazzini, *Life and Writings*, vol. II, p. 248; see also King, *The Life of Mazzini*, pp. 60, 191–2.

50   Mazzini, 'The Duties of Man', *Life and Writings*, vol. IV, p. 278.
51   Amos ix.7 (King James version).
52   Virgil, *Aeneid*, tr. H. Rushton Fairclough (London: William Heinemann Ltd, 1946), vol. II, bk VIII, line 533, p. 96.
53   Mazzini, 'The Duties of Man', *Life and Writings*, vol. IV, p. 275.
54   Ibid., vol. I, p. 176.
55   Ibid., vol. V, p. 150.
56   Silone, *Mazzini*, p. 97.
57   Mazzini, 'Non-intervention', first published in 1851, *Life and Writings*, vol. VI, pp. 301–2, 303, 304.
58   Ibid., vol. III, p. 204.
59   Ibid., vol. VI, pp. 306, 305.
60   Ibid., vol. VI, p. 307.
61   Ibid., vol. VI, p. 308.
62   Ibid., vol. V, p. 151.
63   Ibid., vol. I, pp. 366–8; King, *The Life of Mazzini*, pp. 50–1.
64   D. Mack Smith, *Cavour and Garibaldi 1860* (Cambridge: Cambridge University Press, 1954), p. 247.
65   King, *The Life of Mazzini*, p. 179.
66   Silone, *Mazzini*, p. 104.
67   Mazzini, 'The Duties of Man', *Life and Writings*, vol. IV, p. 281.
68   Mazzini, 'The Holy Alliance of the Peoples', *Life and Writings*, vol. V, p. 274.
69   King, *The Life of Mazzini*, p. 309.
70   Mazzini, 'The Holy Alliance of the Peoples', *Life and Writings*, vol. V, p. 272; and 'Faith and Future', *Life and Writings*, vol. III, p. 129.
71   Ibid., vol. V, p. 274.
72   Ibid., vol. V, p. 278; and King, *The Life of Mazzini*, pp. 310–11.
73   Isaiah xix.23–5 (King James version).
74   Mazzini, 'The Holy Alliance of the Peoples', *Life and Writings*, vol. V, p. 275.
75   Mazzini, 'Letter I on the Crimean War', *Life and Writings*, vol. VI, pp. 314–15.
76   Mazzini in J. E. E. Dalberg-Acton (first Lord Acton), *Historical Essays and Studies* (London: Macmillan and Co. Ltd, 1907), pp. 190, 192–3.
77   Mazzini, 'The Duties of Man', *Life and Writings*, vol. IV, p. 272; 'Faith and the Future', vol. III, p. 129. [Compare Kant: 'I ought

never to act except in such a way *that I can also will that my maxim should become a universal law.'* Immanuel Kant, *The Moral Law; or, Kant's Groundwork of the Metaphysic of Morals*, tr. H. J. Paton (London: Hutchinson's University Library, 1948), p. 70. –Eds.]
78 Mazzini, *Life and Writings*, vol. I, pp. 369–70.
79 King, *The Life of Mazzini*, p. 133.
80 Mazzini, *Life and Writings*, vol. V, p. 222.
81 G. M. Trevelyan, *Garibaldi's Defence of the Roman Republic* (London: Longman, 1907), p. 103.
82 Mazzini, *Life and Writings*, vol. V, p. 391.
83 Ibid., p. 381; and Trevelyan, *Garibaldi's Defence of the Roman Republic*, p. 135.
84 King, *The Life of Mazzini*, p. 134.
85 Mazzini, *Life and Writings*, vol. V, p. 210.

Appendix I:
A Philosophical Genealogy

Appendices

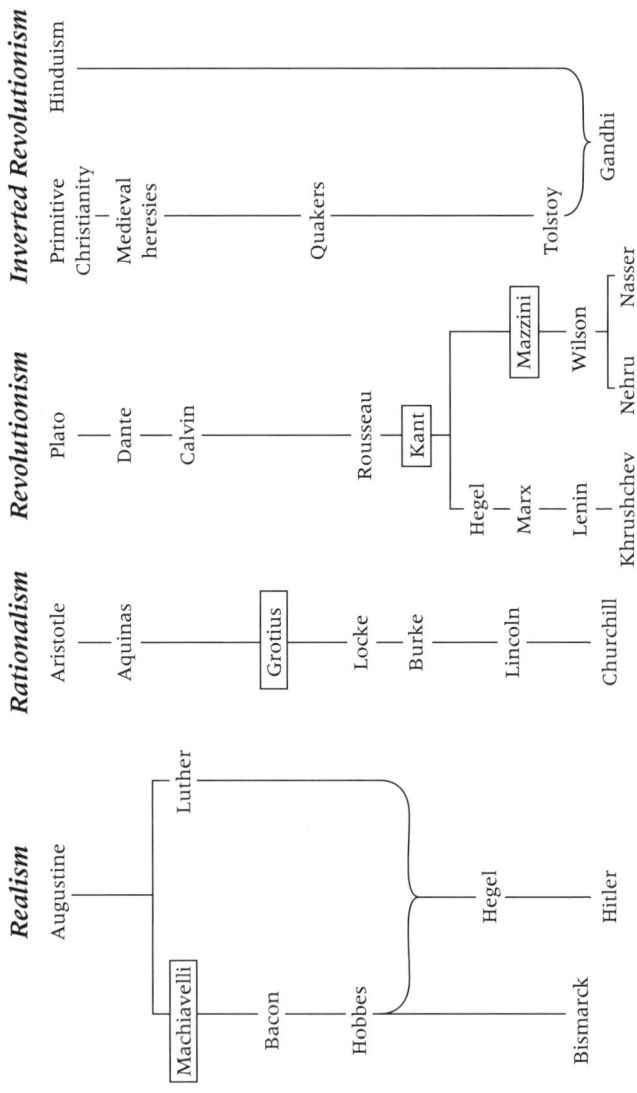

122

Appendix II: The Three Traditions in Christianity

Machiavellian	Grotian	Kantian
St Paul	St Peter = Mark	St John
Augustine	Thomism	Joachism[4]
State exists because men are evil		Spiritual Franciscans
Compelle intrare[1]		
Nominalists	neo-Scholastics	Calvin
Luther[2]	Hooker	Puritanism
Niebuhr[3]		Quakers
Erastianism		Evangelicals[5]

[1] 'Compelled to enter', a phrase taken from Luke xiv.23 and used as a maxim by St Augustine to justify the resort to coercion by the Christian authorities (church or state) for those in error, confusion, or doubt. Since the Fall, Man is a moral invalid and may need harsh medicine. –Eds.

[2] Lutheranism is the Christian equivalent of Machiavellianism.—M. W.

[3] Niebuhr is a Christian Machiavellian—M.W.; of Lutheran background –Eds.

[4] St Joachim (*c.*1145–1202), Italian mystic who proclaimed the reign of the Holy Spirit. See above, pp. 94–5.

[5] Intense American evangelical missionary activity in the former Soviet Union, and especially Russia, home of the historic Orthodox Church for over a thousand years, may be seen as religious counter-revolutionism. –Eds.

Appendix III: The International Theory of Grotius

De Jure Belli ac Pacis (1625)

I Law:
  (a) What is Natural Law (*Jus Naturae*)?
      Prolegomena
      Bk I, ch. I, secs. X–XII
  (b) What is the Law of Nations (*Jus Gentium*)?
      Bk I, ch. I, sec. XIV, paras. 1–2

II International society:
  (a) What is the nature and extent of international society?
      Bk II, ch. I, sec. IX, paras. 2–3
      Bk II, ch. XV, secs. VIII–XI
      Bk II, ch. XX, sec. XLIV, para. 4
      Bk II, ch. XXII, secs. IX–X
  (b) Are there regional societies within international society?
      Bk I, ch. I, sec. XVI; c.f. Bk II, ch. XV, sec. IX, para. 3
      Bk I, ch. I, sec. XV, para. 2
      Bk II, ch. XV, secs. XI–XII
      Bk II, ch. XXIII, sec. VIII, paras. 3–4

Bk III, ch. VII, sec. IX
Bk III, ch. XII, sec. VIII, para. 4
Bk III, ch. VII, sec. IX, paras. 1–2
Bk III, ch. X, sec. III
  (c) What kinds of political associations of states are there?
Bk I, ch. III, sec. VII, para. 2
Bk II, ch. V, sec. XXV
Bk II, ch. XII, sec. IX, para. 1
Bk II, ch. XV, secs. II–III

III International order:
  (a) Is world government attainable?
Bk II, ch. XXII, sec. XIII
  (b) Who is the executive in international society?
Bk I, ch. V, sec. I
Bk II, ch. XXV, sec. I
  (c) Who is the judge in international disputes?
Bk I, ch. III, sec. I, para. 2
Bk II, ch. XXIII, sec. VIII, para. 4
  (d) Is the balance of power a valid principle of policy?
Bk II, ch. I, sec. XVII
Bk II, ch. XXIV, secs. VII–IX
  (e) Has a Power international responsibilities towards others, such as the right or duty of participating in punitive war against a criminal state?
Bk II, ch. XX, sec. VII, para. 2
Bk II, ch. XX, sec. VIII
Bk II, ch. XX, sec. IX, para. 2
Bk II, ch. XX, sec. XL, para. 1
Bk II, ch. XX, sec. XLIV, para. 1
Bk II, ch. XXV, sec. I, para. 1
Bk II, ch. XXV, sec. VII
  (f) What are the duties of neutrals?
Bk III, ch. XVII, sec. III, para. 1

Appendices

IV War:
  (a) What ways are there of averting war by peaceful settlement?
      Bk II, ch. XXIII, secs. VI–XII
  (b) What is the nature of war?
      Bk I, ch. I, sec. II, paras. 1–2
      Bk II, ch. XXII, secs. I–IV
      Bk II, ch. XXIV, secs. IX–X
      Bk II, ch. XXV, sec. IX, para. 2
  (c) Should Christians be pacifists?
      Prolegomena, secs. XXVIII–XXIX
      Bk I, ch. II, secs. VII–X
      Bk I, ch. III, sec. III
  (d) What is a just war?
      Bk II, ch. I
  (e) Can a war be just on both sides?
      Bk II, ch. XXIII, sec. XIII
  (f) The just conduct of war:
      Bk III, ch. X, sec. I
      Moderation (*temperamenta*): Bk III, chs. XI–XVI
  (g) Is fear a just cause of war?
      Bk II, ch. I, sec. XVII
      Bk II, ch. II, sec. XIII, para. 4
  (h) Is it 'better to be Red than dead'?
      Bk II, ch. XXIV, sec. VI

V International morality:
  (a) Self-interest transcended:
      Bk II, ch. I, sec. IX, paras. 2–3
  (b) The limits of necessity:
      Bk II, ch. II, secs. VI–IX
      Bk III, ch. XVII, sec. I
      Bk III, ch. XX, sec. XXXVII

Appendices

(c) The limits of utility:
    Bk II, ch. XXII, sec. VI
(d) Choosing the lesser evil:
    Bk II, ch. XXIII, secs. I–II
(e) Do the ends justify the means?
    Bk II, ch. XXIV, sec. V
(f) The motive of fear:
    Bk II, ch. I, sec. XVIII, para. 1
    Bk II, ch. II, sec. XIII, para. 4
(g) The motive of shame:
    Bk III, ch. X, sec. I, para. 2
(h) Good faith:
    Bk III, ch. XIX

M. W.
October 1971

Bibliography I

From Martin Wight's Notes and Reading Lists, 1959–72

Machiavelli

1. Works

Il Principe, Burd, L. A. (ed.) with an introduction by Lord Acton (Oxford: Clarendon Press, 1891). Standard English edition of the Italian text, with full historical introductions and notes.
The Discourses, tr. with introduction and notes by L. J. Walker (London: Routledge and Kegan Paul, 1950). 2 vols.
The Discourses, edited with an introduction by Bernard Crick (Harmondsworth: Penguin Classics, 1970).
The Prince, tr. W. K. Marriott (London: Everyman, 1908), with an introduction by H. Butterfield (London: Everyman, 1958). This edition also contains two of Machiavelli's shorter works, as well as notes.
The Prince, tr. G. Bull (Harmondsworth: Penguin, 1961).

2. Biographical

Anglo, Sydney, *Machiavelli: A Dissection* (London: Gollancz, 1969; London: Paladin, 1971).
Hale, J. R., *Machiavelli and Renaissance Italy* (London: English Universities Press: Teach Yourself History, 1961).
Ridolfi, R., *The Life of Niccolò Machiavelli*, tr. C. Grayson (London: Routledge & Kegan Paul, 1963).

Bibliography

3. Historical and Critical

Acton, Lord, Introduction to *Il Principe* [see above] reprinted in *The History of Freedom and other Essays* (London: Macmillan, 1907), ch. vii.

Burd, L. A., 'Florence (II): Machiavelli' in *Cambridge Modern History* (Cambridge: Cambridge University Press, 1902), vol. I, ch. vi.

Burnham, J., *The Machiavellians* (London: Putnam, 1943).

Butterfield, H., *The Statecraft of Machiavelli* (London: Bell, 1940).

Chabod, F., *Machiavelli and the Renaissance* (London: Bowes and Bowes, 1958).

Jensen, De L. (ed.), *Machiavelli: Cynic, Patriot, or Political Scientist?* (Boston, MA: D.C. Heath and Co., Problems in European Civilization, 1960).

Meinecke, F., *Machiavellism: The Doctrine of Raison d'Etat and its Place in Modern History* (London: Routledge & Kegan Paul, 1957). A translation of *Die Idee der Staatsräson* (Munich, 1924).

Morley, J., 'Machiavelli' in *Miscellanies: Fourth Series* (London: Macmillan, 1908).

Plamenatz, J., *Man and Society: A Critical Examination of Some Important Social and Political Theories from Machiavelli to Marx* (London: Longmans, 1963), vol. I.

Strauss, L., *Thoughts on Machiavelli* (Glencoe, IL: Free Press, 1958).

Grotius

1. Works

De Jure Belli ac Pacis Libri Tres, tr. F. W. Kelsey et al. (Oxford: Clarendon Press, Classics of International Law, 1913–27), 2 vols.

Prolegomena to the Law of War and Peace, tr. F. W. Kelsey, with an introduction by E. Dumbauld (Indianapolis: Bobbs-Merrill Co. Inc., Library of Liberal Arts, 1957).

2. Biographical

Basdevant, Jules, 'Hugo Grotius' in A. Pillett (ed.), *Les Fondateurs du droit international* (Paris: Giard et Brière, 1904), pp. 125–267.

Knight, W. S. M., *The Life and Works of Hugo Grotius* (London: Sweet and Maxwell, Grotius Society Publications, 1925).

Lee, R. W., 'Hugo Grotius' (Annual Lecture on a Master Mind), in *Proceedings of the British Academy, 1930*, (London: Humphrey Milford), vol. xvi, pp. 219–79.

3. Historical and Critical

Brierly, J. L., *The Basis of Obligation in International Law* (Oxford: Clarendon Press, 1958), ch. 1.
Bull, H., 'The Grotian Conception of International Society', ch. 3, and Wight, M., 'Western Values in International Relations', esp. pp. 102–7, in H. Butterfield and M. Wight (eds.), *Diplomatic Investigations* (London: Allen and Unwin, 1966).
d'Entrèves, A. P., *Natural Law* (London: Hutchinson's University Library, 1951).
Lauterpacht, H., 'The Grotian Tradition in International Law', *British Year Book of International Law, 1946*, (London: Oxford University Press), vol. xxiii, pp. 1–53.
van Vollenhoven, C., *The Three Stages in the Evolution of the Law of Nations* (The Hague: Nijhoff, 1919).
—— *The Framework of Grotius' Book De Iure Belli ac Pacis (1625)* (Amsterdam: Noord-Hollandsche Uitgeversmaatschappij, 1931).

Kant

1. Works

Critique of Practical Reason (1788), tr. T. K. Abbott (London: Longmans, Green and Co., 1948).
Idea of a Universal History from a Cosmopolitical Point of View (1784), in W. Hastie (tr. and ed.), *Kant's Principles of Politics* (Edinburgh: T. & T. Clark, 1891) and in C. J. Friedrich, *The Philosophy of Kant* (New York: The Modern Library, 1949).
Immanuel Kant's Critique of Pure Reason (1781), tr. Norman Kemp Smith (London: Macmillan, 1933).
Kant's Principles of Politics, supra.
Perpetual Peace (1795), Lewis White Beck (ed.) (Indianapolis: Bobbs-Merrill Co. Inc., 1957).

Bibliography

The Philosophy of Law: An Exposition of the Fundamental Principles of Jurisprudence as the Science of Right (1797), secs. 53–62, 'The Right of Nations and International Law (Ius Gentium)', W. Hastie (tr. and ed.) (Edinburgh: T. & T. Clark, 1887).

2. Biographical

Lindsay, A. D., *Kant* (Oxford: Oxford University Press, 1934, 1936; London: Benn, 1934), ch. i.

3. Historical and Critical

Cassirer, E., *Rousseau, Kant, Goethe*, tr. J. Gutmann et al. (Princeton: Princeton University Press, 1945).
Friedrich, C. J., *Inevitable Peace* (Cambridge, MA: Harvard University Press, 1948).
—— *The Philosophy of Kant* (New York: The Modern Library, 1949).
Kant's Principles of Politics, supra.
Klinke, W., *Kant for Everyman*, tr. Michael Bullock (London: Routledge & Kegan Paul, 1952).
Lindsay, A. D., *Kant, supra.*

Mazzini

1. Works

Life and Writings of Joseph Mazzini (London: Smith, Elder & Co., 1890), 6 vols.
The Duties of Man and Other Essays (London: J.M. Dent & Sons, 1907).

2. Biographical

King, Bolton, *The Life of Mazzini* (London: J.M. Dent & Sons, 1912).
Mazzini, J., *Life and Writings, supra.*
Silone, Ignazio, *Mazzini* (London: Cassell & Co. Ltd, Living Thoughts Library, 1939).
Trevelyn, G.M., *Garibaldi's Defence of the Roman Republic* (London: Longmans, 1907).

Bibliography II

Selected Publications since 1972

We are indebted to Professor David Yost for compiling these lists into which have been incorporated a few further suggestions by Professor Howard Williams (Kant) and Professor Denis Mack Smith (Mazzini) –Eds.

Machiavelli

Barlow, J. Jackson, 'The Fox and the Lion: Machiavelli Replies to Cicero', *History of Political Thought*, vol. 20, no. 4 (1999).

Berlin, Isaiah, 'The Originality of Machiavelli', in Isaiah Berlin, *The Proper Study of Mankind: An Anthology of Essays*, (eds.) Henry Hardy and Roger Hausheer (London: Pimlico, 1998).

Berridge, G. R., 'Machiavelli', in G. R. Berridge, Maurice Keens-Soper, and T. G. Otte (eds.), *Diplomatic Theory from Machiavelli to Kissinger* (Basingstoke, England and New York: Palgrave, 2001).

Bock, Gisela, Skinner, Quentin, and Viroli, Maurizio (eds.), *Machiavelli and Republicanism* (Cambridge: Cambridge University Press, 1990).

Bonadeo, Alfredo, *Corruption, Conflict, and Power in the Works and Times of Niccolò Machiavelli* (Berkeley and LA: University of California Press, 1973).

Bondanella, Peter E., *Machiavelli and the Art of Renaissance History* (Detroit: Wayne State University Press, 1974).

Boucher, David, 'The Duplicitous Machiavelli', *Machiavelli Studies*, vol. 3 (1990).

Colish, Marcia L., 'Cicero's *De Officiis* and Machiavelli's *Prince*', *Sixteenth Century Journal*, vol. 9, no. 4 (Winter 1978).

Bibliography

Colish, Marcia L., 'The Idea of Liberty in Machiavelli', *Journal of the History of Ideas*, vol. 32, no. 3 (July–September 1971).
—— 'Republicanism, Religion, and Machiavelli's Savonarolan Moment', *Journal of the History of Ideas*, vol. 60, no. 4 (October 1999).
de Grazia, Sebastian, *Machiavelli in Hell* (Princeton, NJ: Princeton University Press, 1989).
Dietz, Mary G., 'Trapping the Prince: Machiavelli and the Politics of Deception', *American Political Science Review*, vol. 80, no. 3 (September 1986).
Donaldson, Peter S., *Machiavelli and Mystery of State* (Cambridge: Cambridge University Press, 1988).
Eldar, D., 'Glory and the Boundaries of Public Morality in Machiavelli's Thought', *History of Political Thought*, vol. 7, no. 3 (Winter 1986).
Fiore, Silvia Ruffo, *Niccolò Machiavelli: An Annotated Bibliography of Modern Criticism and Scholarship* (New York and London: Greenwood Press, 1990).
Fleischer, Martin (ed.), *Machiavelli and the Nature of Political Thought* (New York: Atheneum, 1972).
Forde, Steven, 'Varieties of Realism: Thucydides and Machiavelli', *Journal of Politics*, vol. 54, no. 2 (May 1992).
Garver, Eugene, *Machiavelli and the History of Prudence* (Madison, Wisconsin: University of Wisconsin Press, 1987).
Gilbert, Felix, *Machiavelli and Guicciardini: Politics and History in Sixteenth Century Florence* (New York: W. W. Norton, 1984).
Hulliung, Mark, *Citizen Machiavelli* (Princeton, NJ: Princeton University Press, 1983).
Mansfield, Harvey C., *Machiavelli's New Modes and Orders: A Study of the Discourses on Livy* (Ithaca and London: Cornell University Press, 1979).
—— *Machiavelli's Virtue* (Chicago: University of Chicago Press, 1996).
Mindle, Grant B., 'Machiavelli's Realism,' *Review of Politics*, vol. 47 (1985).
Newell, W. R., 'How Original Is Machiavelli?' *Political Theory*, vol. 15, no. 4 (November 1987).
Orwin, Clifford, 'Machiavelli's Unchristian Charity', *American Political Science Review*, vol. 72, no. 4 (December 1978).
Parel, Anthony (ed.), *The Political Calculus: Essays on Machiavelli's Philosophy* (Toronto: University of Toronto Press, 1972).

—— *The Machiavellian Cosmos* (New Haven and London: Yale University Press, 1992).
Pitkin, Hanna, *Fortune Is a Woman: Gender and Politics in the Thought of Niccolò Machiavelli* (Berkeley and LA: University of California Press, 1984).
Pocock, J. G. A., *The Machiavellian Moment: Florentine Political Thought and the Atlantic Republican Tradition* (Princeton, NJ: Princeton University Press, 1975).
Price, Russell, 'Self-Love, "Egoism" and *Ambizione* in Machiavelli's Thought', *History of Political Thought*, vol. 9 (1988).
—— 'The Senses of *Virtù* in Machiavelli,' *European Studies Review*, vol. 4 (1973).
—— 'The Theme of *Gloria* in Machiavelli', *Renaissance Quarterly*, vol. 30, no. 4 (Winter 1977).
Rebhorn, Wayne A., *Foxes and Lions: Machiavelli's Confidence Men* (Ithaca and London: Cornell University Press, 1988).
Scott, John T. and Sullivan, Vickie B., 'Patricide and the Plot of *The Prince*: Cesare Borgia and Machiavelli's Italy', *American Political Science Review*, vol. 88, no. 4 (December 1994).
Skinner, Quentin, *Machiavelli: A Very Short Introduction* (London: Oxford University Press, 2000).
Strauss, Leo, 'Niccolo Machiavelli', in Leo Strauss and Joseph Cropsey (eds.), *History of Political Philosophy*, 3rd edn. (Chicago and London: University of Chicago Press, 1987).
Sullivan, Vickie B., *Machiavelli's Three Romes: Religion, Human Liberty, and Politics Reformed* (DeKalb, IL: Northern Illinois University Press, 1996).
Tarcov, Nathan, 'Quentin Skinner's Method and Machiavelli's *Prince*', *Ethics*, vol. 92, no. 4 (July 1982).

Grotius

Berridge, G. R., 'Grotius', in G. R. Berridge, Maurice Keens-Soper and T. G. Otte, (eds.), *Diplomatic Theory from Machiavelli to Kissinger* (Basingstoke and New York: Palgrave, 2001).
Bozeman, Adda B., 'On the Relevance of Hugo Grotius and De Jure Belli ac Pacis for Our Times', *Grotiana*, new series, vol. 1 (1980).

Bibliography

Bull, Hedley, Kingsbury, Benedict, and Roberts, Adam (eds.), *Hugo Grotius and International Relations* (Oxford: Clarendon Press, 1990).

Cox, Richard H., 'Hugo Grotius', in Leo Strauss and Joseph Cropsey, (eds.), *History of Political Philosophy*, 3rd edn. (Chicago and London: University of Chicago Press, 1987).

Cutler, A. Clare, 'The "Grotian Tradition" in International Relations', *Review of International Studies*, vol. 17, no. 1 (January 1991).

Donelan, Michael, 'Grotius and the Image of War', *Millennium*, vol. 12 (1983).

Edwards, Charles S., *Hugo Grotius, The Miracle of Holland: A Study in Political and Legal Thought* (Chicago, IL: Nelson-Hall, 1981).

Forde, Steven, 'Hugo Grotius on Ethics and War', *American Political Science Review*, vol. 92, no. 3 (September 1998).

Gellinek, Christian, *Hugo Grotius* (Boston, MA: Twayne Publishers, 1983).

Haakonssen, Knud, 'Hugo Grotius and the History of Political Thought', *Political Theory*, vol. 13, no. 2 (May 1985).

—— (ed.), *Grotius, Pufendorf and Modern Natural Law* (Aldershot: Darmouth, 1998).

Johnson, James Turner, 'Grotius' Use of History and Charity in the Modern Transformation of the Just War Idea', *Grotiana*, new series, vol. 4 (1983).

Keene, Edward, *Beyond the Anarchical Society: Grotius, Colonialism and Order in World Politics* (Cambridge: Cambridge University Press, 2002).

Kingsbury, Benedict, 'Grotius, Law, and Moral Scepticism: Theory and Practice in the Thought of Hedley Bull', in Ian Clark and Iver B. Neumann (eds.), *Classical Theories of International Relations* (London: Macmillan, 1996; and New York: St. Martin's Press, 1996).

Landheer, Bart, 'The Grotian Model of a World System', *Grotiana*, new series, vol. 1 (1980).

Murphy, Cornelius F., Jr., 'The Grotian Vision of World Order', *American Journal of International Law*, vol. 76, no. 3 (July 1982).

—— 'Grotius and the Peaceful Settlement of Disputes', *Grotiana*, new series, vol. 4 (1983).

Onuma, Yasuaki, (ed.), *A Normative Approach to War: Peace, War, and Justice in Hugo Grotius*, tr. Sakamoto Mikio (Oxford: Clarendon Press, 1993; and New York: Oxford University Press, 1993).

Rabkin, Jeremy, 'Grotius, Vattel and Locke: An Older View of Liberalism and Nationality', *Review of Politics*, vol. 59 (Spring 1997).
Tuck, Richard, 'Grotius, Carneades and Hobbes', *Grotiana*, new series, vol. 4 (1983).
—— 'Grotius and Seldon', in J. H. Burns and Mark Goldie (eds.), *The Cambridge History of Political Thought 1450–1700* (Cambridge: Cambridge University Press, 1988).
—— *The Rights of War and Peace: Political Thought and the International Order from Grotius to Kant* (New York: Oxford University Press, 1999).
van Eikema Hommes, Hendrik, 'Grotius on Natural and International Law', *Netherlands International Law Review*, vol. 30 (1983).
Vermeulen, Ben, 'Grotius on Conscience and Military Orders', *Grotiana*, new series, vol. 6 (1985).

Kant

Anderson-Gold, Sharon, *Unnecessary Evil: History and Moral Progress in the Philosophy of Immanuel Kant* (Ithaca, NY: State University of New York, 2001).
Arendt, Hannah, *Lectures on Kant's Political Philosophy*, Ronald Beiner (ed.) (Chicago: University of Chicago Press, 1982).
Aune, Bruce, *Kant's Theory of Morals* (Princeton, NJ: Princeton University Press, 1979).
Booth, William James, *Interpreting the World: Kant's Philosophy of History and Politics* (Toronto: University of Toronto Press, 1986).
Cavallar, Georg, *Kant and the Theory and Practice of International Right* (Cardiff: University of Wales Press, 1999)
Donaldson, Thomas, 'Kant's Global Rationalism', in Terry Nardin and David R. Mapel (eds.), *Traditions of International Ethics* (Cambridge: Cambridge University Press, 1992).
Doyle, Michael W., 'Kant, Liberal Legacies, and Foreign Affairs', Parts 1 and 2, in *Philosophy and Public Affairs*, vol. 12, no. 3 (Summer 1983), and vol. 12, no. 4 (Fall 1983).
Gallie, W. B., *Philosophers of Peace and War: Kant, Clausewitz, Marx, Engels, and Tolstoy* (Cambridge: Cambridge University Press, 1978).
Galston, William, *Kant and the Problem of History* (Chicago: University of Chicago Press, 1975).

Bibliography

Guyer, Paul (ed.), *The Cambridge Companion to Kant* (Cambridge: Cambridge University Press, 1992).

Hassner, Pierre, 'Immanuel Kant', in Leo Strauss and Joseph Cropsey (eds.), *History of Political Philosophy*, 3rd edn. (Chicago and London: University of Chicago Press, 1987).

Hinsley, F. H., 'Immanuel Kant and the Pattern of War and Peace Since His Time', in Helmut Berding et al. (eds.), *Vom Staat des Ancien Régime zum Modernen Parteienstaat* (Vienna and Munich: R. Oldenbourg Verlag, 1978).

Hurrell, Andrew, 'Kant and the Kantian Paradigm in International Relations', *Review of International Studies*, vol. 16, no. 3: 183–205 (July 1990).

Kuehn, Manfred, *Kant: A Biography* (Cambridge: Cambridge University Press, 2001).

Laursen, John Christian, 'The Subversive Kant: The Vocabulary of "Public" and "Publicity"', *Political Theory*, vol. 14 (November 1986).

O'Neill, Onora, 'Kantian Politics I: The Public Use of Reason', *Political Theory*, vol. 14 (November 1986).

Riley, Patrick, *Kant's Political Philosophy* (Totowa, NJ: Rowman and Littlefield, 1983).

Saner, Hans, *Kant's Political Thought: Its Origins and Development*, tr. E. B. Ashton (Chicago and London: University of Chicago Press, 1973).

Schneewind, J. B., 'Kant and Natural Law Ethics', *Ethics*, vol. 104 (October 1993).

Scruton, Roger, *Kant: A Very Short Introduction* (London: Oxford University Press, 2001).

Shell, Susan Meld, *The Rights of Reason: A Study of Kant's Philosophy and Politics* (Toronto: University of Toronto Press, 1980).

Sullivan, Roger, *Immanuel Kant's Moral Theory* (Cambridge: Cambridge University Press, 1989).

Walker, Ralph, *Kant and the Moral Law* (London: Phoenix, 1998).

Williams, Howard, *Kant's Political Philosophy* (Oxford: Basil Blackwell, 1983, and New York: St. Martin's Press, 1983).

—— (ed.), *Essays on Kant's Political Philosophy* (Cardiff: University of Wales Press, 1992, and Chicago: University of Chicago Press, 1992).

—— *Kant's Critique of Hobbes: Sovereignty and Cosmopolitanism* (Cardiff: University of Wales Press, 2003).

Bibliography

—— and Booth, Ken, 'Kant: Theorist beyond Limits', in Ian Clark and Iver B. Neumann (eds.), *Classical Theories of International Relations* (London: Macmillan, 1996; and New York: St. Martin's Press, 1996).
Yovel, Yirmiahu, *Kant and the Philosophy of History* (Princeton, NJ: Princeton University Press, 1980).

Mazzini

Claeys, Gregory, 'Mazzini, Kossuth, and British Radicalism, 1848–1854', *Journal of British Studies*, vol. 28, no. 3 (July 1989).
Delzell, Charles F. (ed.), *The Unification of Italy, 1859–1861: Cavour, Mazzini, or Garibaldi?* (Huntington, NY: R. E. Krieger Publishing Company, 1976).
*Griffith, Gwilym, *Mazzini: Prophet of Modern Europe* (London: Hodder and Stoughton, 1932).
*Hales, Edward E. Y., *Mazzini and the Secret Societies* (London: Eyre and Spottiswood, 1956).
Mack Smith, Denis, *Mazzini* (New Haven and London: Yale University Press, 1994).
Mastellone, Salvo, *Mazzini and Marx: Thoughts upon Democracy* (London: Praeger, 2003).
Roberts, William, *Prophet in Exile: Joseph Mazzini in England, 1837–1868* (New York: Peter Lang, 1989).
Sarti, Roland, *Mazzini: A Life for the Religion of Politics* (Westport, CT, and London: Praeger, 1997).
Srivastava, Gita, *Mazzini and His Impact on the Indian National Movement* (Allahabad, India: Chugh Publications, 1982).

---

*Although published earlier than 1972, these still repay reading (–D. Mack Smith).

An Anatomy of International Thought

This is the text of a lecture that Martin Wight gave at the Institut Universitaire de Hautes Etudes Internationales in Geneva in February 1961. It was first published in the *Review of International Studies* (vol. 13, no. 3) in July 1987. In this reissue the opportunity has been taken to correct textual errors and misprints and to provide fuller references. Although these few pages encapsulate ideas the author had first set out in his famous lecture series of the 1950s, posthumously published in 1991 as *International Theory: The Three Traditions*, they do throw further light on the development of his thinking.

G. W.
B. E. P.

An Anatomy of International Thought

This is an attempt at analysing the political philosophy of international relations in a very short span of time, so I do not propose to discuss questions of method. Indeed I may sound dogmatic, but that is merely because I shall not have the time to exhibit my diffidence.

You might say there is no such thing as the political philosophy of international relations; I have therefore played safe and called it 'international thought' in my title to use the least pretentious phrase describing speculation about international relations. International thought is what we find in the discussions of the man-in-the-street or in the popular press. International theory is what we find in the better press and hope to find in diplomatic circles and foreign offices. The political philosophy of international relations is the fully conscious, formulated theory, illustrations of which you may find in the conduct of some statesmen, Wilson, probably Churchill, perhaps Nehru; and it may be expressed by serious writers, for example, Kant or Kennan, Machiavelli or Morgenthau. The differences between thought, theory, and philosophy are partly in the precision with which they are formulated, and partly in the degree of their profundity. But I am not concerned with these and ignore them.

To help us examine international thought let us first consider international relations themselves, the state of affairs which produces international theory. As a preamble to our philosophical analysis, a sociological analysis will ask the following question: what *is* this condition which we study under the name of international relations? What does it consist of, what are its ingredients? It has three component social elements:

1. *International anarchy:* the multiplicity of sovereign states acknowledging no political superior. Politics here are not 'government'; they presuppose the absence of government.
2. *Habitual intercourse:* expressed in the institutions of diplomacy, international legal rules, commerce, etc.

3. *Moral solidarity:* the communion deeper than politics and economics, it is psychological and cultural, expressed in such phrases as the 'society of states', the 'family of nations', 'world public opinion', and 'mankind'.

To each of these elements there corresponds a way of looking at international relations. It may be by temperament and bias, it may be by intellectual conviction. Everybody is inclined to give greater importance and value to one or another of these three elements and in consequence one can trace three—at least three—coherent patterns of thought about international relations, two of which are indeed self-conscious intellectual traditions. To illustrate this, let us enquire into the nature of international society.

The First Pattern

The most fundamental question you can ask in international theory is, 'What is international society?', just as the central question in political theory is, 'What is a State?'. Thinkers who emphasize the element of international anarchy in international relations answer this quite simply: Nothing. A fiction. An illusion. *Non est.* The first to make it explicit is probably Hobbes. Hobbes was certainly the first to make the equation between international relations and the state of nature. In the famous ch. 13 of *Leviathan* he anticipates the question whether the state of nature, as he describes it, ever existed. He points first to American Indians, and second to 'Kings, and Persons of Soveraigne authority, [who] because of their Independency, are in continuall jealousies, and in the state and posture of Gladiators'.[1] This equation, that the state of nature = international relations, that sovereign states in their mutual relations are in a pre-contractual condition, passes from Hobbes into the general stream of public law and political theory.

But there is a second equation: international relations may = the state of nature, but what is the state of nature? *Bellum*

An Anatomy of International Thought

omnium contra omnes. The state of nature = international relations = the war of all against all; therefore there cannot be an international society. Society is established by the contract; international relations is pre-contractual; the term 'Society of Nations' is contradictory. This is implicitly the position of Machiavelli and Bodin and explicitly that of Spinoza, Rousseau, Kant, Hegel, Fichte and most legal positivists.

Bismarck, for example, showed impatience when the words 'Christendom' or 'Europe' were introduced into diplomatic language. Once, when Gorchakov was urging on him the view that the Eastern Question was not a German or Russian but a *European* question, Bismarck replied: 'I have always found the word Europe on the lips of those politicians who wanted something from other Powers which they dared not demand in their own names.'[2] At the core of this pattern of thought is the doctrine that power is anterior to society, law, justice, and morality. E. H. Carr in *The Twenty Years' Crisis* restates the Hobbesian position: 'Any international moral order must rest on some hegemony of power.'[3] Here is Hobbes: '... before the names of Just, and Unjust can have place, there must be some coërcive Power.'[4] This position is also expressed by Morgenthau, when he says: '[a]bove the national societies there exists no international society so integrated as to be able to define for them the concrete meaning of justice or equality, as national societies do for their individual members.'[5] For this line of thought the question: 'What is international society?' admits of only one answer: Nothing!—until there is a world state.

This was the governing conception behind the United Nations Charter. The essentials of the Charter were agreed and drafted at the Dumbarton Oaks Conference in September 1944, when international relations were a state of war. The Third Reich and Japanese Empire were raging undefeated and nobody was confident of peace within a year. Hobbes argued that the only remedy for the state of war was an unlimited contract, whereby we all reduce our wills to one will, and appoint one man, or assembly of men, to act on our behalf in those things which concern the common peace and safety.⁶ This is precisely what signatories of the Charter did by Articles 24, 25, and 48. The Smutsian preamble to the Charter, which is in another tradition of thinking, was tacked on later; and it was only later again that it appeared that the Hobbesian sovereign of the United Nations was a schizophrenic paralytic incapable of action, so that the United Nations has never worked as it was intended. [Written in 1961 –Eds.]

The Second Pattern

But the two Hobbesian equations I have mentioned are not inseparable. It is possible to accept the identification of international relations with the state of nature without accepting the description of the state of nature as *bellum omnium contra omnes*. This is what Locke apparently does in the *Second Treatise of Civil Government*. He repeats Hobbes' argument that if you are sceptical about a state of nature ever having existed you need only look at interstate relations,⁷ but he goes on to argue, for a whole chapter, that whereas the state of war is a state of enmity and mutual destruction, the state of nature is a state of goodwill and mutual assistance. I say 'what Locke *apparently does*' because Professor Richard Cox's book on Locke⁸ has placed a large question mark over the traditional interpretation of Locke, but perhaps we may still accept the public Locke at his face value.

Grotius likewise conceded that the social condition was inaugurated by the social contract but argued that the pre-contractual state of nature was the condition of sociability—the capacity for becoming social. Suarez argued that although every state is a perfect community, it is none the less a member of a universal body, this membership being the basis of international law, and with nice precision he described the universal body as *'unitas quasi politica et moralis'*.⁹

This is the sort of answer you will expect from those who emphasize our second component of international relations, habitual intercourse, institutions of diplomacy and law. Sovereign states, they will say, do form a society; they do not exist in a political or cultural vacuum, but in continuous political relations with one another. It is a society which must be understood on its own terms and not by comparison with domestic society, a society governed less by force, as the thinkers of the first group may hold, than by custom. It is a society with a system of law that is crude and not centrally enforced but still true law, a society without a government but regulated by certain special institutions such as diplomacy, the balance of power, and alliances.

Locke's conception of the state of nature leads to a different kind of contract from Hobbes'. If the state of nature is not so beastly, civil society need not be so severe, and the social contract can be limited as was the Covenant compared with the Charter. The men who drafted the Covenant (excluding Wilson) did not think international life had broken down, only that it had suffered unusual interruption, and had shown it was deficient in means for the pacific settlement of international disputes, and what was needed was (in Locke's words) 'umpirage... for... ending all differences that may arise amongst' states.[10] For this a limited contract was sufficient. Signatories did not surrender their natural liberties, their sovereignty; states simply undertook to limit the exercise of their sovereignty, the unanimity rule was not abrogated. If we can detect the sardonic smile of Hobbes between the lines of the Charter, in the Covenant we may discern the more bland and amiable assumptions of traditional Locke.

The Third Pattern

Now there is a third, quite distinct way of conceiving international society and it is related to those who tend to emphasize in international relations the element of moral solidarity. They will answer the question, 'What is international society?' in such a fashion as this: international society is none other than mankind, encumbered and thwarted by an archaic fiction of an international society composed of sovereign states. States are *not* persons, they have no wills but the wills of the individuals who manage their affairs, and behind the legal façade of the fictitious Society of Nations is the true international society composed of men. Now, this much is not in contradiction with the second complex of ideas which we have just been noticing: you will find Grotius speaking of *societas generis humani* more often than of *societas gentium*.

But this third pattern of ideas is distinguished by two master-premises: first, that the existing state of affairs, the existing arrangements of international life, are invalid and illegitimate; second, that they are going to be modified or swept away by the course of events itself. Both these premises are religious in nature. The first expresses the impulse to eradicate sin and suffering, which are condemned by being identified, or that austere moral concern which made Kant argue, in *Rechtslehre*, that if nations were in the state of nature it was their duty to pass out of it, and 'all international rights... are purely *provisional* until the state of nature has been abandoned'.[11] The second premise, that the course of events itself is tending to bring about desired change, shows a desire for a theodicy. Every age has wanted to vindicate the justice of the universe in view of the existence of evil, but it is a peculiar modern manifestation of this desire to believe that the vindication will be accomplished by the historical process itself. The belief in progress, historical inevitability, and the linear development of human affairs, whether evolutionary or catastrophic, is now often named 'historicism'.

'Historicism' is a word that has changed its meaning since Meinecke wrote the history of *Historismus*. Then it had its original sense, of the doctrine that all values are historically conditioned, that reality itself is a historical process, and that history can teach nothing except philosophical acceptance of change. Now it has a new sense: the doctrine that history has a purpose and direction, that its movement is largely predictable, and that it can (under proper interpretation) teach everything we need to know about life and prescribe our duties. In this new sense it is a label for Hegel and Marx, Spengler and Toynbee.

There are two historical agencies which, in this pattern of thinking, promote desirable international change. Kant, who is responsible for so much else in modern thought, was as far as I know the first to describe these historical agencies in this context.

First was what he called 'the commercial spirit', 'which cannot exist along with war, and which sooner or later controls every people'.[12] We should probably translate it as the growing material interdependence of mankind, due to the economic unification of the world and industrialization. Its greatest English prophet was Cobden, whose motto was 'Free Trade, Peace, Goodwill among Nations' and in whose political writings and speeches the expected consequences of growing material interdependence are made plain.

Second was what Kant called 'the spirit of enlightenment'. 'Enlightenment...must ever draw mankind away from the egoistic expansive tendencies of its rulers once they understand their own advantage.'[13] We might translate it as the growing moral interdependence of mankind due to education, cultural exchange, and intellectual standardization. It is manifested in the formation of a world public opinion, which some see as the animating principle of the United Nations.

Kant's imaginary treaty of Perpetual Peace contained a secret article, that before going to war, governments must consult the maxims of the philosophers. It is not to be expected (he says) that kings should philosophize or philosophers become kings, but kings can let philosophers speak freely, 'because this is indispensable for both in order to clarify their business.'[14] Kant was the subject of a Prussian monarch whose minister of education had not allowed him to speak freely: he himself would have liked to be on the Brains Trust of a President F. D. Roosevelt or on the Democratic Advisory Council, Committee on Foreign Policy, of a President Kennedy. This 'secret article' is the expression and possibly the direct inspiration of the Wilsonian belief that enlightened public opinion, instructed public opinion in all countries, will promote peace and goodwill in international affairs.

It must be noticed here that this third pattern of ideas is not characterized by *recognizing* these two historical agencies. The growing material and moral interdependence of mankind as historical tendencies or trends would scarcely be denied by any thinker. But while a thinker of the first class might suppose that these trends would lead to more savage internecine conflicts culminating in a world despotism, and a thinker of the second class would believe that they posed continually new and agonizing problems, the historicist believes that these trends carry within themselves the solution of the problems they pose and will lead in the desired direction.

Given these premises, our question 'What is international society?' appears foolishly academic: 'The philosophers have only *interpreted* the world, in various ways; the point is to *change* it.'[15] Very well then: change it how? By bringing out its essential nature, by making explicit what is implicit, by eradicating evil and making it virtuous, by clearing away the irrelevant historical clutter of states and forms to produce the regularity, uniformity, and homogeneity of virtue. That is, by redrawing the map.

What kind of uniformity? Here there are two answers. First, to assimilate all existing states, members of international society, to a pattern of conformity which alone confers legitimacy, and to eradicate inconsistencies. An early example is Kant's *Perpetual Peace*. He works out an ideal, make-believe treaty of eternal peace. Its first definitive article is that the constitution of each state should be republican, that is, what we should call constitutional. But the principle that members of international society should be doctrinally uniform can be used by ideologists of more than one kind.

Kant's principle was put into effect in a counter-revolutionist sense by Alexander and Metternich in the Holy Alliance, and for purposes of political theory it is necessary to define counter-revolutionism as a mode of revolutionism. Mazzini gave the principle a violent push in the opposite direction, so that it swung to a more extreme point than with Kant: that there would be no valid international society till all its members were nation-states. This was the principle of national self-determination which triumphed in 1919. It was connected with Wilson's original demand that the League be a league of democratic states, which had its counterpart in the initial idea that the United Nations was to be a league of peace-loving states. This produced as a by-product the attempted international ostracism of Spain in 1946. Both the League and the United Nations were originally exclusive and limited bodies, whose membership depended on a qualifying test; but both became inclusive and unlimited bodies, admission to which depended on no scrutiny, and thus became degraded.

The same principle gave its driving force to Afro-Asian anti-colonialism. As Sukarno, host at the Bandung Conference of 1955, said then: 'Wherever, whenever, and however it appears, colonialism is an evil thing, and one which must be eradicated from the earth.'[16] One is not surprised to learn that Mazzini was held in respect by Nehru, and is widely read in south-east Asia. But there is an alternative to the Kantian and Mazzinian line of reducing all members of international society to uniformity.

A more radical change and more drastic uniformity lies in the direction of the Cosmopolis. A Cosmopolis too is immanent in the existing state-structure. Behind the empirical historical members of international society lies mankind, the City of Man, the City of the World, the Great Society, *Civitas Maxima*, the Parliament of Man, and the Federation of the World. The supreme exponent of this view is Dante. *De Monarchia* presents a tight argument, a completely satisfying piece of intellectual architecture:

1. Mankind is a unity, united by the faculty of reason, capable of pursuing the same ends through the same channels: 'humanity'.
2. Mankind can only fulfil itself under a single government.
3. Providence designed for this rule the Roman Empire.

Today we accept the first two points, and can easily substitute for the Roman Empire either the United States or the Soviet Union. If we accept Gilson's view, Dante was the first person to conceive of mankind as a universal *temporal* community, a universal community capable of and requiring a World Federation or the World State.[17]

This idea, whether directly from Dante or not, has haunted international thought. In Vitoria, the earliest international theorist after Machiavelli,[18] and Alberico Gentili[19] you have the idea of mankind as a great society whose majority vote can override individual nations. In Calvin and the *Vindiciae contra Tyrannos* you have the idea of this great society having a right of intervention against a non-conformist member,[20] and Christian Wolff (1679–1754) who was Professor at Halle made the fiction of the *civitas maxima*, of which states were citizens and which could exercise authority over them, the basis of his theory of international law.[21] Kant too finds the idea of human progress in a 'continuously growing state consisting of various nations' to which the 'federative union' of states of the *Perpetual Peace* is a second-best.[22]

Philip II of Spain believed it his duty to suppress heresy and impose doctrinal uniformity not only in his own vast dominions but throughout Christendom as well, and there hovered before the eyes of some of his diplomats and propagandists the mirage of a *'monarquia del mundo'*. The first French Republic imposed Rights of Man wherever its armies could conquer. Hitler and after him Stalin did the same [with their ideologies] in the parts of Europe they conquered. The same aim, of imposing uniformity on the state-system by transforming it into a universal satellite state-system, and this as a preliminary to absorbing the satellite state-system into a universal state, has inspired, however dimly, the successive waves of doctrinal imperialism that have characterized international history from Philip II of Spain down to Mr Khrushchev.[23]

Patterns and Traditions

If we speak of each of these three types of international theory as *patterns of thought* we approach them from a philosophical standpoint. We shall be likely to note the logical interrelation, the logical coherence of the complex of thought, and how acceptance of any one unit-idea is likely to entail logically most of the others, so that the whole is capable of being a system of political philosophy. If we speak of them as *traditions of thought* we consider them historically as embodied in and handed down by writers and statesmen. Here we are more likely to notice illogicalities and discontinuities because exigencies of political life often override logic. We shall find all kinds of intermediate positions. Interesting academic questions arise, such as whether Rousseau's international theory is contradictory to his political theory; how Kant, starting from acceptance of the Hobbesian doctrine of the state of nature, reached totally opposite conclusions; why it is that you so often find the jump from a shrewd realistic appraisal of international politics to a sentimental idealism, even pacifism, in Tolstoy, Kennan, or Butterfield.

It is tempting to develop a psychological typology supposing that each pattern of thought corresponds to a temperament. Coleridge has a tripartite distinction between the politics of sensation (Hobbes), of reason (Rousseau), and of understanding (S. T. Coleridge and Woodrow Wilson). Max Weber analyses three qualities in a politician: a passionate devotion to a cause, a feeling of responsibility, and a sense of proportion. If we brought all this in we might speedily have a comprehensive psychological theory on which to base the understanding of international relations. But I speak of this as a temptation. I only feel capable of analysing political ideas—not psychologies—and when I scrutinize my own psyche I seem to find all these three ways of thought within me.

All I am saying is that I find these traditions of thought in international history dynamically interweaving, but always distinct, and I think they can be seen in mutual tension and conflict underneath the formalized ideological postures of our present discontents. It may be that China is passing out of her first revolutionary fervour into the phase where Machiavellian postulates of national interest will predominate over revolutionary expansion. The USA may yet prove itself a more Kantian society than the Soviet Union in its formal policies, as it seemed to be doing in Dulles' time. The Russia of Khrushchev may show itself more Grotian than the USA or Britain in its acceptance of the principle of seeking a common interest in the limitation of war. Perhaps the mere formulation of such hypotheses implies a faint ray of hope.

February 1961.

Notes

1 Thomas Hobbes, *Leviathan* (London: J.M. Dent and Sons, 1914), p. 65.
2 Quoted by A. J. P. Taylor in *Bismarck: The Man and the Statesman* (London: Hamish Hamilton, 1955), p. 167.
3 E. H. Carr, *The Twenty Years' Crisis, 1919–1939: An Introduction to the Study of International Relations* (London: Macmillan, 1939), p. 213.
4 Hobbes, *Leviathan*, p. 74.
5 Hans J. Morgenthau, *In Defense of the National Interest: A Critical Examination of American Foreign Policy* (New York: Alfred A. Knopf, 1951), p. 34. Cf. Hans J. Morgenthau, *Dilemmas of Politics* (Chicago: University of Chicago Press, 1958), pp. 80–1.

6 Hobbes, *Leviathan*, p. 89.
7 John Locke, *Two Treatises of Civil Government* (London: J.M. Dent and Sons, 1924), para. 14, p. 124.
8 Richard H. Cox, *Locke on War and Peace* (Oxford: Clarendon Press, 1960).
9 Francisco Suárez, *Tractatus de Legibus, ac Deo Legislatore*, 1612, bk II, ch. XIX, in *Selections from Three Works of Francisco Suárez, S. J.*, ed. James Brown Scott (Oxford: Clarendon Press, 1944), vol. I, p. 190. [The translation of this phrase as 'a moral and political unity (as it were)' may be found in vol. II, p. 348. –Eds.]
10 Locke, *Two Treatises*, para. 212, p. 225.
11 Immanuel Kant, 'The Metaphysics of Morals', sec. 61, in *Political Writings*, ed. Hans Reiss and tr. H. B. Nisbet (Cambridge and New York: Cambridge University Press, 1970), p. 171; italics in the original.
12 Immanuel Kant, 'Perpetual Peace', first published in 1795, in *Kant's Principles of Politics*, tr. and ed. W. Hastie (Edinburgh: T. & T. Clark, 1891), first supplement, p. 115.
13 Immanuel Kant, 'Idea for a Universal History with Cosmopolitan Intent', 8th principle, in *The Philosophy of Kant: Immanuel Kant's Moral and Political Writings*, ed. Carl J. Friedrich (New York: Modern Library, 1949), p. 128.
14 Kant, 'Eternal Peace', second addition, in *The Philosophy of Kant*, ed. C. J. Friedrich, p. 456.
15 Karl Marx, 'Theses on Feuerbach', no. 11, in Karl Marx and Friedrich Engels, *The German Ideology* (London: Lawrence and Wishart, 1938), p. 199, and ed. C. J. Arthur (New York: International Publishers, 1970), p. 123.
16 President Sukarno's opening speech at the Bandung Conference, 18 April 1955, *Keesing's Contemporary Archives*, 1955/6, p. 14181.
17 Étienne Gilson, *Dante the Philosopher*, tr. David Moore (London: Sheed and Ward, 1952), pp. 164–6.
18 See James Brown Scott, *The Spanish Origin of International Law: Francisco de Vitoria and his Law of Nations* (Oxford: Clarendon Press, 1934), p. 165 and appendix C.
19 Alberico Gentili, *De Jure Belli Libri Tres* (Hanan: Guilielimus Antonius, 1598).

20 See Otto Gierke, *Natural Law and the Theory of Society, 1500–1800*, tr. Ernest Barker (London: Cambridge University Press, 1934), vol. II, p. 283, note 62.
21 Christian Wolff, *Institutiones Juris Naturae et Gentium* (Halle: Prostat in officina Rengeriana, 1754).
22 Immanuel Kant, *Perpetual Peace*, ed. Lewis White Beck (Indianapolis and New York: Liberal Arts Press and Bobbs-Merrill Company, 1957), pp. 19, 31.
23 See Elliot R. Goodman, *The Soviet Design for a World State* (New York: Columbia University Press, 1960).

Index

G. = Grotius, K. = Kant, M. = Machiavelli, Mz. = Mazzini

Accra Conference (1958), 4
Alexander I, Czar, 151
Alexander VI, Pope, 19
Alexander, Samuel, 64
Altruism, 10
American Revolution, welcomed by K., 64, 71
Aquinas, St Thomas, 122; on law, 42; K. comparable to, 63; influenced by Aristotle, 81. *See also* Thomism
Aristotle, 13, 63, 122; G. on, 6; on slavery, 37–8; on success, 48; a 'culture uncle', 52; K. comparable to, 63; phenomenal and noumenal united in, 66; influence on Aquinas, the Whigs, Hegel, 81
Arnold of Brescia, 115
Augustine of Hippo, St, 122; and *compella intrare*, 123
Augustus, Emperor, 47

B.B.C., motto of, 74; Reith lectures, 91
Bacon, Sir Francis, 122
Bakúnin, Mikhail, 90; an Hegelian, 12; belief in destruction, 12–13; finds Mz.'s patriotism detestable, 99
Bandung Conference (1955), 4, 73, 151
Beethoven, Ludwig van, 13; influence of K. on, 63
Bell, Coral, on Wight, xviii–xix
Bentham, Jeremy, 38; discounts ancestral wisdom, 45
Berlin, Isaiah, explains slaughter for ideals, 81
Bismarck, Otto von, 12, 96, 99, 122; on grabbing God's garment, 23; disliked use of 'Christendom' or 'Europe', 145
Bloch, Marc, 80
Bodin, Jean, 145
Bolingbroke, Henry St J., Viscount, 6
Bond, James, on good defined by evil, 10
Borgia, Cesare, overtaken by accident, 19
Bright, John, 111
Britain, Grotian because secure, 16
Broad, C. D., 64
Browning, Robert and Elizabeth, 91
Buckle, Henry Thomas, 97
Bull, Hedley, on Wight, xviii
Burke, Edmund, 47, 76, 115, 122; on balance of good and evil, 35; favours prescription, ancestral wisdom, 45
Burnham, James, 8
Butterfield, Sir Herbert, vii; from realism to idealism in, 153

Calvin, John, 122, 123; world society's right of intervention, 152

Index

Calvinism, 96
Capella, Martianus, 29
Carbonari, Mz. joins, their character, 100–1; they look to France, 101
Carlyle, Thomas, 91
Carneades, 9
Carr, E. H., v, 7; on law, politics and power, 15; moral order rests on power, 145
Castlereagh, Robert Stewart, Viscount, 7
Categorical imperative, in K.'s moral passion, 67
Catholicism, relation of Mz. to, 92
Cavour, Camillo, Conte di, 99, 114; his *realpolitik* disliked by Mz., 108; letter from Mz. to, 112
Cecil, Lord Robert, 17, 18
Cecrops, mythical king of Athens, 100
Chamberlain, Neville, on the magnanimity of the strong, 16
Charles V, Emperor, 68
China, Communist, and United Nations, 48; passing from revolutionism to realism?, 154
Christ, seen by Mz. as supreme moral revolutionary, 92, 95
Christendom, G. advocates reunion of, appalled by lawless warfare in, 34; Mz.'s international society limited to, 109; use of in diplomacy dismissed by Bismarck, 145; doctrinal uniformity throughout, 152
Christian scholasticism, phenomenal and noumenal united in, 66
Christianity, K. accused of undermining, 64–5; Mz. repudiates theology of redemption, 93; Mz.'s view of, religion of the second age, 94; Primitive, 122
Churchill, Winston, 122, 143; angered by proposal to shoot German officers, 54; incensed by lynching of Mussolini, 55
Cicero, on justice and reverence, 50; on preferring honour to expediency, 54

Cieszkowski, August, Poland as messiah-nation, 104
Cobden, Richard, 109; held trade reduces war, 78, 149; an evolutionary Kantian, 83
Coleridge, Samuel Taylor, on theory and temperament, 153; and politics of understanding, 153
Collective vocation, Mz.'s doctrine of, 103–4
Collenbusch, Dr, on K.'s morality, 68
Columbus, M. compares himself to, 5
Communists, 7, 96; revolutionary Kantians, 83
Comte, Auguste, 94, 97
Conciliar Movement (1409–49), 115
Condorcet, Marquis de, 97
Congress System, 7
Copernicus, influence upon K., 65
Cox, Richard, reinterprets Locke, 146
Crimean War, Mz. on, 111
Crispi, Francesco, 114

Dante, 115, 122; G. rebuts, 35; holds a right valid for all time, 46; on imperial mission, 75; on peace and potentiality of men, 80–1; used by Mz. in political struggle, 90; role in nation-building, 102; advocated universal monarchy, 151–2
Darwinists, social, 7
Democritus, 64
De Jure Belli ac Pacis, 47; its character, 31–2; Lauterpacht on, 32; analysis of, 124–7
D'Entreves, A. P., on K. as among greatest natural law theorists, 42–3; on radicalism in natural law, 44
Descartes, René, 64
Dostoevsky, Fyodor, quoted (Ivan Karamazov), 77
Dulles, John Foster, U.S. foreign policy moving towards revolutionism under, 154
Dumbarton Oaks Conference (1944), 145
Dutch East India Company, 31

Index

Eden, Sir Anthony, 19; intervention in Egypt, 21–2; Machiavellian aim, Grotian instincts, 22
Eisenhower, President Dwight, 68
Eliot, George, 90
'English School', v, vii, liii
Erasmus, 34
Erastianism, 123
Evangelicals, active in former Soviet Union, 123

Fabricius, his decency, 21, 54
Fascism, Lassalle a forerunner of, 12; and primacy of contradiction, 14
Ferdinand, King of Aragon, Castile and Naples, on bird behaviour, 9
Feuerbach, Ludwig, 13
Fichte, Johann Gottlieb, 145; on the will, 70; primacy for Germany, 104
First International, Bakúnin v. Marx over control of, 12–13; Mz. represented at, 98
First World War, causes of, 20; repercussions of, 48
Fortuna, second Machiavellian principle, eludes calculation, 22; how defined, 22–3
Foscolo, Ugo, used by Mz. in political struggle, 90
Fox, Charles James, warns Talleyrand of plot, 53–4
Francis I, King of France, 68
Frederick the Great, King of Prussia, praised by K., 64
Frederick William II, King of Prussia, rebukes K., 64–5; his minister puts gag on K., 149
French Revolution, philosophical repercussions of, 47; welcomed by K., 64, 71; goal of a world state, 75; worshipped by the Carbonari, 101; Mz. believed corrupted France, 102; and doctrinal imperialism, 152
Freud, Sigmund, 3
Freudians, 7

Gandhi, Mohandas (Mahatma), 16, 122; his humanity, 35, 82
Gellius, on disobeying unjust orders, 34
Genoa Conference (1921), 114
Gentili, Alberico, mankind as society, 152
Germany, Mz.'s threefold destiny for, 95–6
Gilson, Étienne-Henry, on Dante, 152
Gioberti, Vincenzo, primacy for Italy, 104
Giolitti, Giovanni, 114
Gladstone, William Ewart, 103; intervention in Egypt, 21
God, represents harmony as ultimate reality, 11; 'aware of himself', 12; M. tempted to believe guides human affairs, 22; Bismarck grabs garment of, 23; principles valid irrespective of, 28–9; G. believes in, 39, 79; natural law unchangeable by, 40; acts through conscience and society, 42; in realm of the noumenal, 66; beyond reach of knowledge, 66–7, 79; in K., as reason, 69; in moral experience, 69–70; Dostoevsky on, 77; compassion of, 82; linked with the People in Mz.'s slogan, 91; Mz.'s view of, 92–3; kingdom on earth through revolution, 94–5; man owes duty to, 96; progress in law of, 96; dictators mistaken for, 98; sovereignty in, 99; created nations, 102, and assigned them missions, 104; shall bless the nations, 110
Goebbels, Joseph, 80
Goethe, J.W. von, influence of K. on, 63
Gorchakov, Prince Alexander, use of terms faulted by Bismarck, 145
Gorki, Maxim, on Lenin, 82
Gospel, The, forbids certain things natural law permits, 37
Green, Joseph, English friend of K., 64
Groot, Hugo de, *see* Grotius, Hugo

159

Index

Grotians, harsh conditions, nuclear warfare, pose problems for, 16; tragedy a category of, 17; do not understand irony, 19; find moral problems complex, 33; assert variety of political virtue, 49

Grotius, Hugo, 29–61 *passim*; Wight on, xxxiff; not a Grotian, 3; sociability, altruism of man, 9–10, 146; morality overrules power, 16; career, 29–31; father of International Law, 31; his *De Jure Belli ac Pacis* difficult and ambiguous, reflects a moral maze, 31–3; and golden mean, a reconciler, 34, 52; need to canalize war, lessen suffering, 35; and Natural Law, 36–44, 51; and International Law, 41–2, 45, 51; and prescription, 45–6; a political conservative, 47; his moral precepts, 49–50; on war, 51–2; influential with European 'Establishment', a 'culture-uncle', 52; and individual moral responsibility, 53–5; in Rationalist tradition, 122; International Theory of (from *De Jure Belli ac Pacis*), 124–7; on international society, 148

Guerrilla bands, Mz. on, 113

Guicciardini, Francesco, 5

Guizot, François, primacy for France, 104

Hague Peace Conference (1899), 31

Hannibal, his ruthlessness, 21

Hegel, Georg Wilhelm Friedrich, 64, 76, 81, 94, 122, 145, 149; links M. with K., 11; on contradiction, 11; influence on Lenin, 13–14; greatest disciple of K., 63; detested by Mz., 93

Hegelian dialectic, misunderstood by Proudhon, 13

Hegelians, M.'s influence on, 14

Heine, Heinrich, on K., 64, 67

Henry IV, King of France, 29

Heraclitus, 64; on change and conflict, 11; Lassalle on, 12, 13

Herder, Johann Gottfried, influence on Mz., 93

Herzen, Alexander, 12, 90

Hinduism, 122

Hirzel, Bernhard, primacy for Switzerland, 104

History, M.'s cyclical view of, 6; Bolingbroke on 6; Meinecke on, 148–9; doctrine that it has purpose and direction, 149

Hitler, Adolf, 17, 18, 122; irony in policies of, 20; as 'sleepwalker' under Providence, 23; and ideological imperialism, 152

Hobbes, Thomas, 43, 64, 122, 147; on quest for power, 9; on power as basis for justice, 15, 145; state creates morality and law, 15; equates international relations with state of nature, 144, 146; unlimited contract to counter war, 145; and politics of sensation, 153

Holy Alliance, 7, 47, 107; Mz. advocates 'of the Peoples', 110; counter-revolutionist, 151

Hooker, Richard, 42, 97, 123

Howard, Sir Michael, influence of Wight on, vii–viii

Human nature, as supreme datum of politics, 8; behind ambition, 8, desire for power, security, 9; altruism, 10

Humanism, Renaissance, emphasis on man, 5

Hume, David, 64; influenced K., 65, 70; abolished metaphysics, 65

International Law, derived from power, 15; G. father of, 31; slavery in, forbids poison, 38; why states obey, 41–2; may permit what honour forbids, 51; Mz. held moral considerations must override, 107; Suarez on basis of, 146; not enforced but true law, 147; Wolff's theory of, 152

Index

Irony, a Machiavellian category, 17; examples of in history, 18ff; as accident, 19; as cumulative causation, as paradox, as self-frustration, 20
Isaiah, on harmony of the nations, 110
Islam, 96
Italy, Mz.'s hopes for, 93, 103–4, 115; debt to Dante, 102

Jacobins, 7; revolutionary Kantians, 83
James I, King of England, 30
Jefferson, President Thomas, on rights of man, 44
Joachim of Flora and Joachism, 123; his 'three ages' influence Mz., 94
John, St, 123
Jowett, Benjamin, 91; character of man determines character of state, 55
Judas Iscariot, his unwitting role in redemption no justification, 98
Julius Caesar, 98
Julius II, Pope, 19
Justice, M. on origins of, 15; distributive, 36
Justine Martyr, St, on living by nature, 37

Kant, Immanuel, 63–87 *passim*; Wight on, xxxviiff; greatness of, 63; career, 63–5; revolutionary in philosophy, 65–6; his 'two worlds', 66; metaphysical matters 'unknowable', 66–7; his acute moral consciousness, 67; the categorical imperative od duty, 67–8; moral direction from within, 69–70; influence of Rousseau, 70–1; status quo not morally tenable, 71–2; looks to future world body, 72, 75; and federation of republican states, 72–4; draws up articles for this, 73; his cosmopolitanism: men as world citizens, 74–5; harmony of interests, 75–6; unconscious progress in history, 76; injustice in this, 77; commerce encourages peace, 78; desperate hope of better world, 78–9; 'as if-ness' of God, 79; belief in Reason despite his pessimism, 80–1; a puritan, a stoic, 81–2; his followers, 83; his comprehensiveness and universality, 83; and universal law, 119; in intellectual tradition of Revolutionists, 122; philosopher of international relations, 143; these pre-contractual, 145; and must be superseded, 148, through spirits of commerce and enlightenment, 149; and *Perpetual Peace*, 149–50, 152; in relation to Hobbes, 153
Kantians, characteristics of, 7, 11; find moral problems simple, 33; hold rights not annulled by prescription, and precedents, 46; and political legitimacy, 48; assert unity of political virtue, 49; evolutionary and revolutionary, respective characteristics of, 82–3
Kedourie, Elie, 103
Kennan, George F., 44, 143; from realism to idealism in, 153
Kennedy, President John F., 150
Keynes, J. M., 3
Khrushchev, Nikita, 68, 122; and doctrinal imperialism, 153; his Russia becoming more Grotian than U.S.A. or Britain?, 154
Kipling, Rudyard, poem 'If' exudes M.'s spirit of *virtù*, 27
Königsberg, life of K. at, 63–5
Kossuth, Lajos, 90, 111

Lammenais, Félicité de, 116
Lassalle, Ferdinand, 13, 90; an Hegelian, 12
Lauterpacht, Sir Hersch, on G. and *De Jure Belli ac Pacis*, 32, 51
Law of nature, *see* Natural Law
League of Nations, 17; and Manchurian Crisis, 18; criteria for membership, 48, 151; Covenant of compared with U.N. Charter, 147
Leibniz, Gottfried Wilhelm, 64

Index

Lenin, Vladimir Ilyich, 122; his understanding of contradiction, 13–14; attitude to suffering, 82
Leo XIII, Pope, 31
Lessing, Gotthold Ephraim, 94
Lincoln, President Abraham, 122
Lindsay, A. D., on K.'s morality, 68
Linguistic analysts, 7
Livy, M. writes commentary on, 6
Lloyd George, David, eulogizes Mz., 114
Locke, John, 64, 122, 147; on natural law, 42; on state of nature, 146
London, life of Mz. in, 90–1
Louis XII, King of France, mistakes in Italian policy, 20
Louis XIII, King of France, 31, 47
Louis Philippe, King of the French, cautious, 101
Luther, Martin, 96, 122, 123

Macaulay, Thomas B., Lord, 76
Machiavelli, Niccolò, 1–28 *passim*; Wight on, xxviff; reputation, 3; criticizes treacherous, ruthless conduct, 3–4; a passionate patriot, 4; prefers facts to ideals, 4; rejects transcendentalism, 5; draws political laws from history, 5–7; his method uncritical, 7; men bad, 7–8, ambitious, avaricious, 8–9; on need for customs, laws, 14–15; his political view of justice, 15; on complexity of politics, 17; his study of political irony, 17ff; and Cesare Borgia, 19; on harsh v. mild methods, 21; and *virtù*, 21, 24; advocates firm action, 21–2; on role of *fortuna* or chance, 22–3; advocates opportunism, audacity, 23; in Realist tradition, 122, 143, 145
Machiavellians, 11; *see* lessons in history, 6; methodologically uncritical, 7; and 'security', 10; *see* moral values as epiphenomenal, 16; irony a category of, 17; do not understand tragedy, 19; irony determines types of, 19; find moral problems non-existent or delusory, 33
Mack Smith, Denis, 133, 139
Malthus, Thomas Robert, 75
Mandeville, Bernard de, 75
Manning, C. A. W., v
Manzoni, Alessandro, 116
Mark, St, 123
Marx, Karl, vii, 3, 7, 64, 70, 90, 93, 94, 99, 115, 122, 149; quarrel with Bakúnin, 12; quarrel with Proudhon, 13; social existence determines consciousness, 16; greatest disciple of Hegel, 63; seeks to accommodate Mz., 99; on need to change the world, 150
Marxists, M.'s influence on, 14; primacy of contradiction a basic principle for, 14; irony as paradox appeals to, 20
Mazzini, Guiseppe, 89–119 *passim*; Wight on, xliiff; and ideal federation of national democracies, 73; a revolutionary Kantian, 83; confusion in the sources, 89–90; involved in English life, 90–1; dictator of Rome (1849), 91; profoundly religious, 91–2; theory of moral progress, 93, 96–8, 99–100; dislike of German philosophy, 93; and the 'three ages', 94–5; destiny of Rome, 95; apostle of duty, 97–8; moral flaw in Caesarism, 98; a democratic socialist, 98–9; outbid by Marx and Cavour, 99; government by the virtuous, 99; and the Carbonari, 100–2; anti-French, 102; 'division of labour' in European nationalism, 102; nationalism and moral purpose, 103; to each nation its mission, 103; Italy as nation-messiah, 104; hostile to settlement of 1815, 105–6, 111; his anti-imperialism, 105–6; and principle of non-intervention, 106–8; hostile to Cavour's *realpolitik*, 108, 112; Eurocentric, a colonialist, 109;

Index

'Holy Alliance of the Peoples', 110; an uncompromising moralist, 111–12; and Crimean War, 111; guerrilla bands as servants of nation, 113; his moral dictatorship of Rome, 113–14; drew strength from past, 115; in Revolutionist tradition, 122; his nationality principle realized in 1919, 151; admired by Nehru, 151

Mediæval heresies, 122

Meinecke, Friedrich, and historicism, 148–9

Melos, destruction of, 17

Mendelssohn, Moses, on K., 66

Metaphysics, discounted by K., 66–7

Metternich, Clemens L. W., Prince, 151

Mickievicz, Adam, and Poland as martyr-nation, 104

Mill, James, 91

Mill, John Stewart, on altruism, 10

Milton, John, 46

Molotov, V. M., 54

Montgomery, F.-M. Bernard, Viscount, advice on Suez, 22

Moore, G. E., 64

Moral order, derived from power, 15

Morellet, André, 75

Morgenthau, Hans J., v, 7, 143; on Hobbes' view that state creates morality, law, 15–16; on natural law as ideology, 44; no international society to define justice or equality, 145

Municipal law, 35; utility in, 38

Mussolini, Benito, lynching of disgusts Churchill, 55; Silone attacks through Mz., 90

Mutual involvement, Mz. preaches principle of, 107

Napoleon I, Emperor, on luck, 23; plot to assassinate, 54

Napoleon III, Emperor (Louis Napoleon), 101, 102, 108, 112, 115; his creed attacked by Mz., 98

Nasser, President Gamel Abdul, 22, 122

Nation-messiah, myth of, 104

Natural law, G. on, 36ff; *pacta sunt servanda* in, 36; not necessarily Christian, 37; principle of utility in, 38–9; known by reason, rational, 39, 43; self-evident, unchangeable by God, codifiable, 40; proofs of, 40–1; Locke on, 42; becomes natural rights, 43; replaced by progress, 43–4; classic form presupposes timeless moral order, 44; ethics extend beyond, 49; laws of Christ transcend, 50; West lives half in world of, 52

Nazis, and primacy of contradiction, 14

Nehru, Jawaharlal, 35, 122, 143; democracy not enough, 50; an evolutionary Kantian, 83; held Mz. in respect, 151

Neo-scholastics, 123

Newton, Sir Isaac, 43, 71; influenced K., 65, 70

Nicholas I, Czar, 107, 115

Niebuhr, Reinhold, on the nuclear deterrent, 18; a Christian Machiavellian, 19, 123

Nominalists, 123

Non-intervention, doctrine of attacked by Mz. when it preserves an unjust status quo, 106–8

Nuclear disarmament, a popular illusion, 5

Nuclear warfare, moral complexity in, 33

Oakeshott, Michael, 8

Oldenbarnevelt, Johan van, 29–30

Paine, Thomas, 96

Palmerston, Henry John Temple, Viscount, 113

Panizzi, Sir Anthony, 91, 116

Paris Commune, enraptures Bakúnin, 13; counterpart and opposite of Mz.'s Republic, 114

Paul, St, 123

Peter, St, 123

Philip II, King of Spain, and doctrinal uniformity, 152–3

Index

Philosophers, philosophically contemporaneous, 1; married and unmarried, 64
Pius IX, Pope, 116
Plato, 7, 11, 64, 122; on unity of virtue, 48; just man prior to just state, 55; K. comparable to, 63; phenomenal and noumenal united in, 66; father of mystical quietism and also Communism, 81; comprehensive and universal, 83
Polybius, 15
Porter, Brian, ix, lii
Prescription, favours existing political forms, need for international validity of, 45; cannot annul a right, 46
Progress, doctrine of, 76ff; inhumanity in denounced by Dostoevsky, 77; and K.'s desperate hope from history, 78–80; Mz.'s moral criterion of, derived from Herder and Vico, 93, and from Joachim of Flora, 94–6; as law of God, 96–8
Proudhon, Pierre-Joseph, fails to understand dialectic, 13
Puritanism, 123
Pyrrhus, King of Epirus, 21, 54
Pythagoras, on essence of universe, 11

Quakers, 122, 123

Raglan, F.-M. Lord, 111
Rathenau, Walther, 80
Rationalists, Wight on, xxff
Realists, Wight on, xxff
Revelation, Book of, on compassion of God, 82
Revolutionists, Wight on, xxiff, inverted, xxiv
Ricasoli, Bettino, 116
Richelieu, Cardinal, stops G.'s pension, 30
Rienzi (Cola di Rienzo), 115
Roberts, Sir Adam, on Wight, xvii
Rome, M. worshipped Ancient, 7; and danger of despotic imperialism, 74; Mz. dictator of the Republic (1849), 91, 113–14; need for moral mission for, 93; idea of the third, 94–5, 104; as seat for Mz.'s 'council of the nations', 110; Mz.'s Republic last flicker of Roman city-state, 115; designed by Providence for government of mankind (Dante), 152
Roosevelt, Elliot, 54
Roosevelt, President Franklin D., 150; and proposal to shoot German officers, 54
Rossetti, Gabriele Pasquale and Dante Gabriel, 91, 116
Rossini, Giocchino, 116
Rousseau, Jean-Jacques, 6, 7, 122, 145; and General Will, 53; influenced K., 65, 70; on conscience, 70; how differs from K., 70–1; theoretical contradiction in?, 153; and politics of reason, 153
Ruskin, John, 90, 91
Russell, Bertrand, 64

Santayana, George, 64
Sarpi, Paolo, Mz. uses him in political struggle, 90
Savonarola, Girolamo, 115
Schelling, Friedrich Wilhelm Joseph von, 94
Schiffer, Walter, on G., 32
Schiller, Friedrich von, influence of K. on, 63
Schopenhauer, Arthur, on philosophers not marrying, 64; his pessimism influenced by K., 81
Second World War, irony in cause and outcome of, 18; moral complexity of bombing in, 33
Selden, John, 31
Seneca, on law v. shame, 50
Seton-Watson, R. W., 114
Shaw, George Bernard, 82, 114
Silone, Ignazio, politician, novelist and writer on Mz.'s thought, 89–90
Smith, Adam, 75
Smuts, F.-M. Jan C., and U.N. Charter, 146
Socrates, 64

Index

Spencer, Herbert, 76
Spengler, Oswald, 149
Spinoza, Benedict de, 64, 145
Spiritual Franciscans, 123
Stalin, Joseph, 4, 17, 18, 46, 70, 105; proposes shooting German officers, 54; and ideological imperialism, 152
Stevin, Simon, 29
Stoics, 36; and pain, 82
Suarez, Francisco, on international society, 146
Suez Crisis, 19; irony in, 20–2; invasion a bungled middle course, 21
Sukarno, on colonialism, 151
Swinburne, Algernon Charles, 91

Talleyrand, Charles Maurice, Prince de, alerted by Fox, 54
Taylor, A. J. P., 23
Tehran Conference (1943), shooting of 50,000 German officers proposed at, 54
Temperamenta, Grotian doctrine of, 52
Thirty Years War, 34
Thomism, 123
Thucydides, on harsh imperatives of necessity, 16
Tocqueville, Alexis dé, Mz. justifies himself against, 113–14
Tolstoy, Leo, 122; on happy families, a Platonist, 49; from realism to idealism in, 153
Toynbee, Arnold, 91
Toynbee, Arnold J., 149
Tragedy, Burnham, Oakeshott, on, 8; a Grotian category, 17; in history, 17–18
Trotsky, Leon, 113
Truman, President Harry S., 19
Turgot, A.-R.-J., Baron de, 94, 97
Tyche (Τύχη), pagan goddess of chance, 23

UNESCO, an evolutionary Kantian body, 83
United Nations, criterion for membership, 48, 151; ostracizes Spain, 48, 151, Communist China, 48; desire for weighted votes in General Assembly, 74; germ of in K., 75; designed to be Hobbesian sovereign, 145–6; significance of Articles 24, 25 and 48 of Charter, 146; a schizophrenic paralytic, 146; and world public opinion, 149
United States, policy of over Manchuria, 18; as potential universal empire, 152; becoming more Kantian than Soviet Union?, 154
Usucaption, *see* prescription
Utilitarian theory, on altrusim, 10

Vasquez, Gabriel, 9
Vatican, Mz.'s banner floats over, 91
Versailles settlement (1919), Mz. prophet of, 103, 115
Vettori, Francesco, 5
Vico, Giambattista, influence on Mz., 93
Vienna settlement (1815), attacked by Mz., 105–6; 111
Vindiciae contra Tyrannos, world society's right of intervention, 152
Virtù, a leading Machiavellian principle, 21; definition of, 21, 24, 27
Vitoria, Francisco de, mankind as society, 152
Voltaire (François-Marie Arouet), 75

Wallace, Henry A., Vice-President, 19
War, father of all things, 11; G. appalled by unbridled nature of, 35; G. on just and unjust, 51, 59; K. on, reason repudiates, 72
Webb, Beatrice, wanted to abolish the poor, 82
Weber, Max, sees three qualities in a politician, 153
West, Rebecca, on harsh imperatives of necessity, 16
Westphalia, Europe after, G.'s *De Jure Belli ac Pacis* a textbook for, 31, and prophetic of, 47; *Ancien Régime* of, a Christian family, 47

165

Index

Whigs, influenced by Aristotle, 81
Wight, Barbara, xi
Wight, Gabriele, lii
Wight, Martin, life and achievement, vff, xviiff, lii-liii; publishing lecture notes of, ix-xi; his distinctive approach to International Relations, xixff; what he meant by 'traditions', xxiiff; on M., xxviff; on G., xxxiff; on K., xxxviiff; on Mz., xliiff; merits of his approach, xlvff; reviews Morgenthau on Hobbes, 16; scrutinizes his own psyche, 154
Wight, Susannah, xi
William II, Kaiser, campaign to hang, 55
Williams, Howard, 133
Wilson, Edmund, on Lassalle, 12
Wilson, Hugh R., 18
Wilson, President Woodrow, 115, 122, 143, 147; on membership of League of Nations, 48; his ideas compared with K.'s, 72–3, an evolutionary Kantian, 83; on public opinion, 150; and politics of understanding, 153
Wittgenstein, Ludwig, 64
Wolff, Christian, *civitas maxima* basis of his International Law theory, 152
World Council of Churches, 30
Wycliffe, John, dominion founded on grace, 99

Yost, David S., xi, 133

Zeno of Citium, 64